DISASTROUS SUBJECTIVITIES

Romanticism, Modernity, and the Real

DISASTROUS SUBJECTIVITIES

Romanticism, Modernity, and the Real

DAVID COLLINGS

UNIVERSITY OF TORONTO PRESS
Toronto Buffalo London

Toronto Buffalo London
utorontopress.com

ISBN 978-1-4875-0614-8

Printed on acid-free, 100% post-consumer recycled paper with vegetable-based inks.

Library and Archives Canada Cataloguing in Publication

Title: Disastrous subjectivities: Romanticism, modernity, and the real / David Collings.
Names: Collings, David, 1959– author.
Description: Includes bibliographical references and index.
Identifiers: Canadiana 20190151196 | ISBN 9781487506148 (hardcover)
Subjects: LCSH: English literature – 19th century – History and criticism. | LCSH: Romanticism. | LCSH: Civilization, Modern. | LCSH: Subjectivity.
Classification: LCC PR461.C65 2020 | DDC 820.9/008–dc23

This book has been published with the assistance of Bowdoin College.

University of Toronto Press acknowledges the financial assistance to its publishing program of the Canada Council for the Arts and the Ontario Arts Council, an agency of the Government of Ontario.

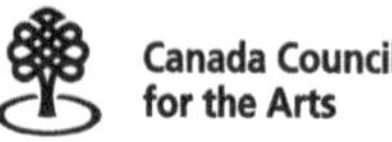

Funded by the Government of Canada
Financé par le gouvernement du Canada

Contents

Acknowledgments

This book has been in gestation for many years. The questions at its core have haunted me for two decades now, arising out of my earlier books, giving way to another (one on climate change) that has ultimately contributed to this book as well, and thus it represents my best attempt to understand some of the abiding stakes of Romanticism's formulation of modernity. As a result, it necessarily arises out of a long, rhizomatic conversation with colleagues and friends across several disciplines and in many settings, constituting in some measure my reply to an untold number of questions and insights, conversations, and acts of kindness, for which I am supremely grateful.

I owe my biggest debt to Tilottama Rajan, fellow traveller in unusable negativity, who read the manuscript of this book for the press, saw its value, and made perceptive suggestions for revision. Since her presence in the field helped define it for me from the start and her generosity to all of us in Romantic studies has been legendary for decades, I must single her out for special gratitude: her consistently inspiring model of professional commitment and her own brilliant work helped me find a home in the study of Romanticism, and her insights about this project helped me immensely as I strove to sharpen this book's arguments.

I am grateful to William Galperin, who invited me to give a presentation that eventually formed the basis for this book's third chapter, and to Thomas Pfau and Rob Mitchell for asking me to present a later and expanded version of that presentation as a seminar at the North American Society for the Study of Romanticism (NASSR) conference at Duke University. I especially thank Colin Jager for his response on the first occasion, for it helped me find my way into this book's response to recent work on the secular, and to the participants in the seminar at Duke for their cogent, wide-ranging suggestions. Nancy Yousef kindly invited me to present a paper that became the core of chapter 2, bringing me into the spirited group of Romanticists at the Graduate Center of the City University of New York – Nancy, Alan Vardy, Josh Wilner, and Alexander Schlutz – who on this project and more have been among my most indispensable interlocutors and friends.

Since so much of this book arose out of presentations at NASSR conferences and took its present form thanks to conversations there, I must honor a host of colleagues with whom I've conversed in those settings and elsewhere over the years: Frances Ferguson, David Clark, Orrin Wang, Rei Terada, Jacques Khalip, Karen Swann, Vivasvan Soni, Ian Balfour, Theresa Kelley, Marc Redfield, Chuck Rzepka, Christoph Bode, Elizabeth Fay, Joan Steigerwald, Arkady Plotnitsky, Anne-Lise François, Richard Sha, Nick Halmi, Mark Canuel, Joel Faflak, Tres Pyle, Daniela Garofalo, Adam Potkay, Deborah Elise White, Daniel O'Quinn, Celeste Langan, Miranda Burgess, Scott Juengel, Jennifer Fay, Noah Heringman, Samantha Webb, Eugene Stelzig, David Baulch, Ron Broglio, Brian McGrath, Julie Murray, Katey Castellano, Alex Dick, David Ruderman, Tobias Menely, Andrew Warren, George Erving, Andy Burkett, Eric Lindstrom, David Sigler, Anne McCarthy, Allison Dushane, Chris Washington, Soelve Curdts, Jonathan Crimmins, Jamison Kantor, Jennifer Horan, Christopher Bundock, Jared McGeough, Anahid Nersessian, Elizabeth Effinger, Jacob Risinger, the late and lamented Stephanie Dumke, Hannah Markley, Aaron Ottinger, and Megan Quinn. Their ideas, comments, suggestions, and incitements have perpetually challenged and deepened my thoughts on this project, prodding me at every stage. I can only express my great joy at belonging to one of the most dynamic and welcoming groups in all of contemporary humanistic scholarship.

This book owes much to the stimulating presence of so many gifted scholars at Bowdoin College. I thank my colleagues in the English, Environmental Studies, and Gender, Sexuality, and Women's Studies programs, whose work as scholars and teachers creates the lively environment in which my endeavours can find a home. I owe heartfelt homage to those friends who have sustained me through thick and thin – the late Celeste Goodridge, Liz Muther, and Mark Foster, extraordinary presences all. I gratefully acknowledge the financial assistance that the Faculty Development Committee and the Dean for Academic Affairs, Elizabeth McCormack, provided to enable this book to reach publication.

An earlier version of chapter 2 appeared as "The Romance of the Impossible: William Godwin in the Empty Place of Reason" in *ELH* 70 (2003): 847–74, and of chapter 3 as "After the Covenant: Romanticism, Secularization, and Disastrous Transcendence" in *European Romantic*

Review 21 (2010): 345–61. I thank these journals for permission to publish new versions of this work.

I am delighted to acknowledge my debt to the staff at the University of Toronto Press, who stand out for their exemplary professionalism. I wish to thank Mark Thompson, my editor, for seeing the value of this book and shepherding it through the process with such grace; the copy editor, Barbie Halaby, for her astute assistance in editing the manuscript; and the production and publicity staff, including Christine Robertson and Breanna Muir, for handling the later phases of this book's publication with remarkable ease.

My greatest thanks go to Terri Nickel, extraordinary partner, colleague, and friend, who with her talent for happiness and her immense generosity – not to mention her acute eye as critic and editor – has made the entire adventure of writing this book a delight. I owe to her the joy in life that makes all my scholarly efforts possible.

DISASTROUS SUBJECTIVITIES

Romanticism, Modernity, and the Real

Introduction

By the end of the eighteenth century, over the course of the late Enlightenment, an array of pivotal assumptions previously held within the early modern West had altered so much that they began to modulate into a set of alternative premises, bringing about the transition to what we might now recognize as no longer an early but a mature modernity. This development took place in part because those living within a broadly religious tradition began to demand the fulfilment of that tradition's millennial promises within this actual world, within the terrain of a lived history. A certain demand that people need not wait until the afterlife to receive justice – that it be realized on *this* side of death – began to make itself felt across the West, a demand that at least some political, legal, social, and economic arrangements be changed for the benefit of all. Such a demand, of course, implied a shift as well from the sense of awaiting the end of history, an apocalyptic judgment carried out by God, to the promise of doing justice *within* history through collaborative action among human beings. Such attitudes have long since become a fundamental, unstated premise of modern societies, which now assume that their task is to achieve justice for all – if not through a singular, sweeping transformation, then at least through the progress that the incremental reforms arising from within the modern democratic process might make possible.

These premises may seem so obvious that they scarcely deserve comment. Yet because they are so fundamental to modernity, their implications so far-reaching, they cry out for careful scrutiny. What exactly does a society – or the broader array of mutually implicated societies inheriting the traditions of Western Europe – set about to do when it brings the notion of a collective justice into history? Can any society achieve justice for all within its flawed institutions, within the constraints of its inheritances? Can such an event – previously consigned to divine action – take place within its midst as part of the ordinary human domain?

The stakes of such questions may be clearest if one considers Immanuel Kant's reflections on whether one may be confident that humanity will eventually reach its goal. Late in his career, over a series of works that substitute for what Jean-François Lyotard describes as his unwritten fourth critique – the critique of the political – Kant takes a position characteristic of him, arguing in *The Conflict of the Faculties* that one cannot directly bridge the gap between empirical experience and the arrival of universal justice, in this case because one cannot predict what human beings will do over the actual course of history.[1] The best one can do, then, is to find *some* sort of indication in experience, such as a "cause" of gradual improvement. Such an indication, Kant argues, may be found less in actual events than in the response of onlookers to those events, and specifically in a sympathy, a "wishful *participation* that borders closely on enthusiasm," among the "spectators" of the French Revolution – a sympathy that "can have no other cause than a moral predisposition in the human race." In his view, "such a phenomenon in human history *will not be forgotten*, because it has revealed a tendency and faculty in human nature for improvement ... that no politician, affecting wisdom, might have conjured out of the course of things hitherto existing." The sign of history gives one confidence, in short, not because of anything one can derive from the flow of empirical events but from a moral capacity that underlies them, a force for good that exceeds the field of phenomenal determinations. This derivation, Kant argues, is thus "a proposition valid for the most rigorous theory."[2]

But it is not entirely clear that Kant's argument holds within the terms of his overall critical philosophy. In his second critique, *The Critique of Practical Reason*, he argues that because "no rational being in the world of sense" may achieve holiness, or "the perfect fit of the will to moral law," only "infinite progress" towards such a state is possible; as a result, for human beings "the highest good is practically possible only on the supposition of the immortality of the soul."[3] Yet this argument collapses: as Lewis White Beck points out, "Presumably the soul upon death, if it is indeed immortal, is no longer a denizen of the world of space and time," in which case "it is not possible to understand" what Kant means by "continuous and unending progress" towards holiness.[4] It seems that the pure good of the moral law is inherently incompatible with the temporality in which the subject finds itself. Such an incompatibility applies as well to the question of human history overall: given Kant's reflections on how one cannot predict what human beings will do, it is clear that even if human societies were to establish a form of universal justice, one could never guarantee that it would endure. Even the achievement of what might pass as the "*final end* of creation itself" would not be so, since such an achievement would still be subject to the vicissitudes of history, time, and what Kant considers to be the inconstancy of human beings.[5]

Thus the Kantian Idea of morality, justice, or the *summum bonum* must necessarily exceed what can take place in time; accordingly, as Lyotard argues, the enthusiasm that spectators feel in response to the French Revolution is "an extreme mode of the sublime," that is, "a presentation for the unpresentable," a sign within history of what history must forever *fail* to bring about.[6] The sign of history marks out a radical gap between it and what it evokes, just as the sublime enables the subject to locate, within the very failure of imagination (the faculty charged with the synthesis of experience), a sign of the subject's supersensible destination. In effect, the sign of history – like the experience of the sublime – enables the subject to posit a destination beyond the reach of a seemingly endless sequence of phenomena. In his discussion of the mathematical sublime, Kant argues that it culminates in the mind's recognition that it can conceive of an Idea of infinity outside the phenomenal realm. In his view, then, the mind overleaps even an indefinitely extended numerical or experiential sequence – any sequence that continues without limit and thereby crushes the capacity of imagination – to apprehend an Idea beyond all number, beyond all possible experience.

Kant's difficulty in bridging this gap arises not from any flaw in his thought; indeed, his achievement in these various critiques – of practical reason, the sublime, and the political – may well be to mark out, more clearly than elsewhere, the structurally necessary impasses of any attempt to bring the end of history into time. His philosophy brings into focus the fact that the orthodox account of history derived its significance from its origin and end in divine action, from a logic that operated beyond the agency and to some extent the comprehension of human beings. The Enlightenment demand to bring about justice for all creates a problem that Kantian analysis specifies with remarkable precision: the writings of his final years make clear that the realization of universal justice within history is inconceivable, that history and its telos are structurally incompatible. Nevertheless, Kant's wish to establish a sign of history – an indication, however tenuous, that humanity may be progressing towards its destination – speaks of his late-Enlightenment wish that justice not simply loom from beyond the reach of history, that it not be consigned entirely to divine action. His appeal to that sign – much like his attempt to justify a belief in the immortality of the soul – shows that he is caught within a contradiction between the demand to realize justice and an awareness of that task's structural impossibility.

Kant's critical philosophy serves as one of the definitive turning points for philosophical reflection because his work delineates with unusual clarity the constitutive impasses of a secularizing reason. Lyotard's exquisitely patient and lucid exposition of Kant's thought shows that it circles interminably around a series of differends between competing phrase regimes, between faculties of mind which can appeal to no supervenient judgment to resolve their disputes. Kant's work provides a signal articulation of the mind's failure to account fully for its situation or to provide a comprehensive architecture for the conditions of mind that one can discern within the limits of reason alone.[7] Accordingly, his critical philosophy is a leading symptom of the dilemmas of the late Enlightenment, the impossible exigencies that befall any effort to outline the contours of the mind's situation in the wake of new scientific knowledges and new forms of awareness of experiential finitude without relinquishing the idea of a telos for the creation.

Insofar as Kant's work speaks of the initial encounter with such impasses, it exemplifies how those who attempted to articulate modernity faced demands that within certain premises – those that largely still obtain even today – must remain unresolvable, that must endlessly reveal a certain failure intrinsic to modernity itself. In doing so, it addresses in its own way exigencies that find no definitive formulation in any single disciplinary formation or any unique project but rather are imposed on a wide range of articulations, including those that belong to what we have come to designate British Romanticism. Arising in the decades around 1800, when what we now call the early modern era edged across into something more like modernity proper – when the departure from prior formations began to seem more definitive – these articulations speak not of the history of modernity as a whole, which extends back several centuries and forward into our own time, but rather of a specific problematic that crystallizes on the threshold of its most visible emergence. Since that problematic necessarily encompasses a range of projects beyond Kant's own, his critical philosophy may best serve as a useful symptom of that problematic, enabling one to discern a wide array of contemporaneous strategies for registering certain impasses and contending with them in ways that, while resonating with the arguments in Kant, greatly enlarge upon and complicate them as well.[8]

Given these considerations, this book takes as its focus not the entire trajectory of modernity but this exemplary moment in its articulation. Rather than embarking on a capacious intellectual history of the West that would both explain the formation of modernity and expose its fissures, this book instead enacts a precise cut across one moment in that narrative, hoping to delineate a specific cross-section of that broader development. Accordingly, it will attend not to the overall architecture of Kant's thought but rather to the problematic that it helps make visible – a problematic that this book will explore in its further ramifications through contemporaneous works in British Romanticism.[9] In short, this book is an instance of what one might call a cultural symptomatology, for it will attempt to illuminate certain characteristic impasses in a particular cultural conjuncture by investigating in Kant and Romanticism alike the formation of what I will designate as the Real.

A powerful example of how literary writing contemporaneous with Kant complicates the concerns evident in his critical philosophy may be found in William Godwin's *Caleb Williams*. In that novel, the servant Caleb, acting on an insatiable curiosity, comes to learn of his master Falkland's murder of a rival; his ensuing experiences under Falkland's vengeful pursuit and the surveillance of others reveal what he eventually takes to be a pervasive, even universal hostility against those who have seen into the violence of existing social relations, inspiring him to oppose that society with what he hopes will be an even more implacable resolve. The emergence of this totalizing contest reveals what is at stake in any appeal to universal justice, for Caleb's fidelity to this ideal of justice forces him into such a desperate isolation that in the novel's initial, unpublished ending, he collapses under the strain and descends into madness. Turning away from such a dire resolution, Godwin revises the ending, describes how Caleb is reconciled with Falkland, and repudiates the fantasy of a total denunciation of society. In doing so, however, Godwin complicates the demand for absolute justice, suggesting that the realization of such justice is not only impossible but also prohibited – that the attempt to force its entry into history would be so morally, politically, or physically violent that it would require more than humanity could bear.

Much as Kant in various ways suggests that history's telos imposes too great a demand on temporal subjects, *Caleb Williams* proposes, somewhat more sharply, that one must protect history or the historical subject from the arrival of that telos, from the violence of that final judgment. The second ending to the novel, which Godwin composes against his initial intention, suggests that although the demand for justice may on some level continue to motivate all ethical and political action, at the same time a due regard for human finitude requires that those who live within history must ward off the realization of that demand. This turn away from the violence of total judgment is consistent with the eventual shift of perspective also evident in the history of the term "apocalypse": where that term once referred to the final revelation, the divine event at the end of history, by the end of the nineteenth century it begins to refer instead to a purely disastrous event, the coming of a violence that leaves nothing positive in its wake.[10] Like the revised ending of Godwin's novel, the redefinition of apocalypse speaks of a preference for mortal experience over the violence of a final judgment; such a preference thus requires the exclusion of the absolute, the formal prohibition of infinite judgment.

This exclusion of the absolute from the temporality within which history takes place constitutes one of the most characteristic gestures of the late Enlightenment. But that move also greatly complicates the hope emerging in the same period to realize justice within history rather than in the afterlife – the hope with which I began. The commitment to bring about justice within history *also* requires the prohibition of what is promised by immortality from entering into the realm of human experience. Therefore the attempt to realize justice must do so in the name of what necessarily exceeds positive content or actual instantiation. It ultimately aims for a justice without content, without any of the characteristics of finite determinations that would attach it too closely to a specific historical moment – a justice to be found and enforced through a perpetual, incremental critique, through an open and indefinitely prolonged process inscribed within a progressive history. Such an arrangement respects at once the location of justice outside history *and* the constraints of historical finitude, as if somehow to coordinate a total justice in the beyond with the vast progressive movement of time. The notion that modern society is to realize some aspect of an absolute justice over time, surpassing any temporary consensus with a better understanding, and then to do so again and yet again in an indefinite sequence, requires that the definition of this justice remain formally empty – even as it also demands that this progressive society keep in view a destination it cannot ultimately name. The logic of this coordination between indefinite progress and empty justice mirrors that of Kant's argument concerning practical reason, which proposes that one might progress towards entire conformity to a structurally empty moral law, in a logic I will discuss further below. But this logic also corresponds to the formal structure of political modernity, complete with what Claude Lefort calls power's "empty place" – the absence of any singular, enduring embodiment of power within modern democracies – and with what Ernesto Laclau describes as the work of antagonism, the contest to fill in the absence constitutive of modern society with a dominant ideological fiction.[11] In the wake of Enlightenment, political antagonism revolves around the site of a constitutive absence that no person and no ideology can permanently occupy.

Thus the overall, complex structure appearing throughout the premises of the modern West incorporates the idea of a universal justice into history – but only negatively, as that ideal which finitude must serve but can never realize. The logic of these developments is captured well by Joan Copjec, who in another context, borrowing from the teachings of Jacques Lacan, provides an exemplary argument regarding the contours of this ensemble – an argument on whose terms I will rely throughout the chapters to follow. "[I]f history has no outside," she writes, "if history is without limit, then it must accommodate or be invaded by the infinite, the never-ending, by undying repetition, or the undead." The authorizing force of divine intention that disappears from creation and apocalypse is reinscribed, in *negative* form, *within* history: "[I]f one wants to prevent the formation of an outside," she writes, one must "inscribe in the interior a negation that says 'no' precisely to the possibility of an outside." Far from allowing this historical ensemble to operate at last without interference, such a move inscribes what Copjec calls "the real as internal limit of the symbolic," an "obstacle that scotches the possibility of rising out of or above the symbolic."[12]

Although in this passage Copjec does not elaborate on her insight, her argument strikingly reinterprets the contours of an apparently secular or modern settlement. Where a familiar narrative holds that a secular history internalizes God into the deep-structural coherence of historical progress, bringing about a positive absorption of what it cancels, and where the Hegelian dialectic is often understood to propose that what a new phase of world history cancels it also absorbs into a higher or more realized self-understanding of spirit, her account suggests on the contrary that this apparently secular order is haunted by a *negated* principle that perpetually disrupts and *undoes* its functioning. That principle has a complex status: as the mark of the "no" that excludes transcendence, it is *at once hostile to transcendence*, excluding the guarantees of history's foundation, telos, and cosmic significance, *and unsurpassable* and so transcendent in another sense, that is, impossible to evade or escape. This negated, obliterated transcendence – what Copjec, following Lacan in a usage that I will follow as well, designates as the Real – thus becomes the defining characteristic not of a secular framework, that is, a settlement that has truly surpassed the appeal to transcendence, but of a *non*secular framework, one henceforth defined in relation to an obliterated but insistent principle consistently operating through modernity's conceptual impasses.

A particularly legible example of the historiography Copjec proposes in this passage is visible in the late-Enlightenment reception of the history of the earth. Only in the mid- to late eighteenth century do natural philosophers conclude that earth has a history much vaster than anything proposed in previous interpretations of holy scripture, that human beings occupy what Paolo Rossi, in Shakespearean phrase, has evocatively described as "the dark abyss of time."[13] If one applies Copjec's terms in this regard, one might say that if a certain divine agency disappears from the origin and end of earthly history in the creation and apocalypse, if it no longer appears as history's "outside," an obliterated version of that transcendence reappears within that history in the endless natural disasters – earthquakes, fires, floods, volcanoes – which have, together with other forces, shaped the surface of the earth and to which human beings, and all other forms of life, are perpetually vulnerable. An agency no longer outside history thus reappears as the "undying repetition" of motiveless, amoral catastrophe within time, as the operation of an "undead" force.

If this example is any guide, it seems that the cancellation of transcendence does not simply remove it from consideration, for it necessarily retains the *mark of that cancellation*, the intrusions of an alien, *non*-redemptive infinity into time, intrusions so persistent that they ultimately reveal geological history to be the domain of material forces that operate without reference to any eventual justice or even the survival of the human species. Expunging the rainbow covenant whereby God promised to do no further harm to the earth, as William Wordsworth proposes in various allusions in *The Prelude*, this gesture undercuts the practices of symbolic exchange between humanity and the divine, producing the scenario in which human beings confront a now terrifying infinity without the mediations of ritual, theology, or institution, thereby generating the direct, violent disjunction between temporality and infinity that frequently appears throughout Kant's work. Moreover, insofar as natural disaster reveals the inhuman face of nature, it suggests as well that something disruptive and hostile inheres *within* nature itself, that it too suffers from an instance of the Real.

The structure of earthly history can thus serve as a guide to the structure of political history: both are riven *from within* by a Real that radically disrupts any settled functioning. Much as the history of the earth takes shape without any nameable destination, operating in part through the unpredictable interruptions of natural disaster, so also political history transpires in relation to a telos that is open, empty, and unknown – an obliterated destination that reappears as the perpetual disruption of an ostensibly secure political order. This structure arises in part from that order's vulnerability to the sway of sheer contingency in which it operates. But more fundamentally, insofar as modernity takes for granted that it comes about through the gesture of expunging prior foundations, it necessarily inscribes within itself the prospect that future attempts of this kind will arise without end. Modernity is as a result forever haunted by further attempts to reimagine the social domain through political, social, economic, financial, sexual, fundamentalist, or ecological revolution. Yet since no such attempt can finally undo historical finitude, none can succeed; as a result, each reveals that history is now endlessly unworked by an unrealizable infinite, by events that in some sense constitute political, social, or historical disasters. Ironically enough, however, modernity can only reassure itself that it enacts perpetual progress by claiming to incorporate these very disruptions into its apparent continuity, as if to craft the fiction of forward movement out of this legacy of interruption.

The absence of any external limit of earthly or political history, any guarantee of its ultimate coherence, has its costs, especially for those who must live within the ensemble that results. The demand for the realization of an absolute justice in history necessarily undercuts all current institutions, showing how they fail to measure up to an infinite demand and thus revealing the ungrounded, disputable, finite element of any historical ensemble. In this regard, modern societies are the heirs of a shift that, according to Reinhart Koselleck, took place in the late eighteenth century, when European political thought breached the limits of a "static mobility" in the notion of progress, which "opened up a future that transcended the hitherto predictable, natural space of time and experience."[14] Henceforth history occurs not within an enduring framework but in a mode that perpetually places that framework into question; history is temporalized, removed from a grounding in nature or the past, breaking through the limits that once contained its mobility within a constant domain, and undergoing irreversible changes as it enters an open future. The unsettled condition that results takes on the cast of a radical historicity, that is, a stunning exposure to history that Heidegger captures a century later in his thematic of Dasein.[15] Such a thematic, however, rather than capturing an ineradicable truth, registers the affective situation arising only under these new conditions, only within a certain modernity. The authority of that thematic since Heidegger indicates that from within modernity, the notion of a radical homelessness seems definitive; all attempts to return to a prior condition, to return to a "static mobility" or an orientation to a determinate transcendence, now appear as efforts to block off an awareness of that historicity, to impose an artificial closure, or ideology, on what remains a constitutively open place. The breach of a secure framework, the undoing of transcendence, now seems irreversible.

Yet that unsurpassable condition, that apparently ineradicable homelessness, is only one side of what also appears as an apparently positive dimension of the subject. If the internal limit is "the obstacle that scotches the possibility of rising out of or above the symbolic," as Copjec continues, then it opens up the possibility of the subject's freedom, for "it is only insofar as [the subject] is held within the internal limit of power, the minimal gap that divides power from itself, that the subject is able to free himself from submission to the forceful pull of his own determined and determinate identity."[16] Ironically, because an empirical history must necessarily fail to account for itself, must forever encounter the absence of a final term through which to capture its overall significance, it cannot reduce the subject to any determinate feature. Obliterating that transcendental term, in short, brings about the internal limit whereby the subject's freedom disrupts or undercuts what it receives from its social and historical situation – but a freedom that in her account also takes on the attributes of an unaccountable, indeed uncanny force.

Copjec's argument here brings to the fore Kant's own insistence on human freedom, an insistence that is perhaps most evident in his account of the subject's relation to the moral law. For Kant, the subject cannot appeal to theological, ethical, or political tradition, for in doing so it evades that law's demands by hiding under the ethical agency of another. Rather than regarding itself as the heir of the ethical reflections of others, the Kantian subject must consider itself entirely accountable for its actions; only if it conceives itself in this way can it abide by an infinite, nonphenomenal demand and show that it is free. In his second critique, Kant illustrates this teaching through a short narrative example:

> [Ask a man] whether he thinks it would be possible for him to overcome his love of life, however great it may be, if his sovereign threatened him with [sudden death on the gallows] unless he made a false deposition against an honourable man whom the ruler wished to destroy under a plausible pretext. Whether he would or not he perhaps will not venture to say; but that it would be possible for him he would certainly admit without hesitation. He judges, therefore, that he can do something because he knows that he ought, and he recognizes that he is free – a fact which, without the moral law, would have remained unknown to him.[17]

Through this little tale, variations on which we will encounter at several junctures in this study, Kant argues that no matter how difficult it may be to do so, one can always comply with the absolute demands of justice at the expense of any number of determinations, such as self-serving (or in Kantian nomenclature, "pathological") motives. But his example ironically makes clear that in his view, such a freedom is unmistakable only when it acts in the form of an absolute violence against every determination, against even the realization of that freedom in a life that will continue or in a project that will endure in the field of mortal endeavour. The subject's freedom, then, constitutes another version of the internal limit of the Real: it forever threatens to disrupt the continuity of a life from within, to annihilate the subject for the purpose of realizing an infinite demand. It thus constitutes a horrific infinity, an undead element forever hostile to those aspects of the subject that comport well within the merely historical domain. It is no wonder that such a freedom has for its ideal what Kant describes as a necessarily empty moral law – a law exactly homologous to the empty telos of modernity.

Elsewhere in the second critique, Kant insists that no subject can attain entire conformity to the infinite demands of the moral law within the bounds of mortality. But this short narrative suggests that perhaps it *can* achieve what one might call an immortal act within the limits of finitude, through the defiant endurance of the punishment of death. Furthermore, the tale suggests that through this gesture of radical freedom, the subject demonstrates that it prefers to reveal the impostures of a fraudulent sovereignty than to conform to an unjust social order. In that case, Kant's theory of moral freedom provides a further instance within what we might discern as a set of homologies between the internal limit of earthly history, political history, and ethical subjectivity: all three domains are now vulnerable to the intrusions of an uncanny infinity, whether in the form of natural disaster, revolution, or ethical self-sacrifice. It is now also clear that in each case, such an infinity appears in the form of a disastrous violence against the status quo, against any apparently stable form of earthly, political, or ethical life. Thus the subject who inherits the new awareness of the dark abyss of time, the prospect of human liberation, and the sense of radical freedom that comes about with historical temporalization exemplifies what I will call *disastrous subjectivity* – a subjectivity disrupted by the logic of the internal limit that henceforth appears in every register of its experience.

Insofar as Kant's little tale also insists on the potential fraudulence of the sovereign's demands, it demonstrates once again that within the terms of modernity there can be no figure who embodies a sovereignty over the field of history, power, or knowledge. That refusal of mastery points us back to a further, pivotal element of Copjec's argument: the subject is free in her account because there can be no final term to sum up the significance of finitude, no *external* limit of the indefinite sequence of terms, claims, or events – that is, in Lacan's formulation, *no metalanguage* that masters the total significance of the symbolic order. The absence of such a metalanguage is already clear in Kant's critical philosophy, which as we have seen can locate no agency that can finally resolve the conflict between the mind's various judgments. Lacan captures that absence at times through reference to Bertrand Russell's mathematical paradox, which holds that one cannot name the contents of a set containing everything without adding one term to the set, the term that names the set itself – creating either an infinitely regressive movement or an awareness that one will never be able to close the set, that it is structurally indeterminate.[18] As we have seen, Lyotard builds on his own rendition of this absence of a metalanguage, a concept he inherits in part from Lacan but even more strongly from his reading of the disjunctions between faculties that Kant insists must remain in place. In these various ways, modern thinkers expose the logical consequences that follow from the emergence of the internal limit, that principle that perpetually undermines from within rationality's attempt to name its own totality.

The resemblance between these various accounts – which point to a central impasse they share but that none can encompass in a definitive formulation – suggests that the deadlocks within Kantian critical philosophy continue to impose themselves even upon recent critical thought, that a Kantian modernity remains continuous with our own. Indeed, the internal limit, far from being a feature of late Enlightenment or Romantic thought alone, is a leading feature of poststructuralist theory – or rather of what Tilottama Rajan has taught us to see instead as post-phenomenological theory.[19] The notion of an ensemble that can never attain totality, that can never name itself or designate its boundaries and is therefore disarranged by an incoherence structurally necessary to its functioning, is formulated in explicit terms across a range of key texts within that strand of theoretical reflection.

We have already encountered two deployments of the internal limit in the theoretical legacy of Lacan and Lyotard. But consider as well the essay "Language to Infinity," where Michel Foucault argues that with "the disappearance of the gods" and the undoing of its capacity to mirror a "real and majestic infinity," language becomes "always excessive and deficient," "fated to extend itself to infinity without ever acquiring the weight that might immobilize it."[20] In this argument, the disappearance of the gods undoes a totalized, self-encompassing infinity – the infinity, proper to the premodern era, that contra Russell manages to name itself and yet remain whole – and produces instead infinity as an indefinitely extended process, an iteration that by definition will never reach its terminus, never become a whole. Or call to mind that passage in "Structure, Sign and Play in the Discourse of the Human Sciences" where Jacques Derrida argues that language "excludes totalization," that its "field of infinite substitutions" operates because "there is something missing from it: a center which arrests and grounds the play of substitutions," the movement of supplementarity.[21] Or ponder the discussion in the first chapter of *Difference and Repetition*, where Gilles Deleuze, rewriting Nietzsche's concept of the eternal return, argues that it functions not through the return of the identical but rather produces "the identity of difference, the identical which belongs to the different."[22] This appropriation of Nietzsche, of course, relies on his attempt to find, in his postulate of the eternal return, an alternative source for infinite significance in the wake of God's death – an infinity that, in Deleuze's rendition, operates through that return's radical non-identity with itself. Each of these arguments links the erasure of an anchoring essence with the infinite play of an ungrounded finitude, figuring the latter as a radically weightless, interminable movement. The infinite ironically becomes a feature of the perpetual, indefinite operation of finitude: the absence of an external term forces this movement to engage in a process of endless iteration, repetition, or supplementation which can find nothing to ground it, revealing the absence of any centre that can arrest its workless labour.

In treating the internal limit with such care, these formulations establish a subtle relation to the Kantian inheritance, for they transform what is for Kant a perpetual difficulty – a conceptual deadlock that arises in the midst of projects oriented to other ends – into a theme worthy of extended treatment in its own right. In effect, they inherit a broadly Kantian impasse but radicalize it, highlighting and foregrounding its features, and thus subtly alter its status in the process.

In doing so, they provide terms with which to trace how the modern disciplines, apparently authorized by their grasp of their objects of knowledge, nevertheless continue to be informed by similar deadlocks. With the loss of a metalanguage by which to name the significance of the social totality, for example, students of the social have little choice but to decipher its meaning from society itself, much as historians attempt to construct the significance of history from a study of history itself, as if to find within various fields of immanent functioning signs of a logic through which to explain them.[23] But since such a task necessarily posits a gap between the surface of social life and its immanent principle, it inscribes within the social another version of the internal limit, locating the significance of the social in relation not to an external telos or a foundational truth but to a truth yet to be determined. Those who embark on such a task attempt to designate a logic for the social that exceeds the merely evident; in doing so, they seek to provide a new metalanguage, to outline a total knowledge of the designated region of the social field, and accordingly carry out the quintessentially ideological attempt to fill in a constitutive gap with a hegemonic term. Any such attempt fails, even within the terms of the disciplines, for any such explanation is necessarily vulnerable to further critique and to the response of further such efforts. The interminable labour of the social, cultural, and historical disciplines thus foregrounds the very gap that also leads to the radical openness of history, making evident the impossibility of capturing in any definitive way what Louis Althusser calls the absent cause of history.[24]

Those who inhabit the disciplines for the most part continue to obey the imperative to fill in the gap, to undo the internal limit, as a matter of fidelity to the inherited imperatives of their respective professions. On this score, one must endorse the interventions of post-phenomenological theory, which is far less confident about the claims of modern knowledge. Here one might do well to extend Charles Shepherdson's broadly Lacanian reading of Foucault, modifying it slightly to accord with the terms in Copjec's argument. In his genealogical works, Foucault argues that modern reason defines itself, for example, over against madness or unreason (a term emphasized in the title of his first major work, *Folie et Déraison*, translated as *Madness and Civilization*), in a gesture that, rather than separating reason from what it negates, stitches them together so that the latter is henceforth inscribed within reason itself.[25] Thus, rather than writing a positive history of psychiatry in that work or endorsing its claims to knowledge, Foucault embarks on a genealogy of this continual reinscription, showing how the discourses of that discipline perpetually retrace the boundaries of unreason.[26] Through this redescription of rationality – and his later genealogies of penal discipline, medical knowledge, and the discourses of sexuality – Foucault attempts to trace the internal limit of disciplinary knowledge, as well as of the secular historical narrative such knowledge uses to justify itself, and thereby to foreground what threatens to undermine the disciplinary authority that such narratives protect. For Foucault, modern rationality takes place through the labour of perpetually reassuring itself that its erasure of any outside to its own sway remains valid, that its reduction of madness, criminality, death, or sexuality to masterable phenomena holds true. The work of genealogy, then, demonstrates that the erasure of the outside – and the production of the internal limit – is an act that must be perpetually reproduced in modern institutions of knowledge.

Such an activity might seem to give the internal limit a "history," but instead of calling for a narrative that assumes the validity and stability of its object, as secular history must do, it takes shape as a *negative* history, a genealogy that hollows out the claims to modernity of the disciplines it treats.

Taken seriously, this critical historiography, in putting the modernizing claims of disciplinary knowledge into question, also undermines the claims of modernity itself. Those committed to the ensemble of modernity might argue, for example, that the developments of the late eighteenth century mark the crossing from a comparatively naive reliance on a metalanguage to a subtler set of premises – to a modernity that does indeed surpass what came before. Yet one who would sign on to such a historiography would in effect take as true what may be no more than a trope, a rhetorical imposition. As Fredric Jameson argues in *A Singular Modernity*, the notion of the "modern" is "a unique kind of rhetorical effect," one quite unlike traditional tropes, for it may "be considered as self-referential, if not performative" and is ultimately "a sign of its own existence, a signifier that indicates itself, and whose form is its very content." In that case, he continues, "what passes for a theory of modernity ... is itself little more than the projection of its own rhetorical structure onto the themes and content in question: the theory of modernity is little more than a projection of the trope itself."[27] The notion of the modern contains no referent; it has no positive content. Rather than recognizing that emptiness, however, theories of modernity attempt to treat it as a historically positive event that determines the shape of virtually everything that follows.[28] In effect, they hope to conceive of a *site* for the emergence of the internal limit of history, as if one might find that internal limit in history's phenomenal field, most likely in the various developments in the late eighteenth century. But that endeavour clearly imposes modernity's own understanding of history *upon* history, hoping to pass off a negative, unlocatable element as a positive one, to provide a necessarily empty trope with a full instantiation, and thereby to ground modernity itself.

A more persuasive account would arise from the sense that the structure of the very claim to modernity closely resembles what Foucault finds in disciplinary knowledge. Much as psychiatry endlessly retraces the form of madness, attempting to know what it nevertheless conceives as an unknowable unreason, so also modernity perpetually retraces the contours of a cancelled transcendence, by that means hoping to supersede a tradition whose negation it nevertheless inscribes forever within its own practices. A certain kind of modernity thus carries out on a more comprehensive level the endeavour already evident in the disciplines, ironically revealing its investments the most clearly when it most fiercely attempts to overwrite the mark of that erasure, the sign of the "no," with an account of what truly and positively grounds the modern. In doing so, it betrays its wish to secure a metalanguage once again – and by this means to carry out in new terms the traditional fidelity it claims to have surpassed. Moreover, insofar as it is caught in the process of *perpetually* obliterating the outside and containing it within its disciplinary gestures, it reveals that the event of modernity takes place only through such endlessly repeated gestures, happening only in the virtual space of that reinscription. Modernity becomes a baffled, reiterated practice, rather than an event, a period, or an overall context that supersedes what went before.

In that case, post-phenomenological thought, by bringing renewed attention to the implications of the internal limit or its analogues, does not carry forward modernity but puts it into question, hinting at a sharply different understanding of the received cultural legacy. One possible approach in this context would be to cultivate what Bruno Latour has called a *nonmodern* approach to Western cultural history, which, in daring to claim that "we have never been modern," puts enormous pressure on the various claims that arise out of modernity's attempts to account for itself.[29] One virtue of this approach is its emphasis on a strong continuity over that entire historical trajectory – one that would take shape in part through the close relation between a tradition informed by classical and Christian thought and a modernity arising in the perpetual cancellation or revision of that thought.

An approach that insists that modernity and tradition are so tightly and mutually implicated might necessarily conclude that modernity as it arises in the West can take its characteristic form only because it emerges from within the premises of the religious and cultural traditions that precede it, only because it inherits a set of deep-structural assumptions it attempts to revise. Gil Anidjar, in a bracing argument, proposes that modern secularism is another phase of Western religion – that it arises, and obtains, only where that religion was once ascendant.[30] In his view, secular modernity is only a modulation of what preceded it. If through its articulation of the internal limit modernity perpetually retraces its negation of transcendence, as I argued above, his work would encourage us to maintain that it does so with reference to a primarily Christian transcendence, setting itself apart as a specifically anti/Christian ensemble, and thereby constitutes another phase in what seems to be a long, nonmodern continuity. Here modernity's incompletion – its never achieving itself as an event – would be found in its imbrication with what it attempts to erase, its interweaving with a tradition it must perpetually invoke and thus maintain. In the logic of the internal limit, then, by which modernity retains the mark of what it erases, it retains as well the tradition it pretends to overcome, sustaining the very continuity it claims to break.

One cannot respond to this situation by proposing that the West return to tradition. The arrival of geological knowledge, for example, permanently bars the way towards a simple revival of prior theological reassurances. The attempt to respond to modernity through a wide-ranging repudiation of its premises and terms from the perspective of what preceded it cannot hold.[31] Yet the attempt to secure modernity, to imagine that one can cover over the Real with an instituted reality, is equally false. The continuity of the West may thus hold together only through the encounter of these mutually failed options, circling around what emerges both as the necessity and impossibility of transcendence. In that case, as Jean-Luc Nancy suggests, the tradition may take shape through the mutual imbrication of a totalizing closure and what he calls dis-enclosure (*déclosion*), that is, through a certain division within transcendence apparent across its entire history, so that the radically undetermined horizon I emphasize throughout this book may arise from within monotheism itself. In this approach, Nancy suggests as he invokes Kant, faith "is the act of the reason that relates, itself, to that which, in it, passes *it* infinitely: faith stands precisely at the point of an altogether consequent atheism." Accordingly, "the atheism that … is inherent in the [Western] mode of knowing and existing, is itself Christianity realized."[32] The opposition of the pre-modern and the modern, of the religious and the secular, may speak of a difficulty that holds all across the history of the West; perhaps one does best today to recognize in the internal limit – in the Real – the complex site of that impasse.

If one approaches the initial articulation of the internal limit within this historiography, as I propose to do in this study, then one must perforce depart from certain treatments of that moment within the study of British Romantic literature, the field to which this book belongs. For one thing, it challenges the narrative of secularization whereby M.H. Abrams and others authorized the return of serious study of Romanticism in the modern academy midway through the last century.[33] A critical practice attuned to the emergence of the internal limit attends instead to a genealogy of the nonsecular, a counterpart of the nonmodern, by considering how the inscription of the apparently secular reveals its constitutive deadlocks and thus its necessary failure. Accordingly, this book participates in the current attempt to propose an alternative to the narrative of secularization, though it does so not by treating that narrative at length in its own right but by considering it as an aspect of the more capacious problematic of modernity itself.

Nor can this critical enterprise embark on yet another historicist reading of Romantic discourse, to reiterate once again the premise that it is best understood in relation to the various contexts that inform its emergence and articulation. Such a premise is itself a product of that period – an insight that even the "new historicism," hegemonic in the field for several decades, reached in James K. Chandler's influential work, *England in 1819*.[34] If adhering to such historicism reiterates an aspect of Romanticism, reproducing Romanticism within the critical enterprise supposedly attempting to interpret it, then one must place historicism itself under interrogation.[35] As my discussion above suggests, Romanticism *already* thematizes concerns more fundamental than those raised by historicism as such, for Romantic texts perpetually suggest that literature cannot evade the trial of suffering a radical disjunction between its contextual finitude and the claim of what exceeds it.[36] Considered in such a light, historicism is only one attempt to encompass the consequences of this logically prior impasse, to narrate and thus to manage an ungrounded condition.

A crucial sign of the limits of historicism in capturing the logic at play in the transition into modernity is visible in the fact that even the field of referential history, most especially that privileged referent, the series of events we have come to call the French Revolution, far from being primarily the trigger for discursive elaborations or the ineradicable criterion for their significance, works out on its own terrain the implications of developments logically prior to it. Kant's second critique and Mary Wollstonecraft's *Mary: A Fiction*, two works discussed in chapter 1, both appear in 1788, a year before the fall of the Bastille, yet both elaborate on conceptual impasses that inform the unfolding of the Revolution as well. Early in his brilliantly nonreductive work, *Romantic Moods*, Thomas Pfau writes in a Heideggerian vein that insofar as literature evokes a period's preconscious but still quasi-cognitive "mood" – that is, what must remain anterior to any mode of representation or knowledge as such – it "does not simply imagine some dreamworld but aims to recover a knowledge occluded by the specious, indeed irrational, fixity and coherence of so-called actual history."[37] Accordingly, the conjunction just mentioned, in which literary and philosophical formulations arise alongside historical projects that similarly work out a logically prior problematic, suggests that all three arenas of endeavour – literature, philosophy, *and history* – evoke what this book will consider not so much a mood but a structural impasse that *precedes* them, a characteristically modern impasse that can never find definitive or proper formulation *even within history*. It follows that to privilege referential history above all, as new historicism did, is to give history too great an explanatory force – and ultimately to evade a far more difficult, if necessary, interpretive task.

But it does not follow that it is sufficient to shift one's ground, with Pfau, from historicism to historicity, as if to place oneself within the Heideggerian problematic he so ably articulates, for if as he suggests this terrain emerges in the late eighteenth century, it does so in tandem with the temporalization described by Koselleck – and thus precisely through the breaching of the framework early modern Europe took for granted, that is, through the dismantling of an external boundary for the play of history.[38] While attention to historicity comes much closer to the signal difficulty, nearly designating the emergence of the Real, it too remains faithful to a certain modernity, failing to attend to the emergence of historicity as a problem in its own right. One might say, then, to extend suggestions I made above, that the task is to carry out what I might cautiously designate as a nonhistoricist (rather than anti-historicist) investigation of the premises embedded in modern, secular history – one that relies on neither historicism nor historicity but rather interrogates their premises.

The approach I have outlined so far clearly owes much to the practices of post-phenomenological theory, whose legacy in Lacan and Lyotard for this book is especially strong. But one cannot simply place this book within a received notion of the deconstructive or Lacanian study of Romanticism. In contrast to accounts that decipher Romanticism through the lens of a particular approach, often anchoring their readings through the authority of that approach, this study does not locate Romanticism in relation to theory (or vice versa) but locates both in relation to what each attempts to articulate, that unassimilable mark of cancellation. Such a perspective, I should emphasize, does not cast either into shadow; it does not, for example, suggest that this strand of theory fails in some crucial dimension. On the contrary, it insists that, insofar as it explicitly thematizes the internal limit across its major works, it already presents itself not as an authoritative articulation but as a mode of attending to the import of a gesture that, taking place in a moment logically prior to theory, inaugurates a problematic that theory itself cannot contain. By the same token, in this study both Kantian and Romantic texts, far from bodying forth a range of authoritative achievements, exemplify the attempt to sort out the implications of that gesture for what appears in a range of disastrous subjectivities. In short, this study conceives both Romanticism and theory in relation to a problematic that precedes and exceeds them both.

In taking up the study of this field in which are arrayed a range of disastrous subjectivities, this book addresses in its own way a further theme now becoming ever more central to the study of Romanticism. The relatively recent work of Anne-Lise François, Jacques Khalip, Anahid Nersessian, and others emphasizes an evacuated or anonymous subject, one that inhabits, at best, a limited utopia.[39] At first glance, the notion of a subjectivity haunted by its infinity might seem to take up precisely the opposite thematic, to enlarge the subject beyond all possible bounds. But precisely because such infinity so radically exceeds what the subject can endure, constituting something alien to it that nevertheless inhabits it to its cost, this book outlines the situation out of which the attenuated subject emerges. Much as Rei Terada writes that if she saw a "real subject" coming, she "would run away," so too do most of the protagonists in the works I explore here: again and again the costs of infinity invite them to explore the possibilities of subjective destitution, to take refuge in a deliberately cultivated finitude.[40] In effect, this book accentuates the sequence that leads to the cultivation of a minimal state, tracing the movement – or the act – whereby the subject, having endured something that endangers its apparent integrity, embraces the prospect of dispossession. In taking up still another broadly Lacanian theme, the ethical stakes of subjective destitution, this study ponders whether the intrusions of the internal limit, too much for the subject to bear, may lead the subject beyond itself into a further phase, into a turn away from transcendence and its obliteration both, a turn towards the radical worklessness of finitude.

A singularly telling site to begin an exploration of this problematic within the precincts of British Romanticism is Mary Wollstonecraft's early novel *Mary: A Fiction* (1788), especially its central episode in which the protagonist insists that the captain of her vessel pause to save strangers from a shipwreck on the high seas. As I argue in chapter 1, the volatile conjunction of themes in this episode – the commitment to saving others, the overtones of the biblical flood in the tempest that caused the shipwreck, the sublime transport the protagonist enjoys after the event, coupled with her distant apprehension of an eventual apocalypse that, through a similarly divine violence, will liberate humanity from the ruined world in which she finds herself after arriving in London – outlines the central deadlocks also evoked in the work of Kant, who similarly juxtaposes a concern with ethical violence, the sublime, and the teleology of history. The scene of shipwreck, however, makes clear that Kant and Wollstonecraft both need catastrophe to call forth the full capacities of the subject, implicating them in a certain Sadean violence as they impose nearly impossible conditions on their ethical protagonists. Yet this novel complicates the Kantian account in several ways. Because it must derive its protagonist's ethical ambition from the circumstances of her life, it must in effect trace its emergence within her development as a finite, pathological human being; in doing so, it ultimately depicts Mary's ethics in pathological terms as well – as the emergence of an erotics of disaster. Yet it confounds the genre in which it is written as well, coming to an end without narrative resolution, instead holding open the protagonist's yearning for an immortal destination. It thus captures within and against narrative form a counterpart of the mathematical sublime, exposing the ethical stakes of conventional narrative expectation for marriage and erotic resolution. As a result, it complicates Kant while carrying out an autocritique of the form of the novel itself, showing how the novel may become a form of critique, an exploration of the limits of mind within the limits of novelistic reason.

The second chapter takes up the pursuit of similar themes in slightly later instances of British radical writing: William Godwin's philosophical treatise, *Enquiry Concerning Political Justice* (1793), and his novels *Caleb Williams* (1794) and *St Leon* (1799). On an initial level, both of these tales inscribe the fantasy that one might gain an insight into the secret of the social sphere, whether through Caleb's discerning the secret of his master, Falkland, or St Leon's gaining access to the philosopher's stone by which he can confer on himself indefinitely prolonged life and coin unlimited quantities of gold. Such fantasies, however, eventually implode, demonstrating either that the claim to mastery over the secret of Falkland leads to a radically dehumanizing contest between Caleb and his master, a contest for ascendancy that Caleb can exit only by renouncing altogether, or that its realization in St Leon's expenditure in Hungary brings about a monetary inflation that undercuts his seemingly benevolent designs. The attempt to realize the infinite is thus not only impossible but, as we have seen, must also be prohibited. This striking development, especially clear in the counterfactual fiction of *St Leon*, leads to a remarkably cogent articulation of the Real; capturing not simply a future unrealized in actual history, a future towards which a politically transformative ethos orients itself, but an inherently impossible one, the book radicalizes that ethos to foreground the exclusions on which a modern history must be based, in effect inscribing in its very form the logic of the internal limit. Yet by allowing readers access to the fantasy of its protagonist, *St Leon* also shows that an orientation to the impossible remains present within that modernity, suggesting that what it formally repudiates it may harbour in another guise.

The explorations of prose fiction in this book's first two chapters foreground how the internal limit, in bringing an uncanny, infinite demand into the domain of apparently finite narrative, forces such narrative to reveal that its own drive to closure is an imposture. Under the pressure of the infinite, narrative can attain a minimal degree of coherence only by incorporating into its form some version of the impossible – of what must remain unattained, outstanding, or prohibited. Although various critics have suggested that Kant's second critique negates the significance of narrative for the ethical life, in fact the little tale of confronting the sovereign maps out an alternative kind of story, creating the template for an unsuspected, seldom noticed genre – the tale of the impossible.[41] Rather than mapping out the coordinates of the realist novel, the scenarios I explore in this book point to the coordinates of a subjectivity caught between finite realization and the infinite. The scenarios on display in each chapter constitute literary mappings of modernity's constitutive deadlock, outlining a variety of forms whereby narrative may encode the shape of its involuntary interruption.

The exigencies that force such literary experimentation suggest that these texts also provide new insights into fundamental conceptual impasses. As the novels mentioned so far reveal, much as the disciplines revolve around the gap between the social and itself, narrative is inevitably undercut by the gap between the questions it attempts to deploy and what it can articulate. In readings of what she calls *autonarration*, especially as written by Godwin, Wollstonecraft, and others in their circle, Rajan emphasizes how autonarration at once evokes and displaces the details of an actual life, making it possible implicitly to open up a space between the questions asked by a life and what it empirically enacts, to bring into view what neither a purely referential nor a purely fictional practice could make legible. This form is a specific instance of a structure she traces elsewhere and that one might describe as the *deliberate* differend, the intentionally articulated disjunction between narrative scenarios.[42] This intentional deployment of mutually implicated yet irreconcilable narrations – in a tactic visible in all three of the Romantic narratives mentioned so far – constitutes a fictional counterpart of the Kantian critical philosophy, which similarly juxtaposes analyses of interrelated, though ultimately incongruent, faculties. If these novels explore genres of the impossible, Kant experiments with a philosophy of the impossible, a mode of thought that, however rigorous, can never attain conceptual closure. All such practices thus point to their knowledge that modern narrative and conceptual analyses attempt to capture what they cannot fully articulate and that they must as a result encode a gap intrinsic to their mode of articulation. To the extent that these tales are constructed to make that gap visible, to foreground what is structurally equivalent to the Real, one may regard them as self-conscious theorizations of the internal limit in literary form.[43]

A much less knowing, but perhaps as a result even more symptomatic, rendition of the Real emerges elsewhere, especially in texts whose narrative momentum is sharply interrupted, indeed invaded, by the traumatic violence of the infinite. In the third chapter, this book shifts its focus from ethical to aesthetic violence, attending at length to the implications of William Wordsworth's hyper-canonic articulation of his crossing of the Alps in *The Prelude* (1805). Initially arising within the context of the poet's meditations on the cancellation of the rainbow covenant, which encode in his terms the consequences of late eighteenth-century treatments of the history of the earth, this episode collapses creation and destruction into the same infinitely extended material process, into a *disastrous transcendence* identical to the operations of nature itself. Moreover, in the famous apostrophe to the imagination through which the poet claims to recover from his encounter with that inhuman process, he encodes a subjective instance of a similar disaster – a desire for the infinite that itself takes on the attributes of infinity, one that brings the inundating, undead force of a tireless desire into the subject. Rather than enabling the poet to recover from this encounter, this inscription of an internal infinity traumatizes him, makes him ill at ease within what he soon depicts as the needlessly vast house that is his subjectivity, and eventually inspires him to abandon this theme altogether as he continues the poem. Far from exemplifying what others have often regarded as the egotistical sublime, the episode reveals instead an uncanny, traumatizing sublime – an exact instance of the radically unsettling, disastrously violent internal limit. In contrast to *Mary: A Fiction*, which explicitly thematizes how an infinite desire broaches the limits of literary form, *The Prelude* attempts in its final episode, the ascent of Snowdon, to reinscribe the traumatic infinite in a sublimity that affirms and authorizes the poet's calling. The poem thus draws attention to a wound it wishes to hide, an intrusion of the Real it wishes to reinterpret in a positive vein. As a result, Wordsworth's treatment of this episode draws attention to the ethical question of how and whether to affirm the invasion of an infinite violence. How should one address that traumatic force – if indeed one can do so coherently at all?

Addressing this very question over the course of several poems, from "Darkness" through *Cain* and beyond, Lord Byron incorporates the awareness of deep time and of solar death into his conception of the modern subject. In his first metaphysical poetic drama, *Manfred*, he clears the ground for his ethical reflections, staging a protagonist who, suffering under the sign of a ruined star, seeks at first to find oblivion or forgiveness but soon learns that nothing can relieve him of his knowledge of disaster. As the book argues in its fourth chapter, Byron dares to translate the general condition of modernity – the sense that natural disaster reigns throughout the history of the stars and the earth and that no external agent can guarantee the significance of human action – into a condition haunting his protagonist, but thereby makes it into *the* condition to which he must forge his own ethical response. In its central movement, the play explores how Manfred, repudiating any appeal to higher powers, in his final gesture passes judgment on himself in an infinite act – what it depicts paradoxically as an immortal act realized in his very death. In doing so, *Manfred* responds to the Real that obtains in the preconditions of the modern subject with what we might call, following Alenka Zupančič's Lacanian reading of Kant, an ethics of the Real.[44] In the final stanzas of his next major poem, *Childe Harold's Pilgrimage*, canto 4, Byron maps out a more capacious stance, swimming on a sea that has the power to drown any human endeavour, trusting to its disastrous billows and identifying with the bubbles that arise from the drowning, thereby turning his groundless state into the basis of a new poetic stance. Over the course of several poems, then, from "Darkness" through *Don Juan*, he attempts to construct a mode of writing befitting his sense of modernity, a poetics of the Real.

While many might regard Percy Bysshe Shelley's final, unfinished masterwork, "The Triumph of Life," as the ne plus ultra of any Romantic exploration of the conditions of finitude, indeed as a summation of the period's most radical insights, I explore how that poem maps out instead the failure of any ethical stance to provide a sufficient *response* to that finitude in chapter 5. Although it incorporates into that triumph themes that often appear in later theoretical formulations – the radical operation of the death drive, the self-subversions of figuration, the universe of materialist figuration (in a mode that, inherited from Lucretius, anticipates later chaos theory), an unauthorized and accidental vitality, a necessary contingency (as if to anticipate the insights of speculative realism), and the perpetual ascendancy across political, religious, and literary history of the impostures of power – it does so not to reduce the domain of human experience to that triumph but to raise with all the greater urgency the question as to how the ethical subject might encompass this scene of devastation in an ultimate orientation to a universal justice. Because Shelley inherits a long-standing tradition of atomistic theism, which weds a sense of the material contingency of life with fidelity to an impersonal, ethical final cause, his ethical orientation is not disrupted by the insights he inherits from Romantic-era astronomy or geology; as a result, he adheres to a stance that does not necessarily conceive of the ethical subject as a subject of disaster, setting him apart from the likes of Wordsworth or Byron. The fact that he retains his fidelity to the final cause is writ large across the poem, evident in passages which invoke, for example, the prospect that one might, in the mode of Lucretius, suspend one's fear of death and thus escape the turbulence of Life's chariot or, with Dante, pursue a higher love whose transcendent music one can scarcely hear behind the noise of that turbulent imposition. Yet in its most telling moves, the poem suggests that such an ethical orientation must eventually collapse. For one thing, the poem indicates that all finite efforts to realize the good through the agency of political action only iterate once again a logic of imposition evident in Life's pageant. But it also suggests that infinite gestures must fail as well, for they cannot alter the logic that operates in finitude itself. In this poem, those who attempt to enact a version of the good in history, to bring about transformation through a radically nonviolent act, exemplify what one might call the divine passivity of the sacred few – those who, like Socrates or Christ, refuse Life's triumph and return to their transcendental origins – but as a result only leave Life to triumph further over the domain of finitude. For Shelley, the ethical subject is left without recourse in the radical failure of every ethical option whatsoever – and so has no choice but to endure a severe ethical destitution, to tarry indefinitely within the space of an ethical disaster.

These various depictions of ethical and aesthetic violence, taken together, foreground a problem that the relatively abstract terms of Kantian discourse cannot easily register: the fact that under the conditions of a certain modernity human beings must remain vulnerable to something they find unbearable, too vast and harrowing to endure. It turns out that the obliteration of transcendence, in crossing out a telos or a metalanguage in which to encompass all its terms, also cracks open the notion of the whole – and thereby exposes human beings to the limitless, the boundless, the infinite.[45] That shift to infinity in some ways imposes on human beings a *greater* violence than before, a force even more difficult to endure. Yet those who operate on the premises of modernity cannot help but consider the notion of a whole under the sway of a divine power or a human sovereign as marking an external limit on what can be thought and enacted, on human liberation itself, creating the perfect conditions for the endurance of dogma and of oppression. This preference for an unbounded history is not arbitrary or naive: it is the structural counterpart of a preference for the realization of a messianic promise in history, that is, a longing that adheres too closely to the promises encoded in Western religious traditions. Modernity's impasses ironically arise out of the longing to realize the hopes of the tradition it apparently repudiates: one cannot simply attempt to adjudicate in favour of one over the other, since they are intimately, perhaps constitutively, intertwined. Yet the result of that contradiction is devastating. Modernity's preference for both fulfilment and a boundless history is contradictory, but the demand that the end emerge from within time disallows any externally imposed terminus, any apocalyptic telos. While the exposure to ethical violence is in part unbearable, then, it also seems unavoidable, for it is a structural consequence of modernity's repudiation of closure.

The fact that such an infinite violence turns out to demand too much of those who endure the conditions of modernity highlights the possibility that infinity, far from being an attribute of nature or indeed of thought, is a radical fiction, a fierce abstraction whose status may be just as disputable as any totality. When in his analytic of the mathematical sublime Kant argues that one may overleap the pain of imagination's failure by seizing on the mind's capacity to grasp the Idea of infinity, he assumes that infinity can attain the integrity of such an Idea. But since infinity can never become a totality, it arguably exceeds anything that one can name or comprehend, even in thought.[46] It may thus exist only in the fiction that one can think it, surviving in as fiercely counterfactual a zone as the philosopher's stone or Manfred's ability to bring about his death through sheer force of thought. Of course, in Kantian terms, that fiction can have no positive form, no visible existence. But these analogues in Romantic literature suggest that it may constitute an entity even more scandalous than Kant supposes, for it may, like the Real, exist only as the name for what destabilizes all names, as the thought of what eludes thought. The term through which Kant hopes to resolve the impasses of the sublime may only accentuate them, revealing what must remain a perpetual scandal for every discourse and practice of modernity. Yet it is equally clear that modernity requires such a figure to name its objection to closure.

Modernity's impasse in this regard, as in so many others, arises only because it forgets that traditional society contests the fictions of closure in another way. That society, as I argue in *Monstrous Society*, knows that the structure of differentiation that composes it is a construction, not the form of reality itself, for through its inversion rituals it enacts a wholesale mockery of its fictions, demonstrating that the collective operates in a domain prior to its constructions – just as it judges the performance of its institutions according to norms that operate beyond them.[47] Traditional society thus accepts its origin and end only provisionally, for it retains the capacity to contest differentiation with *communitas*, power with counterpower. These rituals of inversion symbolically reverse norms; they bring into history its outside, marking an ineradicable knowledge that historical forms are not ontologically binding. Modernity, however, repudiates such symbolic inversion and seeks literal fulfilment, an actual arrival of the promise; it attempts to bring counterpower into the operations of power itself through the forms of modern democratic contestation, hoping to transform society incrementally into a more direct realization of those higher norms. From the perspective of this hope, it cannot understand the logic of symbolic inversion, misreading it as a stratagem whereby power merely reaffirms itself. In its view, only revolution, not symbolic inversion, will do. As a result, it necessarily interprets every instance of reversibility – the demands of counterpower, the alterity of the dead – merely as a feature within the literal ensemble of the state and its history, forcing counterpower to appear henceforth as an obliterated counterpart, a monstrous other. In the logic of the internal limit outlined in the present book, one can trace the exactly contemporary gesture whereby such a modernity also deletes the covenant which recognizes the alterity of the divine – and thus forces it to appear as an obliterated, disastrous transcendence, a horrific infinity, an unbearable ethical violence. The alterity that modernity attempts to expunge returns, forcing modernity to discover that it will henceforth be haunted by the Real.

This delimitation of Western modernity can only reinforce the necessity of pursuing a nonmodern approach to its characteristic discourses. Attending to the complexity of the cultural arrangements that preceded modernity can indeed make visible a certain arbitrariness in its terms. Such an enterprise finds its counterpart in tracing the shape of the cultural formation that comes *after* modernity – that of our own time – in which modernity's fictions begin to appear especially suspect. In its coda, this book takes up the question of how our contemporary sense of catastrophe – the imminent arrival of severe and irreversible climate change, as well as of the planet's sixth massive extinction – undermines modernity's rendition of disaster. As it turns out, climate change melts the glaciers that for Shelley once inspired a sublime apprehension in the environs of Mont Blanc; the disappearance of such glaciers, in dissolving an aspect of the landscape that in Kant's account is necessary for triggering the mind's encounter with its own sublimity, suggests that climate change in some sense eradicates the aesthetics that Shelley and Kant share, the form of disastrous subjectivity encoded in a response to the Alpine landscape. In that case, one must conclude that the use of geological knowledge for the sake of a literal abundance provided by the harvesting of fossil fuels, for objective, economic purposes – and the concomitant colonization of deep time – has made possible a nearly boundless increase in wealth, population, and the consequent human imprint on the biosphere. This process has by now eclipsed what this book traces: the disruptive intrusions of a traumatic infinity into the experience of the ethical and aesthetic subject.

Such a development suggests that modernity's wish to surpass what came before is founded on an illusion, that the very attempt to suspend any external limit to the sway of modern economic systems has only led to the prospect of eradicating the preconditions for human flourishing altogether. But this development reveals as well that under these new conditions no divinity will abide by that ancient covenant. Both tradition and modernity, both the covenant and the post-covenantal condition, are in tatters; the long continuity of which they were a part is now fading away. We endure in a state of more radical impoverishment than anything Shelley could envision: the subject now confronts a power of destruction so great that it threatens to bring even ethical destitution to an end.

1 Catastrophic Benevolence, Ruinous Immortality

Wollstonecraft's Shipwreck

Midway through Mary Wollstonecraft's short novel, *Mary: A Fiction*, the eponymous protagonist, having buried her friend Ann in Lisbon, returns to England on board a ship. During the crossing, she participates in the rescue of passengers on another small vessel from shipwreck. Among those saved is one poor and fainting woman, whom Mary comforts, soothes, and puts to rest. Having witnessed the transports of the saved and inspired by a sailor's comment "that he believed the world was going to be at an end," she gazes over the restless sea, sings a passage to herself from one of Handel's "sublime compositions" – "The Lord God Omnipotent reigned, and would reign for ever, and ever" – and consoles herself with the thought that God "would bind up the broken-hearted, and receive those who [come] out of great tribulation." Retreating to her cabin, she writes in her journal of the "great day of judgment," contemplating the contrast between "the pleasures of life, which are but for a season" and the joys of immortality, which lie "in futurity, in the deep shades o'er which darkness hangs." "Surely any thing like happiness is madness!" she exclaims, as she longs for the moment when "the glad day of an eternal dawn [will] break[]."[1]

Although this episode may seem to be an arbitrary addition to the novel, insofar as it is not woven into any broader narrative development, it captures the novel's ethical scenarios perfectly. Throughout the tale, Mary is engaged in a mode of perpetual rescue as she attempts to protect her mother from the violence of her father, to nurse her romantic friend Ann in her illness, to befriend the dying Henry, and to assist those poor, dirty, or diseased families she encounters. Furthermore, she often meditates on the impossibility of earthly happiness and sets her sights on infinity, immortality, and futurity. These habits of mind are reinforced almost immediately in the novel; after she arrives in London as a "forlorn wanderer" and witnesses "vulgarity, dirt, and vice" on the streets near the Thames, she "mourn[s] for a world in ruins," as if all human affairs transpire within a vast scene of disaster (54).

This volatile array of juxtaposed elements is expanded further if we take into account the episode from Wollstonecraft's life on which the shipwreck passage is based. In that episode, the captain of the vessel initially decided not to pause to rescue the victims of the wreck of a nearby ship, concerned that "he had provisions enough for himself, his crew and passengers, but no more." Wollstonecraft, however, insisted that they rescue those cast into the sea, at first in vain, and succeeded only when she "threatened the captain with a full account when they arrived home."[2] Her wish to save others, in short, required a good deal of assertion on her part and some sacrifice of her own comforts. While she did not choose to incorporate these details into this passage, such a disposition is clearly evident throughout the novel's depiction of Mary's acts, which consistently place the good of others above her own.

Precisely because it captures the novel's overall scenario so well, even where it does not mention its full range of concerns, this episode confronts us with interpretive difficulties we might overlook elsewhere, forcing us to consider the relation between elements not usually brought together. The wish to serve others might well suspend self-interest, but why should it necessarily invoke the prospect of immortality? How can the shipwreck at once inspire the wish to act with benevolence *and* sublime transport at the thought of the deluge? Moreover, why should such thoughts inspire the protagonist shortly afterwards to regard life as a scene of ruins, as a kind of indefinitely expanded shipwreck? This circulation of ethical, aesthetic, and theological responses around an expansive scene of disaster is quite distinctive and raises many questions about the orientation of this episode and the novel as a whole.

An initial glance at these questions hints that the juxtaposition of acting against self-interest with an eye towards immortality, and in relation to a world in ruins, operates according to a scenario in which one might partially realize a higher destination through deeds committed within this life – in acts that defy ordinary forms of self-regard and that can accordingly relieve forms of suffering that others may overlook. Thus despite its marginal status within Wollstonecraft's career and within Romanticism overall, this novel explores a range of concerns closely akin to those that emerge in Kantian ethical theory and to the broader political possibilities emerging in the late eighteenth century. Indeed, because it was published so early – in 1788, the same year in which Kant's second critique appeared – it can reveal what transpires when a certain religiously inspired ethical disposition begins to share the insistent demands of the late Enlightenment, when the longing for the realization of justice cuts more deeply into the terrain of an actual history.

These parallels bear as well on how each version of ethical reflection takes a remarkably explicit form in the central, telling episodes in each text: the shipwreck passage and the Kantian example regarding the subject's capacity to defy the unjust sovereign. Both instances suggest that thought may at times reveal its contours best in the mini-genre of the exemplary episode focused on an ethical decision – that is, the tale of the impossible. The characteristic elements of that mini-genre include a situation with high stakes, the confrontation with a force of great injustice, a decision to act potentially against one's own interests on behalf of others, an orientation to infinity, immortality, or a vast conception of the good, and the evocation, on some level, of a disastrous violence against the current society, the natural order, or the human species itself. Each episode of this kind puts on display a certain disastrous subjectivity, an orientation to a violence capable at last of sweeping away every obstacle to the perfect realization of the infinite.

In several instances that appear in British Romantic writing, this type of episode is embedded in a broader fictional narrative and thus ramifies through the much wider range of concerns and contexts that such a narrative necessarily evokes. Such is the case with *Mary: A Fiction*, where the concerns of the shipwreck episode are writ large throughout the novel as a whole. By virtue of that fact, however, the novel complicates and reframes the core questions at stake in the episode itself. Insofar as it treats this episode as a symptomatic instance within a much broader pattern of action, the novel suggests that one might trace Mary's capacity to act so aggressively for the sake of others back to a particular set of circumstances, to the childhood, youth, and early adulthood that shaped her. The novel's focus on the formation of her character interprets her broadly Kantian ethics within the terms of an affective and erotic disposition specific to the protagonist herself. Anticipating the Lacanian argument that the capacity for Kantian ethical action arises from what Kant would regard as "pathological" elements, it suggests that the ethical life is inherently bound up with the life of emotions and interests – with affect, desire, pleasure, and hope, not to mention loss, fear, and aggression – and that those emotions and interests bear an implicitly ethical charge as well.

While Wollstonecraft's deployment of her protagonist in these terms broaches themes that she will explore four years later in *A Vindication of the Rights of Woman*, gesturing towards a feminist critique of Mary's situation, neither the novel nor *Vindication* rely on a progressive view of history, insisting instead that the ethical life can find satisfaction only in a domain beyond mortality. The scene of shipwreck remains a mark of what must remain outstanding, a justice that may never be realized on the stage of history. Accordingly, the feminist elements of this tale give way to its yearning for a satisfaction beyond the achievements available within history, a satisfaction it figures in religious terms. Yet by marking this yearning through the shipwreck episode and its analogues elsewhere in the text – and by articulating its religious orientation within the framework of a novel – this text proposes its own version of the internal limit within a fictional counterpart of Kantian critique, extending and complicating the tale of the impossible.

One may best begin to decipher the key cluster of concerns evident in the shipwreck episode by attending to the theme of immortality that anchors Wollstonecraft's thought over several years, extending from *Mary: A Fiction* (1788) and *A Vindication of the Rights of Men* (1790) to *A Vindication of the Rights of Woman* (1792). In the view to which Wollstonecraft adheres over this period, anyone who acts on her desire soon discovers that satisfaction is not available in this life, learns that her true destination must lie beyond sense experience in the domain of immortality, and by that means liberates herself from a life of mere sensual or emotional indulgence. In this way, she can define herself through her capacities of mind or spirit and thus as a rational and virtuous being as well.[3] On the basis of this theory, Wollstonecraft attacks a wide range of political beliefs and social practices, such as the confinement of individuals in relations of sexual or economic convenience, for example, and the indulgence of self-interest at the expense of others, as in *Mary*; the prejudicial sentimentality of Edmund Burke, as in the first *Vindication*; and the absence of independent thought in monarchs or the clergy, the self-indulgence of soldiers or women of fashion, the widespread treatment of women as mere instruments of pleasure, and the dubious consequences for them of acceding to such a treatment, as in the second *Vindication*. This use of immortality to radical ends borrows from the strategies of rationalist Dissent, particularly from its attacks on the conformism implicit in adhering to the established church, extending its tone into new terrain. What results is a fairly sharp and wide-ranging critique of late eighteenth-century culture from a perspective at once theological, ethical, revolutionary, and feminist.

These positions may well be familiar to most readers of Wollstonecraft's work over these years. But it is worth pausing over her account, for in a fairly distinctive gesture, she derives a subject's orientation to immortality from the failure of any human practice to satisfy one's inherent demands. One who lives fully and attentively, she argues, must inevitably posit a destination beyond the world of earthly satisfactions.

"The passions are necessary auxiliaries of reason," she writes; "a present impulse pushes us forward, and when we discover that the game did not deserve the chace, we find that we have gone over much ground, and not only gained many new ideas, but a habit of thinking." This sequence, she continues, is "one of the strongest arguments for the natural immortality of the soul," for insofar as "thought" is the "faint type of an immaterial energy," the process that develops such thought orients us to the immaterial or immortal as well.[4] Immortality designates not simply the status of the human soul but also a key property of the aspiring subject. For if, as she writes, "life yields not the felicity which can satisfy an immortal soul," then one perpetually experiences the gap between expectation and satisfaction, enduring in a mode of great tension.[5] This faith in a satisfaction elsewhere can only bear fruit if one loves the resulting virtue "as in itself sublime and excellent, and not for the advantages it procures or the evils it averts" – not for any forms of happiness it may bring about in earthly realms.[6] Such an orientation towards a non-empirical destination ultimately defines the subject in terms other than those provided by a lived social reality, creating a further tension between independent judgment and political context – for example, between Wollstonecraft herself and the Britain in which she writes. Yet as the ultimate aim of expectation, immortality also salvages an ultimate, if deferred, coherence for the subject, promising eventually to resolve the tension implicit in that gap. Thus Wollstonecraft's account of immortality arises within a distinctive theory of the subject, one that resonates with the themes of desire, temporality, virtue, and transcendence.

This dimension of her account already begins to edge across into the terrain of the similarly resonant mode of speculation in Kant, who explores the conjunction of a rationalist religion with a transcendental notion of the subject, an aesthetics of the sublime, and a sharp rendition of ethics. The elements brought together in the novel are conjoined as well in Kant's rigorous speculations, suggesting that certain Kantian arguments may unpack Wollstonecraft's condensed formulations or that Wollstonecraft's literary renditions of certain themes may expose the unspoken implications of Kant's stance. The affinities between them, in short, may illuminate the work of both.

These common elements, however, become much more telling if we examine them not only for the purpose of mutual elucidation but also to uncover a stance they largely share but nowhere state outright. Here again, the notion of immortality must loom large. The import of that notion, I would suggest, is only partly exhausted in any careful overview of the conjunction between rationalist theology, an aesthetics of the sublime, and ethics. In the shipwreck scene, several elements appear side by side, but what is more surprising, they do so in response to an episode of potential disaster. The anomalous element in this picture, it might seem, is the shipwreck itself, this singular image of a "world in ruins." Yet the fact that these particular elements might assemble themselves at this scene suggests that the shipwreck, far from being anomalous, is the feature they most strongly share, the defining element of the entire ensemble.

On one level, discerning the presence of that element may not be all that newsworthy. After all, one who posits the immortality of the soul – as do both Wollstonecraft and Kant – implicitly defines the subject over against bodily death and thus by implication locates an individual version of ruin, or its overcoming, at the most intimate site of subjectivity. Moreover, one who cultivates an aesthetic of the sublime must do so in response to the threat of overwhelming natural forces. The threat or anticipation of disaster seems to be intrinsic to these two dimensions of late-Enlightenment subjectivity. But could one say the same of each author's ethical stance? Does that dimension rely on some version of disaster as well?

In his theory of immortality Kant proposes that only someone possessing an immortal soul could eventually achieve perfect conformity to the moral law. But as I discussed in the introduction, Lewis White Beck argues that in doing so, Kant imagines that someone who is no longer within the constraints of time and space might still embark on a project of incremental progress towards pure holiness and thus must still belong within a temporal order – a contradiction in terms. Building on this point, Alenka Zupančič contends, "*What Kant really needs to postulate is not the immortality of the soul but the immortality of the body*," the immortality of what she calls a *sublime* body, one "that exists and changes through time, yet approaches its end, its death, in an endless asymptotic movement."[7] This requirement, however, places him in surprising company. Drawing from Lacan's insight that one should read Kant with Sade, Zupančič reminds us that for Sade, the "only regrettable and unfortunate thing" about sessions of sexual torture,

> which could otherwise go on *endlessly*, towards more and more accomplished tortures – is that the victims die *too soon* … [T]he problem is that the body is not made to the measure of enjoyment. There is no enjoyment but the enjoyment of the body, yet if the body is to be equal to the task (or duty) of *jouissance*, the limits of the body have to be "transcended." Pleasure – that is, the limit of suffering that a body can still endure – is thus an obstacle to enjoyment.[8]

Much as Kant encounters the difficulty of imagining a potential holiness that a finite subject might achieve, worrying over the disjunction between our inevitably "pathological" or self-interested motives and the absolutely selfless strictures of the moral law, so also Sade is confronted with the difficult articulation between the finite domain of pleasure and the absolute ecstasy of enjoyment.

But Sade's relevance here goes further. Because Kant never explains how a subject riven by pathological motives might adhere to the moral law for its own sake, one might best follow Lacan and postulate that it would do so by submitting to jouissance, to an enjoyment counter to its self-interest and its pleasure. But in that case, Sade is more honest than Kant about the difficulties they both explore, for at least Sade provides an account of how one might overleap the gap between pleasure and enjoyment, or for that matter between pathological motivation and the moral law, pointing out that one might take pleasure in pain, or find a certain benefit in what directly damages oneself.[9]

We might clarify the stakes of this argument if we return to the pivotal ethical tale of the *Critique*, the confrontation of the free subject with the sovereign. For Kant, that tale suggests that the subject's freedom derives from the possibility one might choose a moral course of action even at the cost of one's own life, sacrificing self-interest for the sake of duty. Yet in Kant's account one would never know that one were free unless one encountered this absolutely unjust sovereign and could thus commit a truly free, and wholly sublime, moral act. It follows that Kant must subject us to a quasi-sadistic form of power before we could transcend the realm of sense in the name of an ethical jouissance. The sovereign of this anecdote strongly resembles the hero of a Sadean tale; without a torturer of this kind, one might never leap from one status to another, from self-interest to genuine holiness. In this case, reading Sade with Kant is not difficult, for a figure from the Sadean universe is already present, as it were, within Kant's most telling example.

How might these reflections bear on the stance provided in *Mary: A Fiction*? The fit between this Sadean Kant and Wollstonecraft is in many respects precise. She too argues that pleasure cannot provide what desire demands, postulating the soul's immortality to give it an appropriate sphere of action. The novel, however, radicalizes this prospect, for in its pages the gesture of moving beyond the pleasures of bodily existence goes hand in hand with a practice that repeatedly puts service to others above self-interest. Indeed, one gets the sense that for the novel's protagonist, the pleasure she gives up in the service of something better returns in the form of the jouissance of benevolence itself, the ecstasy of serving and rescuing others. In an episode of her youth, for example,

Mary would at times give up her breakfast to relieve the distresses of beggars at the gate and "feel gratified, when, in consequence of it, she was pinched by hunger" (12). The novel suggests that a version of the Kantian afterlife is already visible, incrementally, in Mary's actual life, in her practice of benevolent self-mortification.

This scenario suggests that Mary, like Kant's ethical protagonist, becomes implicated in a certain Sadean ethos. Much as Kant posits the ability to defy a malevolent sovereign to establish that we are free, Mary posits a "world in ruins" to give herself a space for sublime ethical action. She, like Kant, subjects herself to a toxic form of power so that she can engage in acts of defiant benevolence. If that is the case, however, she makes disaster into a constitutive element of her own ethical project; *she needs catastrophe if she is to orient herself to a supersensible destination*. In the view she exemplifies, only she who fights against the catastrophe of this world may transcend self-interest and realize her immortality in action. This view aligns Wollstonecraft's ethical stance with that in Kant; as we have seen, in the latter's second critique, only the prospect of defying the sovereign at the cost of one's life can establish that one is free. Thus Wollstonecraft, like Kant, creates an ethical version of the internal limit, installing an ethical principle in the subject in the form of an absolute violence against every finite determination, against the ordinary continuity of a life. Much as for Kant the sign of this freedom is the gallows, for Wollstonecraft it is the natural disaster of shipwreck or its extension, the world in ruins; in either case, one must confront a toxic sovereignty to discover one's ethical greatness.

In this passage, then, Mary ultimately performs what one might call a catastrophic benevolence – a form of self-sacrifice that relies upon, and is complicit in, disaster. In an infamous passage in *Juliette*, Sade has the pope argue that we should murder untold numbers of human beings and devastate the natural world as much as possible; his is a truly genocidal and ecocidal ethics.[10] Wollstonecraft, of course, proposes no such thing. Nevertheless, her protagonist cannot proceed unless a Sadean sovereign is in place, devastating the world she knows. She indirectly collaborates with that figure, relying on him to impose his tortures in response to which she may exercise her ethical agency. The depredations of absolute power, it seems, call forth the defiance of an absolute benevolence; the hyperbolic stakes of one cannot be made clear without those of the other.

Yet this novel does differ from Kant in one crucial respect, for here no embodied sovereign is available to impose his will. In his absence, how can one demonstrate one's ethical freedom? If we read the novel within the Kantian framework, it becomes a strikingly original performance, for it expands the short example to novel length, putting her protagonist in the position of fighting back against whatever makes this a "world in ruins" even if, or especially if, she has no life as a result. But to do so, Wollstonecraft must modify the Kantian scenario and suggest that another kind of sovereign is doing murderous work throughout the domain of ordinary experience – the sovereignty, one might say, of disaster itself.

Her gesture in this regard is quite distinctive. For her, such sovereignty cannot take the form of any actual figure of power, for even where one is potentially available, she turns from that singular individual to glance over the sweeping domain of human misery. Her stance is especially palpable just two years later, after the beginning of the French Revolution. In her reply to Burke, having expressed utmost contempt for his sentimentalization of arbitrary power, she outlines her opposition not so much to the Bourbon monarchy as to the principle that allows human beings to devastate each other. In a stunningly indignant paragraph of her first *Vindication*, she dismisses the events of the October days which so preoccupied Burke, writing,

> What were the outrages of a day to these continual miseries? Let those sorrows hide their diminished head before the tremendous mountain of woe that thus defaces our globe! ... Hell stalks abroad; – the lash resounds on the slave's naked sides; and the sick wretch, who can no longer earn the sour bread of unremitting labour, steals to a ditch to bid the world a long good night – or, neglected in some ostentatious hospital, breathes his last amidst the laugh of mercenary attendants.[11]

In contrast to Kant, in this passage Wollstonecraft dares to suggest that a murderous power infects the entire social system, operating especially in slavery, the relations of economic subordination, and the false care given to the indigent and sick. Here a malevolent power reigns over human affairs, subjecting people not to an immediate death at the gallows but a prolonged anguish under the auspices of an entire political order.

Wollstonecraft's perspective is captured best when she writes that "[h]ell stalks abroad," for here she suggests that hell need not be located in the afterlife but may transpire just as well within history. In that case, she brings a demonic, rather than divine, version of immortality into time. She does so, however, not by imagining a singular act but rather by depicting the "tremendous mountain of woe that thus defaces our globe." In effect, she moves from singularity to universality, verging on the notion that the scene of earthly life is already akin to the infinity of a hellish one. In doing so, she finds a figure of sovereignty far more capacious than that visible either in Kant or in Sade. But in that case, she also designates more powerfully than ever the dimensions of injustice required to make possible her contrary assertion of absolute good, a life of action that at every stage invokes an alternative destination.

Through these transpositions, Wollstonecraft takes further the implicitly political stakes of her ethical argument. Although Kant smuggles a revolutionary ethos into his example, proposing that one defy a corrupt sovereign, in his second critique he allows that implication to resonate without further comment. Writing in the transformed circumstances of 1790, Wollstonecraft is not so cryptic; she insists that any individual sovereign is far less dangerous than the many forms of abusive power that operate throughout humankind. One implication of this passage is that if ethical subjects collectively rejected such a sovereign, their action would make possible an ethical revolution, a systematic dismantling of social injustice.

The terms of her argument suggest that one might unpack the political implications of Kant's analysis in yet another respect. This passage's attack on Burke, along with others in both *Vindications*, suggests that the most insidious support of injustice is the logic of self-interest, for it allows one to accept existing social relations as long as one can benefit from them. Kant's pathological subject may thus reappear in the form of a pragmatic collaboration with injustice, one fully on display in a society that accepts enslavement, the abuse of common people, and the subordination of women. In this view, the apparently prudential calculations of self-interest ultimately disguise a willingness to sacrifice the good of others for one's own and thus enable the survival of modes of abuse in the midst of an apparently liberal society.

If we turn back from the *Vindications* to *Mary: A Fiction* and reread it from this perspective, we notice immediately how the earlier text attempts to do the impossible, to address a nearly universal misery through individual action. From this later vantage point, that novel, much like Kant's second critique, seems tendentious: the action of a single individual, however exemplary, simply cannot measure up to widespread oppression. Once one becomes aware that the ethical can ultimately lead to collective political action, any narrowly ethical project seems to fall short. That constraint is evident in the ethical tales on which Wollstonecraft and Kant both rely. One might respond to Kant, for example, by pointing out that even if one defies the sovereign at the cost of one's life, one thereby leaves the sovereign in place. Such an exemplary act may indicate that one is free, but it does so while allowing that sovereign to destroy one's body and enslave the bodies of others. The complicity of ethical heroism with a toxic sovereignty on which I commented above becomes all the more apparent after 1789; an awareness of that complicity now arises from within a political critique of the ethical – suggesting that a truly non-complicitous ethics would insist on dethroning that sovereign, thereby liberating all subjects from his depredations. The Wollstonecraft of 1790 implies that the ethical reflections of 1788 can overcome their limits only if they accept the political developments beginning in France in 1789; ethical thought, in effect, has entered the terrain of actual history in the form of revolution.

This critique would cut sharply into any ethics oriented to immortality. After all, the fantasy in *Mary: A Fiction* is that one can assist the abused, the sick, and the poor in a mode of perpetual rescue. But as the task of salvaging lives from the ruins is seemingly infinite, it restages the story of Kantian immortality in another guise, in the asymptotic progression of one's individual ethical acts towards the ultimate liberation of all humanity. One would indeed need to be immortal to save every person, one by one, from a world in ruins. This critique suggests that one might do better to shift from immortality to an immediate universality, to liberate everyone in a single event.

But that shift towards a unanimous liberation would replicate the original problem on another level, replacing one version of infinity, an endless series of individual tasks, with another – a single, absolute blow against injustice. Both scenarios ultimately retain the notion that human frailty and finitude must go, that pathological interest must be overcome, that hell must be defeated, and that one must achieve a universal and radical selflessness. Such a notion, however, must inevitably run aground on the fact that people do not necessarily want to be liberated from their pathological interests – or, to adopt a more Sadean vocabulary, that they may not wish to be relieved of their pleasures and endure an absolute jouissance. To eradicate injustice in one fell blow would require one to carry out an infinite violence of one's own.

To its credit, *Mary: A Fiction* registers the limits of its ethical scenario by recognizing that resistance. Shortly after Mary completes her voyage from Lisbon to England, she begins to assist a man, his sick wife, and their five children. She helps this family day by day until she contracts the wife's fever, becomes very ill, and even experiences delirium. Once she recovers, however, she discovers that the family no longer treats her with the same respect as before. Because her own funds are getting low, Mary hints to the now recovered mother that she should "try to earn her own subsistence: the woman in return load[s] her with abuse" (57). No doubt this exchange registers a certain class politics endemic to the novel and indeed to contemporary discourses of charity. But it also brings to the fore that most attempts at benevolence throughout the novel fail, in large part because the objects of generosity are unworthy. The novel thus raises another question regarding action on behalf of others. Freud famously rejected the Christian teaching that one must love one's neighbor as oneself. Recent theorists, taking up this remark, suggest that one who attempts to love the neighbor must inevitably love the obscene, inhuman, thing-like aspect of the neighbor as well – in effect, must embrace, rather than eradicate, the neighbor's pathology.[12] In this episode, Mary discovers that her charity does not relieve a sick woman of her selfishness but gratifies it instead. As it turns out, however hard one might try, one can never rescue another from self-interest. Moreover, her attempt to intervene into the world in ruins causes her to fall ill, subjecting her to the very pain from which she released another and ultimately suggesting that she must attend at least minimally to her own interest. The fantasy of pure benevolence, in short, runs aground several times over, suggesting that despite her will Mary is bound on every hand by the selfishness against which she protests.

This exposure of the limits of any attempt at benevolence raises the question as to whether a version of universal justice could ever appear within the limits of an actual history – a question whose contours I briefly outlined in the introduction but into which the intricate evocations of these texts requires us to delve much further here. With this question, the caution Kant voices in his political writings of the 1790s comes to the fore: in *The Conflict of the Faculties* (1798) he writes that one cannot infer from the evidence of human experience that humanity will ever achieve a condition of universal justice; the best one can do is seize on a sign evident in history which indicates that a tendency for progress may exist in humanity as a whole – an event such as the widespread sympathy aroused by the revolutionary events in France. But this argument, so apparently optimistic, may not finally bridge the gap between finitude and the infinite sketched above. The stance in this text shares a great deal with Kant's argument about the incremental progress towards perfect conformity with the moral law: in the latter case, at least, the goal to be achieved is out of reach from within a present defined by the limitations of humanity. If it seems absurd that individual acts could eventually sweep away the mountain of injustice, it may be only slightly less absurd that political action could do so. In these various instances, it seems the constraints of finitude place the realization of justice at an unreachable distance.

Yet precisely in this encounter with the impasses of the incremental, a further possibility comes into play: the aesthetic apprehension of what looms from beyond the realm of sense. The failure of the ethical and the political alike may ultimately lead to the aesthetic. In Kant's account of the mathematical sublime, imagination's inability to apprehend an absolutely large phenomenon points to the mind's capacity to identify instead with supersensible reason, a faculty that in its ability to conceive of infinitude necessarily exceeds any empirical vastness.[13] But the stark contrast between that capacity and any vastness still operating within the world of sense reveals the limits even of an asymptotic progression, and thus of a Kantian immortality. If, as Zupančič points out, an ethical immortality requires an immortality of the body, then it relies on an indefinitely extended human effort, one that by definition would never exceed the determinations of sense. It follows that the subject will arrive at its destination only by overleaping the domain of indefinite extension per se – that is, through the very gesture Kant outlines in his analytic of the sublime.[14]

But this sequence hardly gives the subject what it seeks when it demands justice; on the contrary, it leaves the event of justice outstanding, beyond the range of an empirical history. The infinity it grasps in the sublime, after all, never becomes part of the subject's lived experience, for the mind grasps only the Idea of that infinity and sees, in the possibility of merely having such an Idea, the sign of a higher faculty in itself. One might therefore call this, by analogy with the sign of history that appears in *The Conflict of the Faculties*, the sign of infinity, for it, like pure conformity to the moral law or universal justice, must remain out of reach, only a virtual possibility. Thus it is no surprise that in his analysis of the sign of history in the enthusiasm over the French Revolution, Lyotard argues that for Kant this sign, like the representation of the moral law, is an "extreme mode of the sublime," an instance of the sublime as "'a merely negative presentation,'" of "the impasse as 'passage.'"[15] This sublime feeling, as Jan Plug points out, arises not because the French Revolution is an adequate presentation of the Idea of humanity but precisely because "both it and its guiding principles are the objects before which presentation fails ... [T]he turn to the Idea of humanity that takes place in the feeling of the sublime" in response to the Revolution "arises from a failure to present that same Idea."[16] In other words, no historical phenomenon can adequately signify what people hope for; actual events can only fail to do so, but in that very failure one may find the sign of what one seeks. Here, as in the logic of the sublime, failure is precisely the sign of what surpasses mere experience.

What looks odd here is Kant's tactic of reading the failure of empirical experience as the sign of what can surpass it – of a capacity in human beings that might eventually realize what it hopes. But that is not all; in yet another odd argument, in his analytic of the sublime Kant places something that remains outstanding, beyond any possible experience, *within* the subject, relying on his sense that the grasp of an Idea is a sufficient ground for doing so. Yet as his embedded argument relying on a physical immortality suggests, at times he must admit that it is far more compelling to insist on the actual experience of infinity rather than its idea. Thus, to celebrate the aesthetic apprehension of the infinite when on some level only its actualization will do clearly indicates that the analytic of the sublime is doing far more work than one might suppose; rather than providing an analysis of yet another domain, the aesthetic, it smuggles in under that rubric a new account of the subject's relation to the absolute, allowing its very absence to signify its eventual presence.

Kant's leap in this regard, I would suggest, is nothing less than a rational formalization of what Wollstonecraft would regard as faith. If one steps back from the question of the political to take up Mary's incremental ethical project, where the prospect of realizing the fantasy of universal justice through individual action stands out as clearly impossible, one encounters the Kantian logic in a different idiom – that of the believer's attempt to find some presentation of the idea to which she holds. The shipwreck scene in *Mary: A Fiction* signals that in extremity, ethical effort must give way to divine action, to the day of judgment. But it broaches this possibility in a passage that indicates a remarkable affinity with the Kantian analytic of the sublime. Indeed, the paragraph which quotes Mary's reflections on the shipwreck in her journal – an unusually long paragraph for this novel – could serve as a textbook instance of how, in the Kantian sublime, the mind seeks to grasp what must remain outstanding:

> At this solemn hour, the great day of judgment fills my thoughts ... I have not words to express the sublime image which the bare contemplation of this awful day raises in my mind ... Here we walk by faith, and not by sight; and we have this alternative, either to enjoy the pleasures of life, which are but for a season, or look forward to the prize of our high calling, and with fortitude, and that wisdom which is from above, endeavor to bear the warfare of life ... Our race is an arduous one! How many are betrayed by traitors lodged in their own breasts, who wear the garb of Virtue, and are so near akin; we sigh to think they should ever lead into folly, and slide imperceptibly into vice. Surely any thing like happiness is madness! Shall probationers of an hour presume to pluck the fruit of immortality, before they have conquered death? ... [S]till does my panting soul push forward, and live in futurity, in the deep shades o'er which darkness hangs. – I try to pierce the gloom, and find a resting-place, where

> my thirst of knowledge will be gratified, and my ardent affections find an object to fix them ... Eternity, immortality, and happiness, – what are ye? How shall I grasp the mighty and fleeting conceptions ye create? (51–2)

From a Kantian vantage, one might see here the longing to seize hold of an ethical immortality and of a conceptual infinity both; the passage seems to capture an experience at once ethical and aesthetic. But in Kantian terms it is also an exemplary instance of the sublime: Mary is caught in the moment when the mind flies through vast spaces trying to find a "resting-place," to "grasp the mighty and fleeting conceptions" inspired by the thought of eternity. The passage captures Mary's state of mind as she experiences religious hope, depicting the images that occur to her, her rush into a space of darkness and gloom, her pressing forward with "ardent affections," and her endurance of great but "fleeting conceptions": it articulates her faith in the key of desire, affect, image, and concept – and thus in broadly aesthetic terms. Although she cannot grasp "the mighty and fleeting conceptions" of "[e]ternity, immortality, and happiness" as they loom beyond all possible mortal experience, her very failure to do so authorizes her confidence that they are present there, in effect allowing her to retain her faith in a supersensible destination.[17] In this regard, the logic of this passage is reminiscent of Kant's analysis of the mathematical sublime, for Mary is caught in the midst of a "panting" search for an adequate "resting-place" for her mind, thereby replicating the "displeasure from the inadequacy of the imagination" (that is, to translate from Kantian terminology, the displeasure of the faculty of mind charged with representing the world of sense).[18] Her mode of attempting to apprehend what lies beyond sense experience places this episode well within the Kantian scenario, suggesting that the latter in certain ways parallels the experience of faith.

Yet this struggle to seize on the idea of eternity takes place against the background of the tempest and shipwreck – that is, in the context of the dynamical sublime, of a natural phenomenon that can endanger human life. Kant finds in the response to that threat a sign of the mind's "superiority over nature on which is grounded a self-preservation of quite another kind than that which can be threatened and endangered by nature outside us, whereby the humanity in our person remains undemeaned even though the human being must submit to that domination."[19] In much the same way, Mary finds in her response to the tempest's endangering of many lives the sign of her expectation of redemption. Although this response comports well with Kant's theory of the dynamically sublime, its implications remain striking: *the person who seeks most to save the lives of others is transported by the very event that most endangers them.* Somehow only this danger can constitute the sign of an eventual *absolute and universal care* – the divine capacity to "bind up the broken-hearted" on that day (51); only this kind of violence, it seems, can bring about the leap beyond a merely incremental history (and incremental version of care) to which she is bound.

While this logic confirms the overall unfolding of the dynamically sublime, it complicates the earlier exploration of the limits of ethical and political incrementalism. Evidently the point is not merely that such incrementalism must fail to reach what lies in another domain; rather, the sign of that domain can only be found in a catastrophe in the realm of ordinary experience. In a cosmic irony, the source of violence against human beings is ultimately not a hell that stalks abroad but a catastrophic event that, through its very threat to humanity, signifies redemption. This resort to the discourse of apocalypse thus replicates on another scale the problem of ethical violence we have seen in Kant's tale. Wollstonecraft hints as much when she alludes to the biblical account of the great deluge, writing near the beginning of the episode that the "winds then became very tempestuous, the Great Deep was troubled, and all the passengers appalled," placing "the Great Deep" in capital letters to make the allusion to the biblical floodwaters all the more evident (50). Here catastrophic benevolence gives way to a much vaster scenario, apocalypse as the sign of redemption. It does so, however, because the language of the dynamically sublime – or of apocalypse – places the question of finitude on a basis unlike that we saw in the collapse of incremental effort. Rather than depicting finitude as an inherent constraint on actualizing the demands of the moral law or of universal justice, this episode highlights the inherent vulnerability in finitude, one that exposes it to a vast physical violence. That exposure is evident in the smashing of a ship, the difficult labours of those in the sea, and the possibility of bodies drowning – but also, and perhaps more crucially, it gives rise to the countervailing claim that humanity is superior to the conditions of embodiment and can accordingly lay claim to a higher destination. The violence of the world of sense may lead to the claim that one may ultimately escape its limitations. This entire sequence, then, takes the encounter with the sovereign and expands it into the defiant encounter with nature itself: the dynamically sublime in effect replicates in the aesthetic domain the ethical capacity to face up to an overwhelming challenge and through that encounter to assert a more than finite destination.

If all this is the case, this episode bears as well on the question of the sign of history. As I mentioned in the introduction, Lyotard emphasizes that Kant finds that sign not in the enthusiasm for what is presented in the French Revolution but in the latter's *failure* to present the Idea of humanity. Here the shipwreck episode once again accords well with the Kantian argument, though it takes its suggestion a further, crucial step: as the logic of the dynamically sublime would suggest, Mary's reading of the shipwreck as a sign of apocalypse would suggest that one would find in a historical or political catastrophe the sign of a higher possibility. In effect, then, the shipwreck episode provides an alternative rendition of Kantian themes, blending Kant's formalizations of ethics, politics, and aesthetics into a single complex scenario – one that circulates around a scene of disaster.

Perhaps surprisingly, then, this scene indicates that Mary can seize her faith only as an idea of what remains out of reach – and as an idea inspired by her encounter with a scene of catastrophe. Although this tale seems to offer up an alternative to what is visible in Kant, invoking a belief he attempts to suspend in his rationalist theology, in fact it provides a nearly exact counterpart of the latter, placing its protagonist in precisely the situation inhabited by the Kantian subject. This parallel suggests that both accept the limits of late-Enlightenment discourse: much as Kant works within the constraints of critique, excluding from view what the mind cannot know, Wollstonecraft accepts the constraints of a subgenre of fiction, focusing on the formation of an individual mind, thereby excluding from her narrative what human subjects cannot know or cannot become.[20] In effect, then, where Kant in a later work attempts to frame religion within the limits of reason alone, the novel does so within the limits of fiction alone. As a result, the novel ultimately excludes any direct apprehension of redemption from its frame, capturing it through a sign of natural disaster, and thus in its own way inscribes a version of the internal limit.

It may at first seem that the contrast between these two forms of limitation is quite stark. The imperative to formalize requires Kant to exclude nearly everything from his depiction of the philosophical subject that would be relevant in the analysis of the ethical life: he can regard most aspects of such a life merely as details within the category of the pathological. A novel such as *Mary: A Fiction* does something quite different, for it tells the story of a character, a fictional construct; it too, subjects the person to a certain level of formalization, or rather to the strictures of *literary* form, perforce filtering its concerns through the kinds of explorations narrative coherence can make possible. Even a novel as apparently naive as this one brings its own constraints, not least that of the consistency of theme and character, but thanks to such constraints it is enabled to carry out a more capacious ethical exploration.

Wollstonecraft asks, as Kant does not, how the disposition to adhere to a severe ethical practice might arise, why anyone would enact that disposition through a series of telling decisions, and what the costs and consequences of those decisions might be. In effect, she subjects the dense interplay of concerns she shares with Kant to the non-exclusive concerns of the novel, relying on narrative's capacity to foreground a wide range of ethical concerns that Kant leaves out of view.

But one should not be too hasty in contrasting these two projects. Unlike most novels, *Mary: A Fiction* greatly values the attempt to live a life of radical altruism, to accept the demands of virtue at the cost of one's own happiness; it takes seriously the kind of hyperbolic ethics that appears in late-Enlightenment discourse. While it subjects such an ethics to careful interrogation, it does so not in scorn but in respect. Indeed, it may have no other choice but to do so, since in that novel Wollstonecraft thematizes aspects of her own life. The work is simultaneously autobiographical and critical, blending these modes in what Tilottama Rajan has designated the genre of *autonarration*, in which an author "enters the text ... as a subject-in-process represented by a figure, sometimes a dis-figuration, of the self," creating a form of "self-writing in which the author writes her life as a fictional narrative and thus consciously raises the question of the relationship between experience and its narrativization."[21] By enabling Wollstonecraft to make various features of her own ethical dispensation more explicit on fictional terrain, autonarration allows her to explore possibilities only partially realized in her life, to problematize what they might represent, and thus to carry out a more searching analysis of those concerns than she could otherwise. In effect, it allows her to subject those concerns to an internal critique – that is, to examine them on the basis of their own premises. Much like Kantian critique, which properly speaking attempts to outline the formal constraints imposed on specific dimensions of mind, Wollstonecraft writes a *fictional autocritique* of ethical sensibility, mapping out in novelistic terms its capacities and limitations.[22]

Considering this particular ethical sensibility within the terms of the novel, however, is no easy task, for the novel as a genre takes for granted that it must explain a protagonist's disposition on the basis of ordinary motives alone. In effect, Wollstonecraft sets herself the task of showing how a disposition to push beyond the domain of the "pathological" might arise precisely *from* the field of "pathological" motives, desire, and interests – of how, for example, through her habit of attempting to protect her sick mother from the abuses of her drunken father, the young Mary "exercised her compassion so continually, that it became more than a match for self-love, and was the governing propensity of her heart throughout life" (11). It explores a broadly Kantian ethical stance within a genre that does not typically consider it, binding together imperatives that ultimately conflict. For most of its short length, the novel focuses on Mary's wish to protect her mother, Ann, Henry, needy strangers in London, and potentially a host of others from hunger, the consequences of illness, poverty, or other forms of harm. But it can do so because it has also attempted to provide a compelling account of how such a commitment takes shape in Mary's early years, detailing how Mary responds to the conditions of her youth by forming habits of solitude, self-reliance, intense reading, and the contemplation of immortality.

It pursues this thread as well when it consistently depicts Mary's form of care in erotic terms – as her way of enacting a desire for familial belonging, for affective partnership, and for claiming a power to relieve others of suffering. For Mary, ethical commitment is not opposed to erotic satisfaction broadly conceived; rather, it is the very form that satisfaction takes. Here the opposition on which Kant insists collapses, for the novel adheres to the Lacanian insight that even self-sacrifice can have its erotic payoffs; like Lacan, Wollstonecraft rewrites Kant's moral tale to suggest that one might adhere to one's passion precisely *because* of the threat of punishment on the gallows or, in this case, the threat that one might experience the jouissance one seeks only in the afterlife.[23] Mary enacts her longing through care for her partner – for Ann, for Henry – even if, or especially because, it can never lead to direct erotic pleasure; satisfaction is thus displaced into another zone, into the joy of care itself, as well as into the affective turbulence of what the novel depicts as sensibility. Although Mary's love for Ann opens up the possibility of a queer affect, a form of same-sex passion that resonates throughout this portion of the novel, her emphasis on caring for a partner who is on the verge of death makes it queer in another sense.[24] That longing, similarly present in Mary's relationship with Henry, verges on union with the partner only once – when, at Henry's death, "the soul seemed flying to her, as it escaped out of its prison." As she contemplates this moment soon thereafter, "[e]very event of her life rushed across her mind with wonderful rapidity – yet all was still – fate had given the finishing stroke," as if she too is experiencing death (71). This passage hints that what she seeks is the fusion not of body with body but of spirit with spirit, so that souls, fleeing their prisons, may meet and embrace in a domain beyond them – in a jouissance, one might say, that must remain outstanding, never achieved in the realm of the senses.

This queering of erotics from desire towards jouissance is reinforced throughout the novel as Mary chooses the frail and diseased, such as Ann and Henry, in part because their illnesses show that their bodies are defined in relation to something beyond physical satisfactions. Although neither of them necessarily seeks death, the frailty of each signals an exposure to early death that draws her to them. The logic of this appeal is precisely what we saw in the shipwreck episode, in which Mary is greatly moved by the tempest that most endangers those she wishes to save. Evidently, the pressure that sickness exerts on Ann and Henry makes their frailty a sign of a higher destination, as in the logic of the sublime, transforming them into figures of a more than ordinary erotic power. What draws her to them is this exposure to something that exceeds finitude, this involuntary placement of happiness beyond the grave. The novel as a whole thus constructs a complex, intersubjective erotics of spirit that relies on an exposure writ large in the "world in ruins" she witnesses in London: it ultimately takes the form of an erotics of disaster, a jouissance of the ruins.

The tale frames Mary's queer orientation to disaster by excluding her from what most novels of the period regard as the ultimate sign of earthly satisfaction: a credible, erotically compelling heterosexual marriage. The novel clearly signifies its repudiation of cynical, mercenary abuses of marriage in its depiction of Mary's union with someone previously unknown to her to settle a property dispute. It also suggests that the absence of a genuine marital partner, and the apparent prohibition on her seeking erotic satisfaction from any other partner, reinforces her mode of seeking a jouissance of the ruins. This latter enjoyment, of course, is also painful to her; she experiences it in part as an involuntary imposition, an intense displeasure. But that very displeasure, it turns out, gives her access to another kind of bliss. In retrospect, then, this foreclosure of ordinary sexual satisfaction enables her to cultivate what might be a more powerful alternative, a sublime erotics to which her experiences as a child and youth seem to have destined her. Subjecting Mary to this marriage departs from the facts of Wollstonecraft's own life, on which so much of Mary's experience is otherwise based; it imports into the tale an apparently unmotivated element. One might surmise that, working backward from the erotic scenarios she had in mind for her protagonist's adulthood, Wollstonecraft gave her this botched marriage to motivate and heighten her state in adulthood, to lend coherence and credibility to the erotics of disaster.

Insofar as the novel frames Mary's erotics in relation to a conception of marriage at once foreign to her and imposed on her against her will, one might conclude that Mary's situation arises less from her free decisions than from the constraints imposed upon her by an androcentric society. Mary's entanglement with the strictures of ethical violence and its attendant erotics may speak less about her than about the society that deprives her of an earthly happiness. A reading along these lines might suggest that her erotics is at least in part the result of a forced choice and conclude that where subjectivity is denied, it may as a result choose a self-lacerating ethical project despite impossible odds.

The trouble with this reading is that the alternative it proposes for Mary – a fulfilling marriage – would by implication redirect her passion from the immortality she seeks towards finite satisfactions. While the latter accords better with established conventions of the novel, it would betray Mary's desire for an infinity that is far more important to her than marital love. Where the novel hints that her orientation to catastrophe may arise in compensation for the denial of such love, ultimately it reverses this suggestion, proposing instead that for her, domestic satisfaction must fall away in favour of the more intense satisfactions of a disastrous subjectivity. Within this context, it becomes clear that the foreclosure of marital satisfaction serves as a metaphor for the novel's refusal of finitude; its preference for a contrasting erotics is a figure for the longing for infinity. But the novel can rely on this figure only because it treats a satisfaction in the beyond *as* a form of queer satisfaction – as a mode not only of ethical violence but also of catastrophic jouissance.

It may be worth pausing over this stunning reversal for a moment to tease out some of its implications. The turn towards disastrous satisfactions, after all, seems to fly in the face of Wollstonecraft's feminist politics, classically articulated in *A Vindication of the Rights of Woman*, which followed four years later in 1792. Drawing on this later work, one could conclude against Kant that one finds freedom *not* in subjection to a hyperbolic moral law but by delving into the "pathological" domain of earthly desire and satisfaction. Rather than saving the subject from the field of empirical determinations, freedom may lie within it. Indeed, from this perspective it may be possible that a genuinely human ethics should embrace bad decisions, including erotic error, much as Wollstonecraft herself proposes in an often overlooked passage of this *Vindication*. "[O]ne reason why men have superior judgment, and more fortitude than women," she writes, "is undoubtedly this, that they give a freer scope to the grand passions, and by more frequently going astray enlarge their minds."[25] One finds freedom in this account not by overleaping the realm of sense but by finding one's way through it, negotiating with its manifold strictures and rewards, and in "going astray" ultimately grasping something that only that experience can provide. In place of a violently abstract freedom visible in Kant, here Wollstonecraft may offer us the largesse of a concrete freedom that works itself out in an erotics of finitude. Such a perspective would anticipate Lacan's argument that Kant and Sade, each becoming an "instrument of jouissance," renounced the more difficult "path of desire" at "the price of the truth of man" – a truth that soon thereafter, in his seminar on these themes, Lacan provisionally designates an ethics of desire.[26]

Much of this later argument of the second *Vindication* could be taken to expand on certain implications in *Mary: A Fiction*, further articulating the novel's embedded premises. In the later work, Wollstonecraft argues that even women not forced into false marriages are forbidden from engaging fully in the challenges of life. As that text proposes across a host of arguments, women, deprived of the full opportunity to develop their minds, encouragement to apply their reason within the domestic sphere, permission to test and explore their passions, and rational friendship even with their husbands, are scarcely allowed to become ethical subjects at all. Mary's forced marriage captures well the sense in this *Vindication* that marriage hardly provides a space for women's ethical agency; the novel crystallizes in a single harsh relationship aspects of what the treatise finds in many other forms.

Taking up these aspects of the second *Vindication*, one might conclude that it articulates an ultimately meliorist stance, placing its trust in enlightened progress, under whose auspices women might eventually receive the rights it demands and thus gain access to a finite and mortal happiness. But in fact that work cuts against any such expectation, for to one's surprise it insists at several points that happiness is not available to mortals. As I mentioned early in this chapter, in the period from *Mary* to the second *Vindication* Wollstonecraft maintains that one who seeks satisfaction must eventually discover that it lies beyond this life, that as a result one can never define oneself in the terms of physical satisfaction or emotional pleasure, and through that realization one can instead assume one's status as a rational being destined for immortality. Only on this basis can she demand her rights as a woman. But in that case, Wollstonecraft's feminism is meant to *endorse* the orientation to an outstanding satisfaction that we see throughout *Mary*. Indeed, although Mary is deprived of much that is defended in the later work, she nevertheless exemplifies a form of virtue, a resolute capacity to put her immortality above finite satisfactions, that the later work advocates above all. Hence, what one might take to be a progressivist politics ultimately relies instead on the form of a disastrous subjectivity – one that finds its joy in the anticipation of an event that, for any mortal, is still to come.

No doubt this subordination of feminism to disastrous subjectivity lends the *Vindication* a certain tension, placing it oddly in relation to the later, more secular feminism that claims it as a founding text. But that same subordination has even more visible consequences for the novel *Mary*, primarily because of marriage's importance in the genre of domestic fiction. Insofar as the foreclosure of a satisfying marriage excludes what a novel of the period would normally seek, it deprives this narrative of the most explicit signal of its possible resolution. Neither the author nor the reader can imagine Mary settling down with her despised husband, but neither can imagine how she will be able to forestall the demand for such a fate indefinitely. As a result, the novel ends without any prospect of resolution. The stakes of this gambit are explicit in the novel's final sentence, for when Mary thinks "she [is] hastening to that world *where there is neither marrying*, nor giving in marriage" (73; emphasis in original), she makes clear her preference for immortality over marriage. Yet even this preference is denied its potential narrative payoff: whereas a Kantian subject who defies the sovereign goes to certain death, Mary's dedication to caring for others only makes it possible for her to witness *their* deaths – and live on in a "world in ruins." She has not yet entered the domain of the immortality she seeks.

Clearly, then, *Mary: A Fiction* rests uneasily within the category of the novel, neither entirely repudiating nor entirely accepting its terms. The tale's exclusion of any representation of immortal experience from its narrative obeys a founding principle of its genre. Yet it refuses to limit its protagonist's yearning to the field of human relationships available to her. The story follows the rules of novelistic form insofar as Mary continues to seek happiness; it breaks them, however, when it has her place that happiness beyond what the novel form can convey. At once within the constraints of the novel and oriented beyond them, this fiction stands out as a highly distinctive text, a tale at odds with its own genre. Accordingly, we can now see that in fact it constitutes a rare achievement, an autocritique of the form of fictional narrative itself, for it critically exposes the ethical premises of novelistic closure. Ultimately, Wollstonecraft, like Kant, carries out a critique of the mode of discourse in which she operates – in her case, the formal limits of novelistic fiction.[27]

Thus where some might conclude that this short novel is a failure, a violation of novelistic satisfaction, in fact the novel's conclusion enacts on a narrative level what Kant soon outlines – in *Critique of the Power of Judgment* (1790, 1793) – in his treatment of the non-resolution of the mathematical sublime. Such a formal gambit seems out of place in any novel. But the uniqueness of this ending is not a sign of aesthetic failure.

In choosing a formal scenario alien to conventional fiction, the novel enables the expectations built into novelistic form to protest bitterly against that alternative. In doing so, however, the novel highlights its singular achievement, its formalizing the aesthetics of the sublime (and an attendant ethics, politics, and faith) precisely through the violation of novelistic closure. One could say that Wollstonecraft outlines on the terrain of narrative fiction the very contours that Kant traces in other ways. Insofar as Kant's analytic has become familiar by now, and to some extent has lost what must have been its initially scandalous edge, perhaps only the disorienting effect of this novel's open form can capture for us the supreme strangeness of what these texts share.

In grasping the complex logic of these texts, one might wish to bring them quickly into the domain of political contestation, to see their final level of import as a series of political demands. In doing so, one might then usher them past their invocations of immortality and invite them to partake of the broadly political labour of establishing justice and happiness for all in the field of finitude. But doing so, as I have suggested above, would falsify the logic of these texts, especially those of Wollstonecraft, which certainly make political demands but do so without assuming that such demands might find traction on the field of experience or of history. The form, or anti-form, of *Mary* suggests as much: any narrative closure is simply out of view. What these texts articulate is so powerful and so sweeping, so attuned to the virtually total exclusion of what they seek, that their political intervention seems to be poised instead at the site where an infinite indignation cuts across a merely political temporality, where an impossible demand reveals a "world in ruins." Thus *Mary* exemplifies what takes place when political critique comes up against its limitations, when it too must glimpse only in the distance the justice it has in mind for all. As a result, it cuts through the mode of reading we expect to bring to bear on British fiction, one that takes the domain of finitude – and of political contestation – for granted.

In doing so, this novel opens up a space for what Rajan calls "romantic narrative," a mode that quite often appears in the writing of Wollstonecraft, Godwin, the Shelleys, and their circle. Such texts bring into play a mode of writing that exemplifies what Rajan describes as the disjunction between a radical interiority and ordinary temporality, between lyric and narrative. These later texts, many of which are now enjoying canonic status, are worthy inheritors of its initial explorations of that disastrous conjunction of infinity and finitude, of what cuts across history and of what lives and breathes in its domain.[28]

Despite its marginal status, then, *Mary: A Fiction* constitutes one of the first and clearest instances of that characteristically Romantic genre, the tale of the impossible. It begins an exploration central to its moment, making uniquely evident what is at stake in the juxtaposition of finite human beings with the infinite justice they demand. At the centre of the tradition that has arisen since – and of the texts to follow – one might well place its own central episode, the scene of shipwreck, which captures with special force the contours of a disastrous subjectivity.

2 *Prohibiting the Impossible*

Godwin and the Formation of the Real

In the treatise outlining his version of philosophical anarchism, *Enquiry Concerning Political Justice* (first published in 1793 and revised twice thereafter), William Godwin attacks every possible interference with the individual's private judgment of what best serves the universal good. Every positive law attempts to substitute a contingent and fallible version of justice for its absolute form: "Legislation … is not an affair of human competence. Immutable reason is the true legislator, and her decrees it behoves us to investigate. The functions of society extend, not to the making, but the interpreting of law" (236).[1] Because reason is prior to its historical articulation, the latter is illegitimate. To substitute mere laws for immutable reason is to be confined by potentially false interpretations; it is, in short, to create an imposture, a fiction of justice rather than the real thing. Accordingly, Godwin carries out a systematic critique of every kind of institution, arguing that people should live under the immediate authority of reason itself, enacting an almost total violence against the complex fabric of social life. Because people would justify their behaviour according to reason alone, and because property and sexual relations would be reconfigured to allow for such separate judgment, every form of collective enterprise or identity would disappear. No institution would mediate between people and reason or between people and each other. This philosophy challenges far more than the rule of law or of government, for it also repudiates rhetorical power, prejudice, custom, contracts, promises, cooperative action, gratitude, codes of manners, marriage, the subordination of child to parent, employment of one person by another, and internalized forms of external constraint, as well as the coercion involved in any revolutionary or collective attempt to overturn institutions. Philosophical anarchy is in fact a kind of ratiocracy, a mode of governance even more severe than theocracy, for in this case the immutable principle would never mediate itself in any familiar social form. The same activity – coming to know and enact the judgments of reason – would define every life and every interpersonal relation.

Godwin's philosophy amounts to a uniquely violent conceptual experiment, an attempt to hurl humanity into a space beyond any historical determination. Where Enlightenment thought typically appeals to ahistorical norms such as reason or nature, Godwin tries to make society identical to such a norm. But as a result, his work uniquely reveals the necessary impasses of such an enterprise. The aggression implicit in absolute reason dominates in the relatively unselfconscious *Enquiry*, but the novels *Things as They Are; or, The Adventures of Caleb Williams* (1794) and *St Leon: A Tale of the Sixteenth Century* (1799) expose the costs of such conceptual violence in acute, implicitly self-critical, and progressively more sweeping terms. Total conceptual revolution modulates into a searching critique of the irrational component of rationalist fantasy. While Godwin's anarchist positions made him vulnerable to anti-Jacobin satire in the late 1790s, in these novels he became his own most searching and perceptive critic. As the ending of *Caleb Williams* first demonstrates, when one attempts to oppose immutable reason to established society, it eventually regards the latter as a closed system impermeable to change; only when the total criticism of society recognizes its resemblance to what it opposes, accepting the possibility that it is also shaped by selfish and partial motives, can it break out of the impasse of total accusation. *St Leon* dramatizes this critique even more explicitly, showing that the gift of absolute abundance leads not to universal happiness but to disaster.

By evoking a certain late-Enlightenment ambition – the wish to transform the social order entirely on the basis of an immutable reason that operates outside its institutions – and showing that this form of reason, thanks to its totalizing form, can only be realized in a total violence against what is, these tales ultimately contest that notion of a presocial, immutable reason, negating the ambition that motivated them from the start. But these are not merely tales of failure. On the contrary, they show that the social order cannot survive without cancelling the ideal of immutable reason that could give rise to such violence – and thus without perpetually revolving around that site of cancellation, that negated transcendence. In effect, then, they formulate with unusual force the emergence of the internal limit, the arrival of the Real. Yet they complicate their account of that arrival as well. Insofar as they narrate the formation of this logic in first-person tales that allow the reader to identify with and share in the project of their protagonists, these novels sustain the affect of the very projects they critique. Accordingly, they mark out the constitutive ambivalence of a certain modernity, which perpetually clings to the fantasy of a total social transformation that it simultaneously forecloses. Precisely because these texts start out from a fierce statement of late-Enlightenment ambition, they culminate in extraordinarily telling renditions of the structural impasses and contradictions of a society shaped by the internal limit.

By arguing in the *Enquiry* that society's true basis was to be found in none of its actual forms but only in immutable reason, Godwin posed the crucial question of how to put such a principle into action. One could, for example, interpret those principles exhaustively in an intricately defended deductive system, attempting to give the immutable a final form. Such was the project of Jeremy Bentham, who sought to craft a social order based not in coercion but in utility, not in the punishment of crime but in the design of incentives and modes of surveillance that would bring about the greatest good. To make this design as flawless as possible, he sought to put the general good on a basis more stable and predictable than individual virtue, proposing ways of aligning duty and desire, utility and self-interest, according to which people would serve general utility simply by doing their own will.[2] But in the process of eradicating institutional violence against the subject, he disposed of the ethical subject as such, transforming it into the predictable, malleable creature of utility. Godwin shared much of this project; he also adopted utility as his guiding justification for ethical norms and argued that punishment could be replaced with surveillance and "general discountenance" (659, 644). But he relied directly on individual virtue and would have considered the predictable subject of Bentham's system abhorrent. He also attacked any attempt to reduce reason to a legal code, arguing that no such code could ever anticipate the contingencies of any specific case, that rather than resolving legal disputes it would only give rise to the need for more codification ad infinitum. The only possible standard of justice was uncodified justice itself, whose dictates must be determined case by case in the light of reason alone (686).

Does Godwin therefore rely on the opposite notion that ultimately reason must speak to us directly, ineffably, without articulating itself at all? Consider the ethical theory of Kant, another of his contemporaries. While Bentham hoped to provide ethical theory with ways of arbitrating between competing demands for justice using a utilitarian calculus, Kant argued that one could never determine the contents of the moral law according to the empirical, practical good it might bring about. He argues instead that because the moral law itself defines the good, it cannot be explained or justified according to any external factor; on the contrary, in his account the law makes its demands felt immediately in the voice of conscience. By the same token, one must comply with those demands purely for the sake of duty, rather than from any "pathological" or self-interested motive. As a result of this radical formalization of the moral law, his theory cannot distinguish between moral virtue and radical evil, for both can arise from the attempt to act upon an ethical principle for its own sake, without reference to social utility, even at the cost of life.[3] Godwin would object to Kant on similar grounds, arguing that if we judge only by the intention to adhere to duty, then we would have to give "the palm to some of the greatest pests of mankind," including political assassins, who, like good ethical heroes, "sacrificed their ease, and cheerfully exposed themselves to tortures and death," out of their deep "anxiety for the eternal welfare of mankind." Virtuous intention alone is not a reliable guide, for "self-deception is of all things the most easy" (188–9).[4] Elsewhere he writes, "Pure malevolence is the counterpart of disinterested virtue; and almost all the considerations that prove the existence of the one are of equal avail to prove the existence of the other" (384). As he states quite clearly in the second and third editions of his treatise, "intention is of no further value than as it leads to utility: it is the means, and not the end." In other words, "Duty is the application of capacity to the real, not imaginary, benefit of mankind" (190).

This difference between Godwin and Kant comes through in the contrast between the little moral tales each ponders. Such tales inevitably focus on the confrontation of a tyrant with a powerless man. As we have seen, in his short narrative Kant proposes asking a man what he would do "if his sovereign threatened him with ... sudden death unless he made a false deposition against an honorable man whom the ruler wished to destroy under a plausible pretext." That man might not be able to say for sure what he would do, but "he would certainly admit without hesitation" that it might be possible for him to give his life. "He judges, therefore, that he can do something because he knows that he ought, and he recognizes that he is free."[5] In a slightly different context, a discussion of the necessity of sincerity, Godwin asks whether a man should at the cost of death reveal his own identity to powerful political foes, and he replies that he should do so not only to comply with his duty but also to help free the human race; through his act, he would avoid "contributing his part to the cutting off the intercourse between men's tongues and their sentiments, infusing general distrust," and set an example of "spirited defiance of consequences" that may inspire others (328–39).[6] For Kant, the possibility of complying with the moral law reveals that people are morally free; for Godwin, adhering to the truth demonstrates not only one's freedom but the possibility of creating the conditions which would liberate others as well. Pure freedom, the virtuous intention, is not enough; it must also serve the actual interests of others.

Thus Godwin takes up a fairly unusual ethical stance. Like Bentham, he insists that ethical action must lead to real good for humanity; like Kant, he holds that one must act with a fully virtuous intention. Because he holds to both, he avoids the most coercive aspects of the ethical theories of these contemporaries. Bentham in effect substitutes his own ethical judgment for everyone else's, liberating them from the need to be virtuous through his own ethically heroic enterprise but reducing them to mere instruments of his intention in the process. Kant's theory, while apparently the opposite of Bentham's, replicates its problems on another scale. How, for example, is the law to be imposed without any pathological motive and still find purchase in the mind of an actual human being, riven as he or she must be by countless partial motives of this kind? In reply, as we have seen, Lacan places Kant in the company of the Marquis de Sade to reveal the sadistic dimension of the categorical imperative: by putting oneself under the spell of the moral law, one in fact is "reconstituted from alienation at the price of being no more than the instrument of jouissance," thereby taking up the position confessedly occupied by Sade himself. The law is an alienated will; Kant's inability to specify the object of the law disables his theory, because through that fault he renounces happiness "at the price of the truth of man," the truth of desire.[7] In Bentham's world, we would all become the means of bringing about the greater good, while in Kant, we would become instruments of the law itself.

In contrast to his contemporaries, Godwin argues that people should accept the force only of those immutable principles of which they are truly persuaded, thereby relieving them of the coercions imposed by both Bentham and Kant. But it does not follow that for Godwin they are free to do whatever they please; they would be subject to a somewhat different form of constraint. To ensure that people adhere to the demands of reason, Godwin proposes that people justify their actions before humanity as a whole, who would judge how well they have carried out the obligation to serve the universal good. People faced with ethical choices, he writes, should consider how their decision would appear if they were "to be their own historians, the future narrators of the scene in which they were acting a part … How much better would it be if … every man were to make the world his confessional, and the human species the keeper of his conscience?" (311–12). On the same principle, he writes, "How great would be the benefit if every man were sure of meeting in his neighbour the ingenuous censor, who would tell him in person, and publish to the world, his virtues, his good deeds, his meannesses and his follies?" (313). By making humanity the best judge of how well one safeguarded its happiness, Godwin avoids the impasses of purely external or purely internal modes of punishment. Rather than submitting to the law through the voice of conscience or the sentence of a judge, people would listen to the responses of others to their own accounts of what justice would require (636–42), entering into a chastening debate not only over their actions but also over what right action should be. Just as the law is not the same as its enactment, so also it is not the same as any particular judgment; it would become known best if conscience were mediated through the judgments of others, and those judgments through inner assent, in either case being forced to account for its commands through a process of mutual criticism.

While Godwin's system of conversational enforcement undoes other forms of coercion, it creates one of its own. The theory of internal assent requires a form of moral aggression, the willingness of people to serve as self-appointed embodiments of justice. In reference to the recalcitrant, erring man, he writes, "I must teach him to feel himself, to bow to no authority, to examine the principles he entertains, and render to his mind the reason of his conduct" (692). But in doing so, he will intrude upon his possible preference to remain as he is, a man content with unfreedom. Godwin might argue that people, once taught to be free, would recognize this wish as their own, experiencing it not as coercion but as liberation, but in so doing he would presume that he knows what is best, that without reason such a man "will never rise to the dignity of a rational being" (692). Underlying his philosophy is the coercive demand that people eradicate all coercion: "[T]he dictates of reason," Godwin writes, will bind people "more strongly than with fetters of iron" (660). Although he eliminates every other mode of coercion, he never questions the demand that humanity eventually liberate itself from them or that every virtuous person must be the agent of this demand. In the concluding remarks of the *Enquiry*, he writes, "No maxim can be more suspicious than that which teaches us to consult the temper of the times, and tell only as much as we imagine our contemporaries will be able to bear" (784). But then one must constantly say what is unbearable. In this passage one hears a specifically Godwinian violence, the jouissance of the imperative of liberation: it is as if he wishes to become a hero of a traumatic truth, one who exposes the nullity of the social consensus and reveals that his auditors are as yet only "shadows of men" (601; cf. 205). In the first edition of his treatise, Godwin even contemplates the possibility that such ethical heroism would win the day all by itself: "Nor is it possible to say how much good one man sufficiently rigid in his adherence to truth would effect. One such man, with genius, information and energy, might redeem a nation from vice."[8] These lines reveal the contradiction at the heart of his ethical theory. A single good man who propagates a transforming wisdom is using sincerity to impose his vision on others, rather than allowing a conversation about justice to take place. The coercion Godwin will not countenance elsewhere reappears in his determination to liberate his society from unreason whether people want him to or not. It is not surprising that before long he revealed too much about the life of Mary Wollstonecraft in his *Memoirs*, damaging her reputation and the public sympathy for feminism, or later, in his *Reply to Parr*, discussed infanticide too openly for his readers.[9]

Godwin goes astray in these passages because he forgets that people should live not by their own immediate judgment but by what they discover in conversation with others. If it is so easy to confuse virtue with radical evil, if even assassins think they carry out the dictates of reason, then people should not pretend they have immediate access to truth. In short, he forgets the crucial place of interpretation in the adjudication of duty. Yet if he acknowledges the necessity of such mediation, his system would also contradict itself, for then he would accept the idea that immutable reason is not knowable in its own right prior to its articulation. He is caught between two demands: because he wants to insist on the illegitimacy of all institutions, he argues that reason exists objectively prior to them, but because he also wants to ensure that it does not impose itself without justification, he argues that people must explain their interpretation of it to others. He wants a truth prior to articulation that is known by being articulated. In his attempt to sustain an objective virtue without making it an irrational, immediate principle, he wants a mediated immediacy.

The same tension permeates *Caleb Williams*, the novel Godwin began to write almost immediately after finishing the first edition of his treatise. In the *Enquiry*, he recommends that people act as if they are to become their own "historians, the future narrators" of their lives, that they are to be accountable to "the world" and "the human species," and that their neighbors will "publish" their follies to all. In effect, he asks people to imagine they will write confessional autobiographies that the world might read. Sincerity implicitly operates best on the analogy of mutual textual interpretation; it is an expanded or radicalized form of literacy. In this novel, he tries out what such a book might look like, writing it in the eponymous hero's first-person voice. The problem of articulation posed by the treatise thus bears directly upon the genre of this book. Does the novel simply tell the truth about *Things as They*

Are, the book's original leading title, as if to instruct the reader about the modes of "domestic and unrecorded despotism" referred to in the preface, or is it a confession that will be complete only after the reader has responded with his or her own judgment of Caleb's views?[10] Does it belong to the mode of heroic truth-telling or of conversation and mutual judgment?

The novel does not immediately make clear how it is to be read. The preface suggests that it will merely convey the teachings of the treatise: "It is now known to philosophers that the spirit and character of the government intrudes itself into every rank of society. But this is a truth highly worthy to be communicated to persons whom books of philosophy and science are never likely to reach" (1). The phrase "things as they are" appears several times in the *Enquiry* and is meant to convey, as do many details in the novel, a sense of the overwhelming weight of injustice that the citizens of England must endure (see *Enquiry* 401, 485, 597). The tale of various miscarriages of law and Caleb's imprisonment also bears out points made in the *Enquiry*. Falkland's secretiveness and Caleb's curiosity are instances of the "domestic tactics" of a society in which people do not reveal themselves fully to each other (288). At times the philosophical import of the tale breaks through the surface of the text, as when Caleb, confronted with the choice of whether to keep money given him by his persecutor, calculates the utility of returning it or spending it himself; his reflections in this passage resemble the sort one might find in the treatise (287–8). Similarly, when Caleb decides to tell the truth about his name when he is being sought by bounty hunters or refuses to sign a statement exonerating Falkland although he knows he will be subject to indefinite future persecution as a result, he closely resembles the ethical hero of both Kant and Godwin, one who will risk future suffering to adhere to the truth. Even the stunning paranoia of the novel's third volume, in which it seems that an entire society is bent on persecuting him, echoes the passage in which Godwin denounces the machinations of the tyrant whose eye "is never closed." Here again "no man can go out or come into the country, but he is watched," nor publish without attracting the attention of spies, nor frequent "places of public resort" without becoming "objects of attention"; it is as if Caleb stands in for the English nation, for he too could be "held in obedience by the mere operation of fear" (*Enquiry* 438). It seems that almost every feature of the novel extends or confirms Godwin's previous work.

But at the same time, Godwin signals a certain nervousness about his medium. "If the author shall have taught a valuable lesson, without subtracting from the interest and passion by which a performance of this sort ought to be characterised, he will have reason to congratulate himself upon the vehicle he has chosen" (1). What lesson, exactly, is he teaching? Caleb joins in a single persona two genres of ethical reflection: he is at once the ethical hero telling the truth at all costs about an unjust society and someone confessing his ways to another. Insofar as it solicits readerly interpretation, the novel puts in question the value of that ethical heroism, asking whether in fact such hyperbolic virtue serves its purpose. These competing perspectives finally break the novel open in the two versions of the final chapter. The first ending – in which Caleb encounters Falkland one last time, fails to alter him in any way, and ends up imprisoned and mad – gives Caleb the chance to act out the fantasy that he is the solitary truth-teller in the face of a closed and total system of oppression. But it also exposes the failure of this fantasy, its impotence in the face of what it opposes. The novel is caught between two closed orders, tyranny and resistance, without indicating any way beyond them. In the second, published ending, Caleb encounters Falkland, is moved by his weakness and suffering, repents of his accusation, and accuses himself, while Falkland, moved by this performance, exonerates Caleb and denounces himself in turn. Here the personifications of the closed orders of tyranny and resistance suddenly admit their mutual implication and accept the violence implicit in their own self-righteous claims. In these pages, Caleb indicates that his book does not manifest some prior truth but rather seeks an as-yet-unsuspected truth in the response of the reader. As Rajan argues, "Through Caleb as reader, Godwin inscribes a model of reading as the unearthing of truth and the correction of past misrepresentations. In finally becoming to Caleb what Caleb has been to Hawkins, we recover a truth of a different kind: the truth of what should rather than of what really did happen." In the end, Caleb admits that he did not know what his life actually meant; thinking himself master of things as they are, he never paused to imagine how they might be. Godwin "thus passes on to us the task of applying in our own lives an insight that comes too late to help the characters."[11]

This second ending breaks open Godwin's ethical theory. Godwin might say that his critique of legislation extends to narrative as well: someone who believes that Caleb's narrative tells the whole truth about his life and therefore actually represents things as they are forgets that, just as reason cannot be captured in legislation, the meaning of the life cannot be told in any single mode of articulation. If this were not so, Caleb would be frozen in the role he created for himself and would be nothing more than a character in his tale. But the novel gives this argument a new form. Caleb escapes the first ending not by recovering a truth prior to articulation but by discovering that narrative cannot fully capture who he is, that truth is found in the *failures* of articulation.[12] According to this ending, immutable reason exists not in a domain prior to institutions, but *negatively*, in what they can never fully establish. In effect, by subjecting the fantasy that underlies the *Enquiry* to narrative articulation, the novel exposes a subjective excess that philosophical articulation could never capture, bringing about a narrative critique of a purely philosophical judgment.[13] Because this is so, Caleb exceeds the character he framed for himself and can become other than who he has been. He expresses this insight by stating that his novel vindicates Falkland rather than himself, reversing what he set out to write. Moreover, by admitting to the vast gap between intention and meaning, he implicitly accepts the possibility that the effects of action are never knowable in advance, that one cannot finally tell the difference between imaginary and real utility, and thus that no action can be entirely free from self-deception.

Many readers would object to this account, arguing that the second ending is far too caught up in modes of performance exposed as fraudulent elsewhere in the novel. The rhetoric of sincerity in Caleb's final speech, not to mention in Falkland's response, resembles that used by Falkland to exonerate himself of the charge of murder. Caleb's sympathetic response to Falkland might be no less fictive than Falkland's call upon his audience's sympathy on that occasion.[14] As Randa Helfield argues, early in the novel Caleb tries to construct a legal case against his master and fails to do so in part because his hearers only listen for the confirmation of their expectations. The truth alone cannot win the day. Only after he learns that the telling of the truth, not the truth itself, "establishes its credibility and power" can he become convincing in the final scene.[15] But only through this shift to persuasive telling does the novel relieve Caleb of his solipsistic grandeur. When he relinquishes the self-evidence of the truth and accepts the fact that it must be represented through fiction, he can encounter the world of fictions as other than a closed system of lies. This insight is mirrored in Godwin's own practice in writing the second ending. In the 1832 Preface to the Standard Novels edition of *Fleetwood*, Godwin recounts the stages he went through in composing *Caleb Williams*, writing that he conceived of the breathless anxiety of the third volume first and then worked backward from there.[16] On this account, the entire novel germinated from the idea of a person trying to survive unendurable pressure from a more powerful antagonist. The logical culmination of this sensationalist plot, this fantasy of absolute resistance to absolute oppression, is in fact the madness of the first ending. In writing the second ending, Godwin dramatically changes the import of his text, doing so only at the last moment, in effect discovering the significance of his novel not at its inception but in the process of composition. The same process took place as he composed the *Enquiry*. As Godwin declares in *The Enquirer*, "When a man writes a book of methodical investigation, he does not write because he understands the subject, but he understands the subject because he has written."[17] Godwin's own experience of writing thus contradicts his claims about immutable reason: just as Caleb must submit to rhetoric before he can break out of his narrow identity, Godwin must also write to discover what he has to say.[18]

In accepting representation in this way, the second ending challenges the central premise of the *Enquiry*, that actual legislation falsifies the decrees of immutable reason. Not long after completing *Caleb Williams*, Godwin wrote a pamphlet attacking the way the lord chief justice conceived of "constructive treason" in a case against several members of the London Corresponding Society. Helfield shows that in the pamphlet Godwin argues that the law "is and must remain constant" and have the same meaning in all circumstances, in effect that "it is an objective and self-contained entity that can be apprehended independently of judicial constructions." But this novel's ending demonstrates that the law can be known only through construction.[19] The second ending implicitly undermines Godwin's entire theory of justice, whether or not he appropriates its insights in his future work. Reason, too, needs to enter into a conversation in order to discover its truth; it must speak through positive law or institutions, not because they coincide with it but because they make it possible for it to discover itself.

Because this ending brings about such a pronounced change in Godwin's basic ethical theory, it allows for a retrospective reinterpretation of the entire novel. Consider Caleb's state for much of the third volume. In the aforementioned preface of 1832, Godwin writes that he conceived the novel when he imagined "the fugitive in perpetual apprehension of being overwhelmed with the worst calamities, and the pursuer, by his ingenuity and resources, keeping his victim in a state of the most fearful alarm."[20] But since Caleb remains in this state because he refuses to comply with his pursuer's demands, this third volume vastly expands the little tales of ethical heroism familiar in Kant's second critique or Godwin's *Enquiry*. In those tales, ethical defiance presumably leads to a quick death, but here Falkland, having already deprived his victim of his livelihood, reputation, and place in civil society, wishes to keep him alive and torment him indefinitely, as if he could perpetually undergo a kind of emotional or spiritual death. Furthermore, Falkland's accusation does not remain his alone: sealed by a legal verdict, enforced by prisons and agents of the law, converted into a popular narrative sold on the London streets, passed by word of mouth among the lower ranks, it permeates the social order from top to bottom, pressing against Caleb from every conceivable part of his world and through every form of discursive and textual articulation. Caleb's insistence on the truth thus reveals an even more hyperbolic investment in doing the right thing, this time in defiance of an entire society and potentially over the course of an entire life. The culmination of this logic in the first ending demonstrates that Caleb is willing even to go mad to demonstrate his fidelity to the truth. What was a short and brutal confrontation with unjust power in the *Enquiry* here becomes an extensive negotiation with various kinds of intimidation; the novel translates the battle with an unjust force into an almost Foucauldian reflection on the manifold layers of social power.

It might seem that in this volume Caleb is entirely subject to Falkland's power. Yet Caleb can master Falkland's charge at least on one count: he knows that it is untrue. Having once imagined that he could know Falkland's secret, he now believes he knows the secret of the entire social order, that its power is illegitimate through and through. Although he lives in misery, his perpetual defiance of Falkland's demand allows him to experience that misery as a feature of the jouissance of his absolute ethical heroism, his determination to hold up against the entire creation if need be. Caleb needs a figure such as Falkland if he is to reach this state of heroism; only if the world is a system of total oppression can he become the singular pillar of truth. Of course, since nearly the entire nation is against him, he neither has an audience for his tale nor can he claim his true identity; he must adopt a series of disguises as an Irishman, a beggar, or a Jew to elude his pursuers. It might seem that by using such disguises, Caleb becomes guilty of not telling the truth, but by regarding those identities as not revealing his true self, he keeps himself pure, safeguarding a self entirely outside of the language of social life. Caleb's dilemma is the logical extension of Godwin's ethics: if all legislation necessarily falsifies reason, then all social identities are illegitimate as well. The novel's sensationalist plot originates directly from the premises of the *Enquiry*, for an ethics this hostile to articulation must eventually dramatize its pretensions through a revelation of the world's nullity. The heroic truth-teller of Godwin's fantasy is Caleb himself: he is the singular just man whose truths could transform the world, except that there is no one is listening.

The novel thus makes quite clear that the fantasy of possessing a world-transforming truth implies a similar fantasy that the world could be under the sway of a total falsehood, of what Falkland describes as "so well digested a lie, as that all mankind should believe it true" (135).

If one man could be the hero of truth, another could be equally committed to radical evil. Such is the case with Caleb and Falkland. But then it is not entirely clear whether Caleb himself escapes becoming a hero of evil as well: in the novel's penultimate chapter, just before the second ending, he becomes so incensed at his impossible situation that he explodes in a furious denunciation of his antagonist: "What should make thee inaccessible to my fury! – No, I will use no daggers! I will unfold a tale – ! I will show thee for what thou art, and all the men that live shall confess my truth!" Beneath this fantasy of murder through truth lies the wish for a power to destroy the world: "The elements of nature in universal uproar shall not interrupt me! I will speak with a voice more fearful than thunder!" (315). Here Caleb is not so different from Falkland, who on occasion expresses the wish to "crush the whole system into nothing!" (117). Caleb is willing to destroy the creation in order to save the truth, just as Falkland would annihilate the "system" to safeguard his reputation. What could better represent the sacrifice of actual future good? Thus a sweeping demand leads each of them to express the wish for what Sade calls the "second death," for an annihilation without hope of regeneration.[21]

Caleb is saved from his destructive fantasy when he fails to adhere to his duty. When he at last meets Falkland and, in that man's ravaged and dying body, sees the unmistakable signs of his moral sadism, he realizes that his virtue has no human justification. Falkland is only human, not the source of the world's evil; the enormous power he exercised was the product of Caleb's wish to prove his infinite capacity to resist it. The second ending thus rewrites the ethical fables of Kant and Godwin, suggesting that the sovereign and the ethical hero relied on each other to sustain a useless and disastrous jouissance without ever regarding each other as human beings, that the fantasy of heroic defiance serves the purposes of glory rather than the general good. But then evil is found not only in Falkland but also in Caleb's insistence on a truth and an identity prior to social articulation. The encounter demystifies the fantasy that there could ever be a secret order of the world that Falkland could control or that Caleb could know. Caleb "works through the fantasy," as Lacan would say, when he discovers that the world exceeds any singular truth, any virtuous intention, that there is neither a transcendental law one can use to defy it nor any principle antagonistic to such a law which holds it in thrall.[22] In the excessive self-denunciation that follows, Caleb almost sustains his ethical fantasy by making himself into the prince of evil, as if he wishes to protect himself against his realizations through a different kind of moral aggression. But the novel's final paragraph, in which Caleb writes about completing the tale so that the world might fully understand Falkland's errors, not his own, shows that he rapidly moves to another understanding in which both Falkland and he are to be found not in the tale of their errors but in its interpretation. Moreover, in the penultimate paragraph, Caleb muses on how Falkland was infected in youth by the poison of chivalry and thus finally admits that ethical agency might take shape through forces other than one's own will, that he and Falkland are both implicated in the history of social fantasy, and that the interpretation of their errors must reach beyond their own stories into a more comprehensive critique. In that case, they are also participants in a story whose ultimate import is unknown: much as they exceed their narratives, society exceeds the tale of its errors as well. No longer in thrall to an immutable reason, Caleb finds his place in the domain of mutable and open interpretation, one whose ultimate form must also be retrospective, knowable only in the future perfect tense, beyond reach from within history as it is actually lived.[23]

In these various ways, the second ending makes possible the emergence of a negative definition both of identity and of justice, carrying out its own version of the defining gesture of a philosophy of progressive modernity. In the essay "What Is Enlightenment?" Kant argues that society can enlighten itself only if the public is free to discuss political and religious affairs without fear of punishment. Reason would create a perpetual check to state power in the realm of public opinion, protecting society from the impositions of a state that might otherwise identify itself immediately with ultimate power and dispose of the need to justify its actions. State power would renounce its claim to embody transcendental justice, which would now appear only negatively, in the ideal form to which it would aspire and which reason would invoke in its public criticisms. The society as a whole would thus take shape around an absence akin to what Lefort considers the empty place of power, the form of ultimate legitimacy that would never receive permanent content in any person, doctrine, or law but that nevertheless would shape the social order as a whole.[24] This schema accepts institutional authority only within the context of its perpetual interrogation; it retains external power alongside modes of investigation that would force such power to win general consent. It corresponds to the ethic found at the end of the novel, which proposes that the reader interpret it to discern in its representations of things as they are signs of things as they might be, to find in the gap between representation and being the place for possible enlightenment.

The retrospective approach to justice refigures the novel's first two volumes. If no narrative or institution can directly capture being, reducing the world to its known and frozen terms, then no one could ever capture the essential truth about another person. But then the fantasy at the basis of Caleb's detection is fraudulent. When he listens to Collins's account, he assumes that something is missing in his narrative and that this thing must be the essential truth; he attempts to fill in the lack in the narrative, and in Falkland's subjectivity, with a single, positive act – something he may know and master at Falkland's expense. In this way Caleb enacts the premise of the *Enquiry*: whatever is prior to articulation must be its truth. No doubt Godwin would argue that secrecy and voyeuristic investigation both follow from the lack of sincerity, but the novel suggests that insincerity itself follows from the premise of a presocial essence of consciousness. Both Falkland and Caleb assume that to possess the secret would be to possess Falkland himself. The trunk thus symbolizes a secret and essential knowledge.[25] Through his insatiable curiosity, Caleb enacts a version of his later fantasy, hoping to penetrate Falkland's lies, unmask social power at its source, and reveal a truth beyond its coercive distortion. The novel builds outwards from this fantasy, reversing and complicating it in several stages: Falkland frames Caleb by placing jewels in Caleb's own secret boxes, publicly symbolizing his ironic, second-level mastery of Caleb's mastery; Caleb responds with his own secret knowledge of Falkland's illegitimate power, as I argued above, but does so in a narrative which, like the contents of the trunk, is known only to himself (and to the reader), as if his tale is outside social discourse in exactly the same way Falkland's secret remained untold in Collins's tale. The parallel between the contents of the trunk and Caleb's narrative suggests that positing a prior truth inevitably makes it wholly alien to the social order, even if it also transforms the entire social order into a symptom of this absent intention, a discourse permeated with its possible inadvertent revelation. Falkland's paranoia in Caleb's presence exactly matches Caleb's paranoia in the third volume: both are under the sway of the illusion that their essential selfhood might become visible to the eyes of another. The second ending thus cuts through the novel's entire plot by suggesting that it is no more possible to know the essence of Falkland than to maintain a total social power over Caleb. There are no successful detectives, any more than there are tyrants who know all and see all, because there is no positive essence to the law, to the social order, or to the subject – *only a constitutive lack*. Without that absence, there would be nothing to articulate, no subjectivity that could engage with others. It must remain a constitutive absence, a site of negativity within the field of articulation, or it will become the object of a fantasy of total control and the prize in a game of endless rivalry.

Although the novel culminates in a thorough critique of its early premises and makes possible a fairly rigorous understanding of post-utopian society, it does not conclude by affirming this alternative possibility. Caleb completes the manuscript to provide a full history of Falkland's life, not to speak of himself. It is as if, in renouncing his illusions, he also wishes to renounce himself, to disappear from public view entirely. The novel concludes with a strange tone whose exact import is elusive, divided between a chastened ethic of interpretation and Caleb's wish to disappear. Much as the tension that permeated through the treatise leads to the breakthrough in the novel's final chapter, the elusive tone of that chapter indicates that even in its revised form it has not entirely settled the key questions.

Thus it is no surprise that Godwin addresses those questions in a much more sweeping and comprehensive manner in his next novel, *St Leon*. Once again he writes a first-person romance concerning a protagonist who made a fatal error in coming into the possession of secret knowledge.[26] In contrast to Caleb, who knows the truth about one man's crime and extends that knowledge to the rest of the social order, St Leon gains possession of the secret of the philosopher's stone from a disreputable stranger, learning how to coin gold out of simple materials and to renew his youth indefinitely. He has apparently effortless wealth and something like immortality. But he can possess such magical knowledge only if he does not share it with anyone, not even his wife or family, much less agents of the church or state. As a result, he becomes socially unaccountable, a figure of permanent suspicion; like Caleb, he is hounded out of a rural village, is imprisoned on specious charges, and becomes alone in a world that does not understand him. Because he cannot renew his youth without giving up his name, his property, and all his social ties, he is more fundamentally alienated from a social identity than Caleb. Ironically, his immortality forces him to experience social death: as St Leon laments, "I became prematurely dead to my country and my race, because I was destined never to die!"[27] In a logic familiar from the previous novel, it seems that only those who are mortal can experience the delights of social life.

Although this novel might seem to go even further afield from Godwin's philosophical concerns, the counterfactual premise is right to the point. St Leon's impossible knowledge perfectly represents the access to immutable reason Godwin posited in the *Enquiry*. Just as Godwin's ethical agent gains access to reason by cutting through all social and political mediations, St Leon can draw upon a potentially infinite fortune without participating in economic activity; just as Godwin founds his philosophy on an immutable reason not subject to historical contingency, St Leon acquires the ability to live potentially forever, to become equally immutable. If this reading seems implausible, ponder the appendix "Of Health, and the Prolongation of Human Life" that appeared in the *Enquiry*, in which Godwin speculated that eventually medical science would enable people to live for indefinite periods, freeing them from the need for sexual reproduction and enabling them truly to become exemplars of private judgment. In his celebration of this possible future, Godwin implies that it would bring about the anarchical society he has envisioned throughout the book – one of universal, passionate benevolence (776–7). Like Kant's version of the afterlife, it would free people from the contingencies of mortal existence, giving them access to enormous knowledge and self-discipline, to an impartiality almost impossible in ordinary existence.

Given these overtones, St Leon's decision to accept the stranger's knowledge is partly honourable; he imagines that with great wealth and long life he can do much good in the world. But here again the seemingly utilitarian justification conceals powerful pathological motives, such as the wish never to experience poverty again, to regain noble status, and to pursue a glorious destiny. Godwin makes it quite clear that to possess this secret knowledge is akin to committing a great crime (cf. 143). Early in the novel, immediately after agreeing to his wife's earnest request that he never gamble again, St Leon submits to the impulse to gamble precisely because his love for his wife prohibits it and in a single night loses his entire fortune in a frenzy of transgression (59–71); in almost exactly the same way, he agrees to accept the stranger's offer of secret knowledge, knowing that in doing so he risks losing everyone he loves (149, 168). While it may seem that in acquiring the secret he gambles away everything to gain the world, it turns out that the latter is in fact a curse, for his unique condition actually cuts him off from the world and condemns him to a horrific life. At first, he thinks his knowledge sets him apart, and he briefly regards even princes and kings as his inferiors (163–4). But because he cannot discuss his new condition with anyone, the absolute good to which he has access is indistinguishable from radical evil and his greatness equivalent to a curse. Even worse, the fact that he will never lack gold or life exposes him to the experience that Lacan calls "the lack of the lack": where there should be something missing, some goal or object that he could search for, there is something present instead, blocking off his access to desire.[28] Restless, triumphant, ecstatic, St Leon lives in a continual fever of the soul, a state of solitary jouissance (159, 164–5); having gained immortality, as Lacan would say, "at the price of the truth of man," he later repents of his deed, confessing, "I felt that I was not formed for the happiness of a God" (377).

Perhaps St Leon is cursed simply because he violates the ethic of sincerity in keeping his knowledge a secret when something this powerful should be given to all. But consider what would result if he told his secrets: "Exhaustless wealth, if communicated to all men, would be but an exhaustless heap of pebbles and dust; and nature will not admit her everlasting laws to be so abrogated, as they would be by rendering the whole race of sublunary man immortal" (161). Infinitely abundant, gold would lose all value, as would all paper currency based on its standard; at least for a time, monetary exchange itself would collapse. Total abundance would lead to wholesale destruction. Similarly, universal immortality would destroy the institutions of sexual and cultural reproduction, including the family, which Godwin regards with especial reverence throughout *St Leon*, bringing about not the ideal society of the *Enquiry*'s appendix but an atomized dystopia. To realize pure reason would lead to the disaster that Caleb and Falkland only wish for when intoxicated by the jouissance of self-vindication.

This novel thus departs somewhat from the terms familiar in Godwin's previous works: in the counterfactual scenario, Godwin transforms what was merely fantasized into an actual disaster. Here the disclosure of the secret would threaten not merely social authority, as is the case with Caleb, but social relations themselves. The novel's focus shifts from ethics to an objective social logic: rather than adhering to the absolute as an ideal, St Leon possesses it in the form of a technology. This novel describes society as a system ordered by formal structures distinct from intention or affect. Social structure is a framework for action which depends on the constraint already given in the "everlasting laws" of nature. The implicitly hierarchical confrontation between Falkland and Caleb, which sustains the entire mode of inversion, complete with the ambivalent genres of criminal autobiography and of forest outlawry, gives way to a very different dynamic – the attempt to commit a crime against the laws of nature, one that would, like Sadean crime, attempt "to liberate nature from its own laws."[29] St Leon's magical knowledge constitutes precisely this kind of crime, one that would liberate by bringing about a version of the "second death" through the annihilation either of exchange or of the need to reproduce. While St Leon does not destroy himself with his secret, the fact that he receives it from a stranger who asks that he never "betray to mortal man the place in which [he] shall have deposited [the stranger's] ashes" (157), just as Sade commanded that his coffin be covered in acorns so that the "traces of [his] grave [would] disappear from the surface of the earth," suggests that his indefinitely long life is already a version of such a second death, that he already embodies a principle alien to nature.[30] The shift from the defiance of power to that of nature suggests that Godwin extends the critique of immutable justice carried out in the earlier novel; here he implicitly identifies the attempt to realize perfect reason with a crime against the most fundamental elements of things as they are. To attempt destroying all legislation in the name of reason is to become another Sade.

This shift in focus leads also to a change in form. While Caleb learns that his ethical heroism was socially useless only at the end of his tale, St Leon recognizes the solitude and misery of the stranger even before he gains his forbidden knowledge. The novel never needs to arrive at a moment of self-critique, for it demonstrates that St Leon is pursuing a doomed project all along. Consider the effects of St Leon's attempt to improve life in Hungary. In his account of his sojourn in that domain, where he attempted to revive the nation with his benevolent public expenditures, St Leon writes, "I was aware that, in the strictness of the term, money was not wealth; that it could be neither eaten nor drunk; that it would not of itself either clothe the naked or shelter the houseless"; it could do these things only if he spent the money to employ the most people in the most productive form of labour (372–3). In itself, money has no value. St Leon does not in fact have infinite wealth, only the capacity to command it by exchanging gold for the produce of labour. But in that case, he is caught in a familiar dilemma. On the one hand, when he is abandoned in the dungeons of Bethlem Gabor, he is tormented by hunger (413) since he cannot buy any food. Bereft of its social context, gold is as useless as dust. The pure disinterestedness of immutable reason is represented here as the uselessness of the abstract medium of exchange. On the other hand, when he puts his money into circulation to bring about the greater good, launching a major public works project, the massive increase of specie in circulation leads to inflation and disrupts the conditions for employment for everyone (379). To spend money on this scale brings about a small-scale version of the economic disaster that would follow upon telling his secret. If coining gold in solitude is useless, making the gold useful threatens to undo the actual relations of labour.

A similar logic informs the novel's treatment of St Leon's political position. The more he spends, the more he raises the suspicions of the bashaw, the Turkish authority who administers the region, who regards St Leon's officious interference with the "superintendence of the public welfare" as "blasphemy against the spirit of our religion" and a challenge to the authority of his sovereign, primarily because the person from whom people "have the most to fear and the most to hope, will always be their master." Through his public works, St Leon implicitly challenges the monarch's unique prerogative to be the public benefactor. Furthermore, his attempt to act on purely benevolent motives makes him suspect, since, as the bashaw states, he comes "hither with no apparent motive" (388–90). Whatever his intentions, his actions will have the same effect as if he wished to become the patron and thus the master of Hungary's citizens. The attempt to act upon pure benevolence is indistinguishable from the attempt to seize power. Bringing abstract reason to bear on social problems exposes the fantasy that one might be able to reshape society all on one's own, that one might find a place outside of the world from which one could dictate its transformation.

Godwin's new emphasis on the laws of currency or of social power is less a development of earlier positions than an attempt to refashion them within the context of debate that prevailed after the 1798 publication of Malthus's *Essay on the Principle of Population*. Malthus wrote his essay in response to Godwin, who had in the *Enquiry* and *The Enquirer* devoted significant attention to population, property, poverty, avarice, and other economic questions, and who in 1820 would publish a book-length refutation of Malthus.[31] Insofar as this novel shifts its focus from justice to the social constraints on just action, it accepts Malthus's attempt to change the terms of debate. Yet this novel does not adopt a Malthusian argument against utopia. While Malthus argues that the achievement of an ideal social condition would lead to a rapid increase of population and a return to misery, Godwin demystifies utopia even more directly, showing how its very achievement would destroy society. In effect, Godwin identifies utopia with disaster and dispenses with the need for a demographic argument. The counterfactual premise of his novel allows him to demonstrate that it is forbidden to realize immutable reason in history because it is itself the immediate threat: when forms of justice rooted only in disinterested, abstract reason are realized, they wreak havoc in a world shaped by ordinary human motives. The novel ultimately argues that immutable reason is already the disaster that Malthus fears.

This scenario of disastrous abundance transposes the problem of the lack of the lack onto a social stage, suggesting that a monetary system of exchange, like the desiring subject, also relies on lack. Without death and scarcity, the social order would collapse. The empty place of power reappears here as the empty place of life and wealth: only the gap between what people have and what they might wish to have sustains them. In this novel, the Lacanian subject of desire, the Lefortian empty place of power, and the economic theory of scarcity, all of which emerge at roughly the same historical moment, are strictly homologous.[32] At one point in the *Enquiry*, Godwin argues against the "political superintendence of opinion" by invoking the theories of "speculative enquirers that commerce never flourishes so much as when it is delivered from the guardianship of legislators and ministers" (562), linking philosophical anarchism with laissez-faire economics. While his theory of property does not otherwise conform to liberal economic doctrine, such a passage reveals the basic homology between the development of the individual subject, the general transformation in public opinion, and the flourishing of commerce. All three rely on a progressive model that draws upon on the notion of lack, of something which, while remaining absent, will inspire an endless effort to achieve it.

The possibility of such a productive lack is foreclosed from this novel precisely because St Leon himself embodies what should be missing. As a result, it sketches, as in a negative image, the shape of Enlightenment society as it traces St Leon's path through the world. What prevents St Leon from becoming a benevolent sovereign and dispensing his gold for the public good? Would it not work for him to become the equivalent of the Benthamite legislator, who from a position grounded in ahistorical reason would manipulate the world of self-interest to improve the common lot?[33] This prospect opens up when St Leon learns he can bribe the bashaw to allow him to continue his scheme of public works. But the bashaw will of course ask for more and more bribes, just as people, once they learn of St Leon's endless wealth, will regard him as evil if he does not immediately relieve their distress. As the bearer of an impossible abundance, he rapidly becomes the target of greed or opprobrium. Even worse, the misanthropic Bethlem Gabor captures him and imprisons him, demanding to be told the secret or to be supplied henceforth with gold. These events demonstrate that a society rapidly seizes control of a source of wealth generated outside of it, that St Leon does not in fact master Hungary with his benevolence but is mastered by it. It replicates on another scale the plot of *Caleb Williams*, in which Caleb, having detected Falkland's secret, cannot use his knowledge in any way before Falkland, realizing what has happened, subjects Caleb in turn. The result in each case is not the unilateral imposition of knowledge but rather its capture by those who wish to use it for their own ends. Much as Falkland demands that Caleb exonerate him and thus legitimate the authority of a murderer, Bethlem Gabor demands that St Leon supply him with money to fund his activities as the leader of a marauding band. The public authority of the English magistrate or the Hungarian nobleman is founded in lies and violence, in the attempt to master, rather than serve, true knowledge.

Yet the very episodes which show that knowledge is inevitably mastered by social power also show that the latter is irrational. Here reason and power expose each other's limits, leading not to the progressive interplay of Kant's theory of Enlightenment, in which power accepts the perpetual criticisms of reason, but to a contest that discredits power and enslaves reason. If St Leon's benevolence makes him a despot, as the bashaw implies, those who would use his power to their ends are also despots. As a result, the novel points to the failures of disinterested benevolence and of selfish rule both; it carries out a double negation, emphasizing that the impartial and the partial fail in similar ways. *But such failures are inevitable simply because immutable reason has become actual in the form of St Leon's secret knowledge.* The novel thus everywhere suggests that enlightenment is possible only if society founds itself on the prohibition of what St Leon represents – on the prohibition, ironically, of what is impossible. Insofar as society demands that absolute knowledge never be realized, either in legitimate authority or its critique, it makes their fruitful interplay possible. Power would no longer claim to exercise transcendental authority, reason would no longer regard power as purely illegitimate, nor would reason pretend to have an ahistorical truth that power could either enslave or appropriate. Henceforth, power, reason, and truth – as well as the domains of intersubjectivity and of economic exchange – are all to be conceived as founded in a lack or gap, the internal limit of the Real. If this lack is erased, or if it is filled in by a positive term, a referential content, such as St Leon's secret knowledge, then all is lost: only the foreclosure of the Real makes everything possible.

Thus the novel reveals Godwin to be a particularly astute theorist of the limits of enlightenment. Rather than merely reinforcing the various ideologies and institutions of progressive modernity, he delineates with unusual care their constitutive premises, demonstrating in these first-person narratives what must remain absent, yet perpetually invoked, if subjectivity, truth, power, and social exchange are to survive. He does so in part by bringing certain Enlightenment fictions directly into lived social reality, giving Caleb knowledge of a secret behind the façade of social power and giving St Leon a version of Kantian immortality. In both cases, he allows his readers access to the jouissance of transgressive knowledge, inaugurating one of the most enduring genres of the Real: sensationalist counterfactual tales. But such success demonstrates that these Enlightenment fictions can have effective purchase in that reality *only where they remain unrealized*, only where their *prohibition* becomes a governing principle of collective life. Furthermore, insofar as both protagonists learn that they cannot repudiate or manipulate the entire social order from outside it, from a position of supposed mastery, since they both remain within it and subject to its demands, these novels demonstrate that social knowledge, however powerful, is necessarily *internal* to what it knows and thus can never claim to master the totality, to grasp *all* of the social order. The internal limit, here as ever, points ultimately to the absence of any metalanguage, any external vantage or limit on whose basis one might survey the social field.

These novels outline in surprisingly accessible terms how a society begins to define itself in relation to the Real. In the first move, some aspect of that society attempts to exceed it, to impose upon it a mastery from outside, to remake it according to the demands (for example) of a transcendental justice. But in the second move, such an agent realizes that if that attempt succeeded, it would bring about nothing less than the end of sociality, exchange, reproduction, and possibly history itself; it would lead to wholesale disaster. This second move does not cancel transcendence itself but its realization within the realm of lived experience. Yet rather than leading that society back to its prior condition, in which transcendence constituted the framework of history, its origin and end, this second move incorporates the negated transcendence into itself, installing it as the very principle of its modernity.

As a result, Godwin's novels show us that the Real emerges as the residue of a specific historical process – not a historical development like any other, but rather a quintessentially modernizing process whereby those living within history attempt to surmount it, only to discover that such an enterprise is at once impossible and prohibited. By negating that attempt to surmount history, the agents of this process return to history to install this prohibition into history as the basis of its functioning. The attempt to exceed history, in effect, leads *back* to history, not by plunging into its domain indifferently but by embracing it *tout court*, establishing the notion of history as its supreme value. But this decision for history – this negation of any realization of transcendence – must perpetually exceed history itself, for it is irreducible to anything that history could produce or assimilate. In this way, a particular historical experience – the French Revolution, Kantian critique, Godwinian political defiance – leads not merely to another phase of history but to a new *relation* between history and itself, an incorporation of a decision on its behalf into its own functioning. Through this process can arise the modern sense of a *gap* in history, an event that alters the very form of history – and one for which it cannot account. The arrival of the Real through the prohibition on realizing a transcendental justice or immutable reason *also* produces the Real as the gap in history.

This installation of history as its own supreme value signals an important shift. Where premodern society considered the event variously described as the apocalypse, the day of judgment, or the end of history to be its positive destination – the arrival at last of a perfect justice that it could never realize on its own – modern society regards that final day with horror, for it regards history as far too precious ever to relinquish in this way. From this perspective, apocalypse, rather than promising a resolution to the problems of history, becomes unmitigated disaster, an assault on all that is precious in human existence: establishing history as the supreme value thus leads not only to the cancellation but also to the prohibition of apocalypse. Since modernity affirms finitude, rather than apocalypse, it must also affirm a temporality that runs indefinitely into a future without a final event, without resolution – a temporality that, in never reaching a perspective from which it can make a claim about the total structure of history, in never reaching the day of judgment, can never know itself – except (once again) in the mode of a negative transcendence.

While such reflections may seem to extend the insights embedded in Godwin's tales too far, in fact those tales articulate them with remarkable skill, even if on a smaller scale. Caleb's realizations in his final encounter with Falkland, for example, carry out a certain prohibition on attempting to render final justice on a life – and by extension, to orient oneself to a day of judgment that would do the same for humanity as a whole. Something in Falkland is Real, forever inaccessible to such judgment, just as something in Caleb forever eludes the ubiquitous light of general surveillance. St Leon's failure to bring absolute abundance to Hungary, to take another example, similarly reveals how monetary exchange also rests on a prohibition – this time, on the forbidding of any attempt to abolish scarcity. Something in exchange is Real, forever resistant to any attempt to alter it in the name of immutable reason.

What follows for Godwin's original ideal, the attempt to actualize immutable reason in the relations between people? Once people recognize that such a realization is not only impossible but prohibited, the negated form of that justice perpetually inhabits the domain of positive law, marking out the fact that such law will never attain what it seeks, that it will remain incomplete. That determining absence, that structurally necessary incompletion, is the Real, an exact homologue of what, for Lacan, perpetually makes the symbolic incomplete. Much as history becomes indefinite, extending into the future without any prospect of attaining its finality, so also positive law holds sway in the absence of any final knowledge of what it achieves or indeed any claim that its judgments are true. In effect, then, the endings of these tales do not redeem positive law from the thorough criticism to which Godwin subjects it in the *Enquiry*; they return to it nevertheless, authorizing it even in its indefinite condition, as if condemning modern society to endure under the sway of a legal regime that can never attain – and is forbidden from attaining – its ostensible goal. From the perspective of these tales, at least, modernity serves under regimes of law that can only indefinitely realize an impossible justice.

This development in relation to Godwin's initial stance on immutable justice implicitly bears on Kantian ethical theory, for it suggests that one must impose a prohibition on actualizing the moral law as well. Realizing the demands of the moral law within human experience would lead to no better results than what Caleb or St Leon witness; it would produce in its own domain unmitigated disaster. But Godwin's tales go further. *Caleb Williams* shows that Caleb's attempt to attain total knowledge of another subject – and Falkland's consequent attempt to gain total control over him as subject as well – deprives both subjects of their basic liberty; freedom thus inheres in negating the realization of a perfect freedom through the moral law. The realization of the moral law, in short, decimates freedom rather than establishing it. To be fair, in the story about the unjust sovereign, Kant claims only that a person subject to that sovereign's demand could choose for justice at the cost of his life, and because of that possibility would know that he were free. He for a moment seems to suggest that freedom inheres in the prospect of realizing the moral law rather than in actually carrying it out. But even this stance fails to do justice to the full structural imperatives here; Godwin's tales make clear that it is precisely the mere fantasy of realizing immutable justice that gets his protagonists in trouble, leading them to wish for an enormous violence (Falkland, Caleb) or to seek a form of power that ends up causing widespread social disarray (St Leon). The transcendental capacity Kant posits must be prohibited – but thus must take the form of a negated transcendence inherent in the ethical subject, an ethical instance of the Real.

The extraordinary power of narrative fiction to capture these insights suggests that it, too, can carry philosophical weight – that it is a worthy counterpart of conceptual formalization and indeed may be superior to philosophical argument in discovering the necessity of such self-critique. *Caleb Williams* is especially distinctive for forcing its author to abandon his initial premise; the logic of the narrative, in confronting him with the impasse of a total repudiation of English society, enables him to push further than the mere exposition of rationalist critique and to apply the apparent rigour of that critique to itself. But what should we make of the counterfactual premises of *St Leon*, clearly distinct from the apparently realist mode of *Caleb Williams*? Insofar as its central premise brings into play what is obviously impossible in lived experience, it represents a step beyond the earlier novel, as if to build self-critique into its form from the start. No doubt St Leon learns why gaining access to the secrets of the philosopher's stone cannot give him what he seeks from it; here again first-person narrative invites the reader into a social fantasy that eventually undermines itself. But since that critical operation takes shape over the course of the entire novel, rather than at its denouement, that novel elaborates on a self-critique embedded in the counterfactual situation itself, greatly extending the kernel of insight captured in the final pages of the previous tale.

But why would Godwin write a romance centred in a project that is clearly identified at the start as destructive? If this romance already displays its impossibility, what social purpose does it serve? The fact that such a romance could be entertaining, even fascinating, suggests that it indirectly fulfils the wish to be able to carry out such an impossible enterprise. The novel's mode shares much with that Godwin outlines in the "Essay of History and Romance," written around 1797 but unpublished in his lifetime, in which he argues that a fictional representation is preferable to a factual account of a historical personage's life, for it makes available what is otherwise unknowable in the historical record. In this essay, he defends the attempt to represent an inaccessible subjectivity, replicating the enterprise of *Caleb Williams*. Jon Klancher argues that romance defined in this way could articulate defeated radical projects of the past, especially those of the seventeenth century, preserving such "possible, unrealized futures" from the realist reifications found in the universal history of the Edinburgh Enlightenment.[34] Yet by writing a romance about not only a historical personage but a non-existent one, in *St Leon* Godwin makes the fictional representation of actual and of imaginary people indistinguishable, at once exposing the essay's potentially scandalous argument and reaffirming that scandal, in effect depicting what could never happen rather than what might happen, narrating not only what has been but what will always be unrealized. If, as Klancher argues, in this essay he shifts from the *Enquiry*'s theory of necessity to one of contingency, in *St Leon* he goes further and writes a book of the impossible.[35] The utopian future may never come to pass, but he enacts its impossibility in fictional form nevertheless. Rather than cutting against the reifications of historical narrative, here he breaks through the structural limitations that enable history itself to unfold. Yet at the same time, the novel makes clear throughout that what it explores is not only impossible but prohibited. In all these ways, in this tale Godwin inaugurates a new genre of the Real – one that, potentially quite popular, can henceforth flourish, in tales such as his daughter Mary Shelley's *Frankenstein*, even as it bears significant philosophical weight.[36] Thus if in the *Enquiry* Godwin theorized the conversational, experimental ethos of London radical circles to which he belonged, serving as one of the first organic intellectuals of revolutionary living, and in *Caleb Williams* carried out one of the earliest and most exemplary instances of revolutionary self-critique, in *St Leon* he articulated an absolutely transgressive and impossible project, becoming one of the first artists of the Real.[37]

If, as I suggested a moment ago, *St Leon* allows one the opportunity to live through a certain experience vicariously, to inhabit what is structurally impossible, it not only exposes the fraudulence of its protagonist's project but allows one to identify with it and live it through as well. Embedded within the critique, then, is another level: the novel articulates what it demonstrates to be at once impossible and prohibited, allowing the reader access to an experience of stunning transgression. In effect, the tale renounces the fantasy of immutable reason not to abandon it entirely but to sustain its affect even in the midst of its loss. St Leon occupies the place of the lack not because Godwin wishes to have similar access to immutable truth but because, knowing that this place is empty, he would rather capture a mode of experience that might transpire in that emptiness rather than merely embrace the social order that circulates around it. On this level of the tale, it protests against the traumatic loss of the fantasy, even if it must simultaneously acknowledge that it could never be fulfilled. But since the counterfactual terms of this protest reinforce the realistic premises of the social order, they also demonstrate that negative romance is that order's way of marking out its premises and limits.

Thus it turns out that the negation of the protagonist's project still allows it to speak. Much as the transcendence that modernity seeks to cancel remains effective, *as* negated, within it, here a prohibited version of immutable reason still operates, even though it is crossed out from the start. The form of counterfactual fiction, in short, makes it possible for readers to occupy a position that the novel itself – and the modernity it licenses – has foreclosed; it keeps alive precisely the fantasy that it negates. If that is the case, *St Leon* advertises the fact that the exclusion of transcendence, far from bringing a certain historical logic to completion, allows a certain fantasy to endure, even within a modernity authorized by that fantasy's exclusion. Rather than leading to a new phase of maturity, a new level of insight, self-critique brings in tow the very thing it seems to have repudiated. This survival hints at a wish to carry out the initial project after all, to enact a wholesale revolution, this time for good – whether as a political, financial, scientific, industrial, sexual, technological, or other revolution. In effect, *St Leon* points to the structural ambivalence of modernity; far from taking the form of a Hegelian sequence towards a more advanced knowledge of its condition, it *perpetually replicates the impasses out of which it initially arises*, forever remaining caught within a self-contradictory dynamic. If on the one hand it apparently operates through a knowingly secularized mode, accepting the structure of a history without finality, on the other it attempts to overleap that mode to impose yet another rendition of immutable reason. Modernity, in short, might be yet another version of first-person critique – capable of seeing through its premises on one level while still remaining caught in a fatal identification with its initial fantasy.

Godwin's critiques in these two novels at once exclude and embrace a certain hyperbolic fantasy, crystallizing an ambivalence inherent in modernity. His tales rest on the seam between the social order and what it must foreclose, between intersubjectivity and the romance of the impossible. In Godwin's work one passes not from a discredited social order to one finally authorized by genuine insight, as an ideology of progress would have it, but from a sociality grounded in an external transcendence to one riven by an internal limit. Thus Godwin's project, precisely because it begins with a classic statement of late-Enlightenment ambition, culminates in equally classic statements showing that such ambition leads neither to supersession nor to progress but to the advent of the Real.

3 After the Covenant

Undead Subjectivity in Wordsworth's Alpine Sublime

Midway through *The Prelude*, immediately after recounting the astonishing effect on him of crossing the Alps, William Wordsworth briefly depicts its aftermath:

> That night our lodging was an Alpine House,
> An Inn, or Hospital, as they are named,
> Standing in that same valley by itself,
> And close upon the confluence of two Streams;
> A dreary Mansion, large beyond all need,
> With high and spacious rooms, deafened and stunned
> By noise of waters, making innocent Sleep
> Lie melancholy among weary bones. (6.573–80)[1]

This passage might seem at first merely to describe an unpleasant night. But insofar as it personifies a vast interior space deafened by mighty natural forces, it reveals the consequences of claiming that the experience of the sublime in the encounter with such forces reveals stunning attributes of the mind. If those attributes are truly within an interior space "large beyond all need," then they might perpetually deafen and stun it, making it almost impossible to retain such a mind within a body that requires sleep. In that case, the sublime is not an experience that confirms the self; it is unwelcome, involuntary, even traumatic, splitting open that self and leaving it deafened and exhausted. Thus a narrative that might seem to advertise an egocentric sublime does quite the opposite: it suggests that the very infinity which seems to authorize the poet's vocation in fact makes it nearly unlivable. Where one might suppose that in this epic poem Wordsworth hopes to subsume prophecy or inspiration into a secular understanding of the poet, this passage hints instead that the poem reveals what necessarily undercuts any such understanding.

For Wordsworth, the encounter with such violence takes place at the height of the Alps, in the midst of the jagged, riven landscape resulting from the earth's geological history; accordingly, that traumatic transport bears an intimate relation to the scene of natural disaster. Borrowing from Copjec, I have argued that with the deletion of history's origin and end, transcendence does not disappear but in its negated form unsettles that history, becoming an alien, unpredictable, haunting force. Wordsworth's epic suggests that it becomes a *disastrous* transcendence, one that operates through the natural disasters whose evidence is preserved in the splendid chaos of the earth's surface, most notably in the Alpine mountains – and that intrudes as well in the experience of the traumatic sublime. This rendition of the internal limit thus shifts our focus towards the volatile intersection between Romantic-era understandings of the "history of the earth" and the violence inherent to the aesthetics of the sublime; moreover, in tracing both of these key questions back to a reconfigured concept of transcendence, a concept that necessarily ramifies broadly across many domains – aesthetic, historical, ethical, political – it calls out for a new understanding of the place of an apparent secularization within Romantic poetics.

Wordsworth's poetry may well provide the best opportunity for such explorations. Although his characteristic stances apparently confirm the putative narrative of secularization, in such poems as "Tintern Abbey" or the Prospectus to *The Recluse,* at moments he exposes the costs of this process, especially when he contrasts older certainties with a modern anxiety. Various passages in the thirteen-book *Prelude* are particularly revealing in this regard. The dream of the Arab in book five, the crossing of the Alps in book six, the ascent of Snowdon in book 13, and the "analogy passage" concerning a rainbow immovably fixed above a ferocious storm (a draft written in relation to the five-book *Prelude* envisioned briefly in the spring of 1804) allude to the theme of the biblical deluge, touching in some way upon the anxiety of imagining the consequences of a natural cataclysm. Features of the "analogy passage" resonate with aspects of the passages regarding the rainbow covenant in Genesis 8 and 9, implicitly making clear that such a covenant no longer forestalls the return of the deluge.[2] Although these passages are placed at strategic junctures over the course of the epic, they resonate so well with a series of further passages on sublime inundation or its foreclosure that on some level they constitute one of the leading motifs of the poem. This emphasis is all the more pressing because of the fairly explicit reworking of the covenantal motif of Abraham's sacrifice of Isaac in "Michael" a few years before.[3] The consistent focus on the problem of a covenantal poetics ties these texts together and makes evident that the poet who can pass by Jehovah and his angels unalarmed, or who imagines himself as a prophet of Nature, considers the task of rethinking various biblical covenants to be a central aspect of his project.

What can justify such a sustained attention to this theme? The prologue to the Arab dream provides a clue: there, the poet imagines that a cataclysm might erase human achievements but allow nature itself, and its "soul divine," to persist (*Prelude* 5.16). As many scholars have argued, this unease arises from the poet's readings in the "history of the earth," particularly in those texts that emphasize the vast scope of natural time, the frequency of natural disaster and species extinction, and the contingency of cultural origins and survival. Studies by Marjorie Hope Nicolson, Ernest Bernhardt-Kabisch, Theresa Kelley, and Alan Bewell, among others, chart the significance of seventeenth- and eighteenth-century geological writing to an emergent aesthetics of the sublime, particularly as it appears in Wordsworth's poetry, and more recent studies by John Wyatt and Noah Heringman deepen this analysis, arguing that Wordsworth's poetry is so thoroughly pervaded with geological concerns and tropes that his work influenced the further articulation of geological ideas.[4] The poet's reflections on the undoing of the rainbow covenant register his interpretation of a broadly shared cultural transformation and show that in his view this new understanding of earth's history makes cultural achievement, and perhaps human existence itself, vulnerable. His knowledge of geological processes has clearly undone his confidence that humanity is sheltered by a divine guarantee.

This treatment of human vulnerability is not alone in the Romantic era. A number of other texts in the period juxtapose the representation of such contingency with allusions to aspects of the Christian tradition: a partial list might include the jarring coincidence of the imagery of condemnation, mercy, and penance throughout *The Rime of the Ancient Mariner* with the radical chance captured in the image of Life-in-Death and her game of dice; T.R. Malthus's use of the tale of "Nature's mighty feast" at a telling moment in *An Essay on the Principle of Population* to repudiate and condemn charity; the uses of the "history of the earth" in the contests for the protagonist's soul in Byron's *Cain*; and the severe irony of a performance of Haydn's *The Creation* in the midst of a universal plague in Mary Shelley's *The Last Man*.[5] Judging by these examples, the Marquis de Sade is not entirely out of bounds in blasphemously placing a discourse on nature's infinitely destructive powers, and our duty to imitate them, in the mouth of the pope, as we have seen: the transgressive overtones of this gesture point to a characteristic feature of the period's literature and to a defining element of its response to arriving at a new understanding of the natural world.

Even this brief listing of Romantic texts suggests that the awareness of human vulnerability arises not only from geological discourse but from an array of sources and experiences. The close interweaving of the imagery of deluge with that of revolution in Wordsworth's poetry invokes a radical instability in the history of human institutions. Furthermore, in Malthus a series of apparently random disasters – war, famine, plague – become signs of a constitutive fault, in which the apparently external threat to human flourishing is found in that flourishing itself. In the early nineteenth century, these three depictions of vulnerability – geological, political, demographic – were so familiar, and their terms so analogous, that they could be mutually reinforcing, creating a much more pervasive sense of unease than any could on its own. One cannot help but conclude that the widespread crisis of faith presumably engendered by the publication of *The Origin of Species* in 1859 actually transpired much earlier and in a somewhat different tone; the attempt to think through the materialist underpinnings of the human condition is already well under way in the Romantic era.

The import of these emergent discourses of materiality, not to mention their close ally, historicism, have long been of interest to scholars of British Romanticism. Indeed, they have loomed quite large in the work of critics who wish to establish that Romantic writing, far from repressing or negating historicism, plays a crucial role in making it a privileged mode of comprehension. Yet what remains out of view in such accounts is the specifically delugic aspect of materialism, the post-covenantal edge of secular apprehension. Materialist discourse does not stand on its own, as it were, for by disfiguring the species' foundation in a divinely ordained nature, that discourse does not simply erase the transcendental but redefines it precisely *as* an infinite material process. It follows that Romantic-era discourse, by drawing on the awareness of that process, simultaneously disfigures and refigures divine agency, locating it anew in a post-covenantal yet non-negotiable dimension, one that makes human flourishing radically uncertain.

The theory of the internal limit fits this occasion well, sharply illuminating the limits of familiar notions of secular history. To expel the divine infinite does not expel infinitude itself; the latter reappears as a disruptive, uncanny aspect of finitude which undermines or exceeds it from within. This interior infinite is nothing other than that ungrounding negation, that element that must perpetually intrude and disrupt the functioning of the world as modernity conceives it. In this account, nature does not amplify a fundamental substance, for its ordinary operations include cataclysm and extinction; the overthrowing of natural forms is an inherent part of natural history. Likewise, cultural institutions are shaped by forces that can just as easily overthrow and transform them. The Real names a constitutive incoherence, an uncanny dimension that forever unsettles all that is familiar, that perpetually threatens to undo the known world.

Thus to situate Wordsworth's explorations of a post-covenantal modernity – an account that differs significantly from received versions of his contributions to secularization – one must pause over the question of secularization itself to locate its central fissure and impasses. In this regard, the notion of the internal limit provides a useful fulcrum, for it enables one to see how familiar versions of secularization fail to note the consequences of suspending or negating a ground outside history itself. The idea that secularization might bring about a mere displacement from the biblical to the literary canon, for example, or from apocalyptic to progressive history, must founder on its inability to specify how sacred authority can reappear in a literary canon that is never closed or in an incremental history whose end will never appear.[6] The authority invoked by this model of secularization must remain out of reach, at once insistent and impossible. A different problem arises with the innovative approach of Hans Blumenberg, who argues that secular reason need not borrow from the sacred to legitimate itself but may focus on its capacity to build on relatively modest but demonstrable achievements. Yet for Blumenberg, Descartes cannot inaugurate secular reason without explicitly suspending the question of teleology: the secular project finds its start not by superseding what came before but by bracketing it, leaving it unresolved.[7] As a result, despite Blumenberg's claims, secular history cannot be entirely self-legitimating, for it authorizes itself through its determined ignorance on ultimate questions. Even a successful history of scientific achievement cannot explain what science is for or what concept of the human it is meant to serve.[8]

This logic of suspension reappears in a different guise elsewhere. José Casanova, for example, provides a model not of secularization but of differentiation, whereby religion gives up its power over the state and retains its authority, if at all, through its participation in the normative debates of modern civil society.[9] In a similar vein, Mark Canuel shows how religious toleration in England locates the "indispensable resource for the meaning of beliefs" in liberal "society and its institutions."[10] In both accounts, religious claims are bracketed in favour of the ordinary functioning of civil society, implicitly elevating the latter above those claims and creating an apparatus of management consisting of the rational justification of norms and the suspension of religiously based conflict. But in creating such an apparatus, modern society evidently relinquishes a language in which ultimately to legitimate itself, in which to claim an ontological or divine foundation. On what basis does it assert that suspending conflict is superior to enforcing transcendental claims? In such a settlement, the transcendental does not simply disappear; it inevitably insists, even where the terms meant to figure it have been suspended, making its claims at once pressing and incoherent. As Fredric Jameson has pointed out, the characteristic conflicts of modern politics take the form of contests between political stances that orient themselves to a utopian promise; the hegemonic debates of democratic societies perpetually renew the prospect of a haven outside history, even though, as one might add, they cannot, by virtue of their participation in civil society, ever realize such a utopian hope.[11] Thus it seems that history must perpetually circle around the site of a certain suspension or negation, its internal limit, invoking a transcendental telos that it must perpetually defer and promising the arrival of a future that it endlessly undermines.

Aspects of this crucial impasse are already visible in Romantic-era discourse, especially in those texts that emphasize humanity's geological and demographic vulnerability. Insofar as these texts insist that humanity is entirely circumscribed by nature's functioning, the internal limit makes itself felt in the alien dimensions of the preconditions of life, in the materiality that at once enables and potentially undermines human flourishing. Here the transcendental names not a divinity but the very horizon of our experience – a horizon now at once intimate and inhuman. As a result, the suspension of telos radically alters the collective orientation to time and space, life and death, materiality and spirit, subjecting each to the logic of finitude while finding within that logic the haunting remains of an alienated transcendence. Bracketing the collective's invocation of the divine places it in intimate relation with what cannot manifest intentionality, cannot sustain a relation, and is beyond all appeal. Within the context of Romantic discourse, at least, modernity is not a secular but a post-covenantal condition.

Such claims may appear to impose too strict a coherence on a potential interpretation of secular modernity. As any serious engagement with the many recent studies of the secular suggests, that entire question is so complex, so fraught with competing and inconsistent elements, that it can scarcely be comprehended in any total fashion without sacrificing a rigorous interrogation of its leading metaphors, ironies, fissures, and contradictions. Yet such a knotted field is precisely what modernity's (un)founding in negation must produce: by making that negation into a positive principle, modernity inevitably becomes a scene without any underlying consistency except for this principle, which thereby becomes the unstated, yet endlessly invoked, basis for its practices and institutions. The defining element of modernity, then, is not materiality but the gesture of negation, on whose (anti)basis it can build not only its idea of material process but also its notions of historical aimlessness (shaped by the absence of a telos), scientific investigation (of a reality stripped of ontological import), the delimitation of any "culture," the philosophical critique of metaphysics, and the literary supersession of the religious. Through these institutions, modernity perpetually rehearses its emptying the collective of any positive content, any orientation to a goal. At its most stable, modernity becomes the management of its aimlessness, the routinization of its (un)founding, a practice of perpetual suspension.

Wordsworth's emphasis on the undoing of the rainbow covenant focuses directly on the most symptomatic elements in this negation and as a result cuts against the more complacent renditions of secularization dominant by the early nineteenth century. Recent scholars have emphasized the gradual shift, over the late seventeenth and eighteenth centuries, towards a theology in which divine action is regarded as immanent in the processes of nature and society. Charles Taylor, for example, describes how the emergence of the concept of a self-confirming system, beneficial to its members without requiring them to make an altruistic effort – in short, an "economy" – alongside the practices of the public sphere and philosophies of mutual sympathy and benevolence gradually makes superfluous the theology of sin and grace, atonement and redemption.[12] Colin Jager brings the argument from design back into the orbit of Romantic studies, suggesting that in its best renditions, particularly in David Hume and Anna Letitia Barbauld, it is no longer an argument at all but a polite supposition, a sociable agreement, a practice – one that nevertheless provides a formative context for Romantic discourse.[13] However greatly these readings of secularization differ, they agree that eighteenth-century discourses or practices give the knowable world a certain modest stability, relieving it of cosmological or theological pressures and enabling the collective to sustain a more confident, settled tone in relation to its world.

In seeking to make divine intentionality immanent in natural design, eighteenth-century discourses hoped to downplay the aspect of God that exceeds design. But that transcendental excess is at stake in the biblical tales of creation, flood, and rainbow covenant. By alluding to those stories, Wordsworth emphasizes precisely those features of divinity that natural theology most wished to efface, opening up a breach in the thinking of design which he nevertheless invokes. In doing so, he also foregrounds that moment of scientific investigation which challenged the confidence of a deist natural theology – the moment that Taylor, invoking Paolo Rossi, describes as the encounter with "the dark abyss of time."[14] In that dark abyss, James Hutton famously wrote, he can find "no vestige of a beginning, – no prospect of an end."[15] In Wordsworth's poem, one sees how the response to that vast time inevitably brought with it a new reflection on the entire array of questions associated with the biblical covenant, making newly visible the question of a divine grounding for nature.

To take up Wordsworth's explorations in this regard, one must turn from the late eighteenth-century context and delve into the biblical text itself, if only to examine how alluding to it might serve the poet's purposes in framing questions most relevant to his project. Even a cursory look at the early chapters of Genesis makes clear that the flood is caused by the same deity that creates the world, in which case the God of creation is not necessarily, or not yet, a guarantor of human flourishing but is equally capable of destroying human existence altogether. The juxtaposition of creation and flood suggests a nearly primordial contest within the pre-covenantal biblical God between a will to create and a hatred of creation, between the will to affirm and the will to punish humanity (see Genesis 1:28, 1:31, 6:5–8, 6:11–13). This contest may derive from an ambivalence inherent in the primordial event of creation itself: insofar as creation is conceived as imposing a system of differences (light and dark, waters above and below the firmament, dry land and sea, day and night) or as taming a primordial "earth" that "was without form and void" (Gen. 1:2) by imposing form, the flood may simply be the return of what creation meant to tame – the undifferentiated earth, the void. To impose order on chaos, it seems, might also be to invite chaos to return; to exert a power to create an ordered cosmos may only invite a contrary impulse to undo that order.

Thus it turns out that the biblical God in which humanity can trust does not emerge at creation but rather after the flood, when he repents of his destructive act and, in the form of the rainbow covenant, promises never to repeat it. Although Noah sacrifices to God to seal the covenant, this act does not bind Noah nearly so much as God, who vows to curb his own transgressive tendencies, his own wish to subvert the creation. The rainbow covenant, then, is the biblical tradition's way of regulating divine transcendence. If the God who can create can also destroy, then the tradition needs a supplementary step to ensure that the event of creation is irreversible, that the world is indeed founded for good. Strangely enough, the habitable world does not originate in the act of creation per se; more crucial is the gesture of sacrifice and the covenantal promise, the symbolic exchange between human and divine, which alone guarantees the survival of the cosmos. Because God himself is wayward and transgressive, the cosmos is secured in the covenant. As a result, this act of symbolic exchange subsumes both humanity and divinity through the binding pact of the covenant itself; this sacrificial arrangement contains both parties as well as nature within the order of symbolic exchange. Since symbolic exchange now provides the basis for the creation, nature is not truly other to culture or to the ritual order but is only another division within that order, outside of which can only be chaos or anti-creation.[16]

If all this is so, it follows that the suspension of a covenantal relation to transcendence opens the way not merely for a return of the primordial floodwaters but more crucially for the return of the God of the deluge as well. Suspending the covenant makes humanity vulnerable to the dangers of geological and biological processes, to a nature now conceived as truly other, but it also removes any curb on transcendence, exposing humanity to the actions of an uncontrollable God. It is not possible simply to ignore the emergence of such an alien divinity and focus instead on incremental, secular achievements; if humanity is to conceive of its relation to natural processes, it will inevitably have to raise certain questions, especially about the prospect of its extinction or survival, that can only be considered of transcendental import. It follows that the attempt at secularization or differentiation does not remove the question of God from a central place in modern culture but rather alters his status: *a negated God emerges from this process as alien, disfigured, and utterly unreadable, a mode of disastrous transcendence.*

The persistence of this unreadable divinity suggests that the apparent erasure of transcendence does not truly undo symbolic exchange but gives it a new form, a mode of encounter between a radically ungrounded domain of history, nature, or human existence on the one hand and an alien, unmoored, disastrous transcendence on the other. What Copjec describes as an internal limit takes shape as well through this vexed, unpredictable, and unmanageable encounter between ungrounded domains. This development is homologous with the process that effaces broadly shared understandings of symbolic exchange that obtained throughout the eighteenth century – the exchange between the gentry and plebeians in what E.P. Thompson describes as the moral economy of the English crowd, leading to the impasses of the era of Chartism (when a mass radical movement voiced its demands in the face of the implacable opposition of Parliament), as well as the exchange between the living and the dead, leading to the emergence of a literature preoccupied with figures of the undead.[17] As I have argued elsewhere, these developments ultimately distorted symbolic exchange;

contesting the implicit authority of the crowd led not to a pacified body politic but to the emergence of a negated, monstrous agency.[18] Similarly, the erasure of the covenantal God did not eradicate the deity but produced a disastrous, alien figure. Evidently, the covenant was never simply a matter of belief, for it was part of a strategy in relation to an otherness that persists even after its undoing.

The emergence of geological knowledge is thus only one of a series of transformations in eighteenth-century European society, each of which undermines prior notions of symbolic exchange and accordingly raises anew the question of what might possibly give the collective, history, or nature an appropriate coherence. Within the many attempts to address these unprecedented challenges, Kant's critical philosophy stands out for explicitly incorporating a new modesty about the reach of human reason into an overarching account of its capacities. The Copernican revolution, which undermined the authority of common-sense perception of the phenomenal world, and new geological knowledge, which unsettled prior convictions about the earth's origin and end, undercut the prospect that direct human apprehension might have access to reality and its telos; accordingly, Kant's project sets itself the task of salvaging a credible architecture for reason in the wake of these losses, to describe the mutual relations of rational faculties newly defined by their limitations.[19]

In pursuing this project, Kant demonstrates that he is by no means naive regarding the impact geological knowledge might have on the most fundamental premises of thought; one need only consult his scientific works, written largely in the 1750s on such topics as the formation of planets, the "theory of the heavens," and the Lisbon earthquake, to see that he is remarkably astute, even original, in his contributions in these fields. His work is of equal significance for retaining a basic theodicy despite his grasp of the ultimate consequences of a Newtonian understanding of astronomical and geological matters, for he retains a confidence in God's perfection even as he acknowledges that the physical universe itself must eventually decay – and be reborn – and that earthquakes may strike people despite their status as Christians. In effect, he subordinates human beings, as well as their moral condition, to what he calls the "whole essence of nature," the design of the physical world overall, even as he acknowledges that human beings must be "in the dark" when attempting to guess the ultimate divine intention.[20] In the wake of these reflections, one is not surprised that within the major works of his critical philosophy that emerge later in his life, Kant adopts a remarkably careful approach to the core themes of scientific knowledge and the sense of divine reassurance, accepting the loss of claims to a direct knowledge of reality, the disappearance of certainty regarding the telos of nature, and certain hesitations regarding the specific content of orthodox theology.

Within the context of that more modest approach, Kant's *Critique of the Power of Judgment* remarkably attempts to incorporate the mind's response to nature into a structure that might still have a rational telos of another kind.[21] Rather than routing the coherence of things through a divine terminus for history, he does so through outlining the relations between faculties of mind. In effect, Kant hopes that even if one must shed old certainties regarding nature's origin and end, one might proceed untraumatically to provide a framework for what remains after this process in a capacious, precise description of the mind's finite resources. It is as if Kant hopes to overleap the mark of a negated transcendence and relinquish old certainties while crafting modern, more philosophically conceived alternatives. Giving up a knowable telos for nature as a potential ground for humanity, he hopes that his account of the capacities of and relations between the mind's faculties – including the relations between their various responses to this newly conceived nature – will provide what is necessary to complete the architecture of the three critiques.

According to his own account in the third critique, to bring his system together he requires a bridge between the mind that perceives, oriented as it is to the phenomenal world (the problematic of the first critique), and the subject that is free, oriented to its more-than-phenomenal dignity (the problematic of the second critique); such a bridge he locates in the power of judgment (the problematic of his third critique). Yet this endeavour to craft an overall architecture necessarily encounters a significant obstacle in what Lacan would call the absence of a metalanguage in which to adjudicate between the claims of each faculty. To some extent, of course, this activity of adjudication is proper to the power of judgment itself, which is present in the philosophical interrogation of aspects of reason in the first two critiques. But when judgment sets out to judge *itself* in the third critique, by Kant's own admission the recursive structure of that activity must cause serious difficulty. As a result, Howard Caygill argues, the "outcome of unravelling the problem is not a clear solution … but a statement or report of its difficulty." For Caygill, Kant's emphasis here "on stating a difficulty rather than resolving it" places the third critique "within the tradition of aporetic philosophy," whereby the philosopher is "cast as an arbiter between the conflicting accounts of an issue, and not as a party to the dispute."[22] The philosopher without a metalanguage finds himself charged with the task of articulating as clearly as possible impasses that reason cannot resolve because it can resort to no power higher than itself.[23]

The aporetic nature of Kant's enterprise arises not only with regard to judgment's difficulty in judging itself but also in its task of accounting for the relation between the mind's faculties along the way. The appearance of key disjunctions between faculties of mind across the three critiques testifies to a certain ability to articulate those disjunctions – yet it also hints that the effort to overcome the impasses of a secularizing reason may not succeed. Gilles Deleuze captures this aspect of Kant's thought when he proposes that "the harmony between the faculties can appear only in the form of a *discordant harmony*, since each communicates to the other only the violence which confronts it with its own difference and its divergence from the others," and he suggests that Kant "was the first to provide the example of such a discordant harmony, the relation between imagination and thought which occurs in the case of the sublime."[24] In a similar vein, Lyotard finds in the analytic of the sublime the first formulation of the notion of the differend on which his own major work relies.[25] The concept of the differend is almost exactly the aporia of which Caygill speaks, for Lyotard defines it as a conflict "that cannot be equitably resolved for lack of a rule of judgment applicable to both arguments."[26]

The presence of such a differend in the Kantian sublime is especially significant, for that analytic proposes that the experience of the sublime enables the subject to bridge the gap between its grasp of the world of phenomena and its higher capacity for moral freedom. But since bridging that gap requires such a discord between the faculties, Kant seems to construct one element of his architecture out of a constitutive dilemma, as if to convert crisis itself into resolution. This very attempt to regard the problem as an aspect of its solution can only strike one as dubious, not least because it accentuates a discord that no further critical work can dismantle. Furthermore, insofar as the analytic of the sublime incorporates the encounter with the inhuman materiality of natural phenomena – the vastness of a mountain, the turbulence of a sea – into its conception of the subject's faculties, it risks placing a version of alienated transcendence into the overall structure of modern rationality itself.

The consequences of such an endeavour are especially visible in the poetic counterpart of the third critique, the moment of sublimity in Wordsworth's crossing of the Alps. Indeed, insofar as Wordsworth conceives of such an encounter in part through a reference to the collapse of the rainbow covenant and the emergence of a geological sublime, his account emerges from within a project strikingly akin to Kant's, for

The Prelude similarly sets out to examine the fundamental properties of mind, its capacities and limitations, within the context of the mind's new situation after the cancellation of transcendence. Yet this poem is by no means merely parallel to Kant's texts, for it foregrounds several features that remain implicit in the latter, providing a new point of entry into the question of the mind's description of itself.

Consider a central passage from the account of the Alpine crossing in *The Prelude* regarding the journey of Wordsworth and a companion through the Gorge of Gondo:

The brook and road
Were fellow-travellers in this gloomy Pass,
And with them did we journey several hours
At a slow step. The immeasurable height
Of woods decaying, never to be decayed,
The stationary blasts of water-falls,
And every where along the hollow rent
Winds thwarting winds, bewildered and forlorn,
The torrents shooting from the clear blue sky,
The rocks that muttered close upon our ears,
Black drizzling crags that spake by the way-side
As if a voice were in them, the sick sight
And giddy prospect of the raving stream,
The unfettered clouds and region of the heavens,
Tumult and peace, the darkness and the light
Were all like workings of one mind, the features
Of the same face, blossoms upon one tree,
Characters of the great Apocalypse,
The types and symbols of Eternity,
Of first and last, and midst, and without end. (6.553–72)

This passage collapses apparently opposed modes of temporality into a single flow; in those "stationary blasts of water-falls" the poet sees an apocalyptic violence intrinsic to temporal movement and to nature's endless self-renewal. In this gorge the poet encounters a process whereby nature, in perpetually destroying itself, perpetually endures. Such a mode clearly undoes the rainbow covenant, which ensures nature's endurance by permanently deferring another flood; here chaos is intrinsic to the cosmos, the flood a permanent dimension of creation. That chaos, in the form of earthquakes, may have formed the Alpine scene and may continue to shape it forever; the passage suggests as much in its depiction of the gorge as a "hollow rent," a fissure in the earth, and in its highly dynamic rendition of the elements, as if to suggest that the traveller moves through a kind of earthquake or cosmic upheaval, a rending still taking place. That upheaval may also take on the aspect of an ongoing, primal deluge; after all, the "torrents shooting from the clear blue sky" seem to have a supernatural origin, to be assaulting the earth from another space entirely, even as they are permanent fixtures in the Alpine scene.

This collapse of temporal contrasts makes unusually visible the specific logic of the internal limit. Insofar as the "Characters of the great Apocalypse" and "[t]he types and symbols of Eternity" are "features / Of the same face," much as the "first and last" are here brought together with what is in the "midst, and without end," then indeed, as Copjec would say, the origin and end as initial and final terminus of time have been cancelled and brought into history in the very form of the infinite, of endless repetition. At first this passage seems to deploy a contradiction in terms: How can what is last be without end? How can the first and last appear together in the same moment? But it does so to foreground the temporal disarray that emerges when something intrudes into time from a domain not exactly in the past, present, or future but from *another temporality entirely* – yet that temporality, as this passage makes abundantly clear, *is still this temporality itself*, the very "face" of nature. Here the mere material processes of the earth register the intrusion of an alien temporality into time, yet this intrusion becomes intrinsic to this time, the very logic of the ordinary.

Such a realization can have chilling effects: the forces that are utterly indifferent to human survival and might well eventually eradicate the species are already at work here and now. The infinite, undying repetition takes place in the form of a disastrous material iteration. If Genesis depicts a pre-covenantal God caught between the will to create and to destroy the cosmos, this passage suggests that in this state the two faces of God – creator and destroyer – vanish into the same faceless "face." The scene speaks everywhere of a disastrous transcendence embedded in material processes themselves, in the mere operations of a nature far too powerful, and extending over far too great a time, for any human being to grasp or endure.

The result is a disfiguration of reality by the Real, an event the passage registers in the breakdown of binary oppositions between categories, the oppositions on which Genesis insists both in its account of the creation and in its contrast between creation and deluge. This collapse of opposites takes place as well in the hints that rationality dissolves, that the rocks mutter, the black crags speak, the stream raves – as if the distinction between material process and subjectivity has disappeared, as if the pure process of the natural world has taken on a voice and the mind has taken on the attributes of that process; everything here suggests that both have become "workings of one mind," workings that indefinitely extend subjectivity at the risk of madness.

But the Alpine sequence in book six does not give such madness the last word; in the crucial apostrophe to the imagination, which precedes the passage on the descent through the gorge as if to give the latter a suitably comforting frame, it claims to represent a recovery from that impasse: "And now recovering," writes the poet, "to my Soul I say / 'I recognize thy glory'" (6.531–2). One might think at first that the mind here breaks out of a disastrous experience and lays claim to a higher destination. In this initial rendition of the passage, as in the ethical scenarios in Kant's second critique and in *Mary: A Fiction*, the subject would be confronted by a certain horrific power only to overcome it and thereby claim a higher power of its own. Political or geological catastrophe, ethical or aesthetic sublimity: these scenarios everywhere would share a similar logic. This parallel with the episode in *Mary* would hint as well that the Alpine passage makes the face of nature into a single endless shipwreck, a scene of disaster without limits, one so vast that it is difficult to imagine any form of sufficient rescue. Moreover, much as Mary notes her sublime response in her journal, at some remove from the crisis itself, here the poet records that passage at an even greater temporal distance, suggesting for a moment that a radical disidentification separates him from the traveller who passes directly through cosmic chaos. That apparently secure distance from the deluge imposes itself as well in an associated passage, the Arab dream, where near its end the narrator, glimpsing the "fleet waters of the drowning world," suddenly wakes in terror (5.136).[27] In these two instances, it seems, something like recovery takes place precisely through the tactic of radical separation, salvaging the overall structure of a Kantian sublime.

Yet the claim to recovery may not be all that credible after all. If one reads the sequence out of order, taking up the apostrophe to the imagination after considering the descent through the gorge which follows, one begins to see how greatly the ostensible recovery recapitulates the crisis recorded in the passage on that descent:

> And now recovering, to my Soul I say
> "I recognize thy glory." In such strength
> Of usurpation, in such visitings
> Of awful promise, when the light of sense
> Goes out in flashes that have shewn to us
> The invisible world, doth Greatness make abode,

There harbours whether we be young or old.
Our destiny, our nature, and our home,
Is with infinitude, and only there;
With hope it is, hope that can never die,
Effort, and expectation, and desire,
And something evermore about to be.
The mind beneath such banners militant
Thinks not of spoils or trophies, nor of aught
That may attest its prowess, blest in thoughts
That are their own perfection and reward,
Strong in itself, and in the access of joy
Which hides it like the overflowing Nile. (6.531–48)

On an initial reading, several details may accord with the Kantian account. The poet writes that "our home / Is with infinitude, and only there," as if the experience of the sublime gestures towards our transcendental destination. Yet this destination apparently remains outstanding, unachieved, with "something evermore about to be." Evidently the Kantian awareness of one's supersensible reason belongs to the end of a process that never reaches completion. But on a closer look, this account collapses: the mind is not after all attempting to reach a state beyond it, for it is "blest in thoughts / That are their own perfection and reward," experiencing in its very thoughts – in its endless expectation – its greatest strength. The mind reaches its higher condition precisely through the infinite experience of hope, expectation, and desire. *The destination is the process itself.* In that case, however, this subjective movement begins to look remarkably like nature's endless flow, into which eternity and the apocalypse have also been absorbed, creating once again, as in the passage on the descent through the gorge, a remarkable parallel between apparently internal and external domains. The poem confirms this reading when it attributes to the mind a certain strength "in the access of joy / Which hides it like the overflowing Nile," as if its strength comes precisely in its undoing, its creation in its destruction. Where Milton's Raphael recounts how the deluge "shall heave the Ocean to usurp / Beyond all bounds, till inundation rise / Above the highest Hills," thereby destroying Eden, this passage finds precisely in that usurpation and inundation a sign of the mind's infinitude.[28] Thus, rather than demonstrating how one might recover from an encounter with an alien natural process, this passage finds something homologous to that process in the operation of the mind itself, constructing a potential resemblance between an endlessly self-blasting materiality and an infinitely self-usurping mind.

This homology thus suggests that the overall Alpine passage forces the subject to encounter an internalized agency akin to the endlessly creating and destroying force found within natural process. If anything, then, this passage is even more scandalous than that regarding the gorge; it is one thing to depict an alien iteration of natural force, another to embrace a similarly obliterating aspect of mind as its highest feature. The poem does not restore the subject to unity or integrity but openly declares that the subject's integrity is to be found in its infinitely prolonged state of creation-destruction. Rather than erasing the otherness of the usurping power by claiming a self-confirming authority, the passage crafts a language that redescribes crisis as recovery; in effect, it undoes the logic of disidentification visible elsewhere, proposing a tacit but still visible logic of identification of poet with traveller, sublime subject with drowning man.

But the identification of these two figures is not absolutely direct. The passage insists on a distinction between two levels of mind when it refers to the moment "when the light of sense / Goes out in flashes that have shewn to us / The invisible world." The language of this passage is echoed late in *The Prelude*, where Wordsworth recounts that in his journey across Salisbury Plain, he "called upon the darkness; and it took, / A midnight darkness seemed to come and take / All objects from my sight" (12.327–9). The mind's usurping force, it seems, has the power to obliterate the visible world; it constitutes a subjective version of a divinely destructive power. The poet makes sure to affiliate this destructive capacity with a creative one in the prologue to this episode, seeing it as akin to nature's "Enduring and creative" power (12.311–12).[29] Here again, it seems, we are to understand this higher power as at once creative and destructive, not to mention enduring – all terms familiar from the depiction of natural process in the passage on the gorge. Yet the close links between the Salisbury Plain hallucination and the celebration of the mind's infinitude expose the lethal violence at the heart of the sublime, especially in the moment of identifying with the mind's usurping power: if one's home is with infinitude, perhaps one is quite willing to plunge all finitude into a "midnight darkness." Such a violence outdoes anything in the work of the Marquis de Sade, for while the latter advocates imitating natural destruction, ostensibly to promote nature's creative powers, he does not conceive of a force that might obliterate phenomenal reality itself. Ironically, Sade's materialism prevents him from attempting what we might regard as an even more blasphemous possibility, that of claiming for himself the power to destroy the world. Wordsworth's epic thus exposes what neither Kant nor

Sade fully articulates, the possibility that identifying the mind with a transcendental greatness gives it access to a destructive as well as creative power. What might enable the mind to recover from a traumatic encounter, in other words, may give it access to another version of that same traumatizing power.

But where is the subject in this now very complex scenario? If the poet remains a usurped empirical subject, he also identifies with the force of usurpation. He is in both dimensions, inundated by the Nile and unleashing that flood. What appears at one point to be subjective devastation turns out, on another view, to elevate the subject to a transcendentally destructive status. Thus where the poem seems to confirm the Kantian logic of crisis and resolution, in fact it undercuts that logic directly. Where Kant attempts to read the imagination's displeasure as a sign of supersensible reason, Wordsworth suggests that such a supersensible faculty beckoning from "the invisible world" is yet another horrific power to create and destroy. The movement from the imagination to reason does not lead to a resolution but rather finds a new version of disaster on another level. As a result, the logic of identification between figures of the subject here is complex: the passage insists on the strong parallel between versions of mind and nature that are also opposed, retaining a contrast between the phenomenal and noumenal while constructing a strict resemblance between them. In this regard, it follows the logic of both/neither that it outlines in the passage on the Arab dream ("Of these was neither, and was both at once": 5.126). In turning from an endlessly self-blasting materiality to an infinitely self-usurping mind, the poem rehearses what seems to be a version of resolution but turns out to inscribe one mode in the other, tying together what the Kantian analytic places on distinct levels.

Thus the Alpine passage greatly elaborates and complicates the Kantian analytic of the sublime. In the poet's account, the violence may be found not merely in the discord between the presentations of sense and supersensible reason – in the differend between faculties – but within each domain as well. The erasure of transcendence is felt here in the absence of a metalanguage as well as in redescriptions of natural and subjective processes. But the passage extends these complications a further step when it rethinks the question of the infinite as well. According to Kant's first critique, the infinite can never be the object of perception or cognition; accordingly, in the third critique he treats infinity as an Idea – what we might describe in layman's terms as a powerful, perhaps even transcendental, fiction.[30] In contrast, Wordsworth places infinity in the experience of such affects as effort, expectation, and desire, which persist in the expectation of something "evermore" to come. For him, the infinite is not a mere notion, a kind of mental object, but a dimension of the subject's perpetual experience.

This turn from the Idea of infinity to the infinity of desire is a radical move. After all, how can an affect of a mortal human being be infinite? How can it "never die"? The passage installs something infinitely vast within subjective experience, wrenching it open through a force much too large for it – one that must inevitably traumatize it, as the passage on the bad night in the Alpine inn a few lines later confirms. Moreover, it does so by pointing to an aspect of subjectivity not mentioned in the analytic of the sublime, a form of desire or hope that forever urges the subject onward. At first the passage represents this form of desire in an idealizing idiom, insofar as it associates that desire with "Greatness" and the mind's "destiny," but insofar as the experience of this infinite expectation is akin to inundation, to an endless experience of drowning, it also seems to cut *against* subjective self-authorization. If desire seems to be an attribute of high achievement – higher than the achievement of the Napoleonic armies to which the passage alludes – it also has the attributes of a flooding Nile. It may give the subject a home with infinity, but insofar as the latter becomes the subject's *only* home it also makes the subject otherwise homeless. It is thus self-confirming *and* alien, intimate with greatness and forever hiding the subject from itself. The infinity of desire, it seems, is precisely what the poet wants – except that it forever usurps him as well. It may be nothing other than a redescription of the ghostly unfather that usurped the poet in the passage's opening lines (6.525–30), an uncanny visitation that remains within the subject as the alien logic of its own desire. Its infinity – as a sign of its immortality – may make it akin to a ghost, a figure that, neither exactly living nor dead, survives in that liminal zone of uncanny insistence. If to experience the infinite as endless expectation is to endure, and affirm, the absence of any origin or end, any telos in its own right, then it is to bring into the subject the consequences of erasing transcendence. Thus the erasure of transcendence, discernible in the limits Kant sets himself in his overall project, becomes far more visible and palpable in this passage *in the undead subject itself*. The Wordsworthian subject, one might say, is the living ghost of the expired God.

In these various ways, then, the passage on the infinity of desire dares to go much further than Kant in subjectivizing the sublime. Lyotard points out that in the experience of the sublime, when the imagination has a moment of comprehension via intuition, that moment "is the destruction of the temporality proper to all presentation" and thus "contraven[es] the finality of the faculty of presentation." In effect, "the time of aesthetic feeling is not necessarily the same as the time of cognition," suggesting as well that "the subjective is not the subject." Indeed, Lyotard argues, Kant never affirms that "thought as reflection, as pure faculty of judging, presupposes an 'I think'"; as a result, "it is very difficult to classify Kantism among philosophies of the subject, as is sometimes done."[31] Kant leaves the aporias of the sublime in place; he allows the interruption of sense to remain an attribute of a subjectivity without a subject. The poet works through similar themes in the passage on his journey through the Gorge of Gondo, capturing there an experience of near-madness, a radical disorientation of sense. But when he writes the passage on his ostensible recovery, he brings about a radical *subjectivation* of the sublime along with its attendant destruction of sense, affirming a certain self-usurping power and finding it in the ever-present experience of desire itself. In doing so he expands what one might define as the subject beyond its usual boundaries, incorporating into it aspects of the unconscious subject of desire; the complexity of the mind's self-usurping power I outlined above hints that for Wordsworth subjectivity operates through a volatile interplay of elements that confirm and undermine conscious intention, that intermix (shall we say) Kantian and Freudian elements. Thus where Kant adheres to the discipline of critical philosophy, outlining the attributes of subjectivity in the mode of a conscientious critique, the poet takes up a rather different discipline, what one might call an ethical response to what is revealed in the sublime, embracing it as an aspect of his broader, if traumatized, experience of subjectivity. For a moment, at least, he affirms the uncanny force he encounters there *as an uncanny dimension of his own being*, converting his encounter with the Real of a disastrous transcendence in material and subjective processes into a momentary affirmation of himself as a figure of the Real.

While this passage is largely focused on the lineaments of the sublime in an encounter with the indefinitely vast material processes on view in the Alps, its occasional use of political and military terms – of usurpation and banners militant – suggests that it bears as well on a closely associated array of questions arising from the field of political history. Various historicist readings of the passage have proposed that it reinscribes aspects of Napoleon's crossing of the Alps and indeed of Napoleonic political and military endeavour more generally.[32] These and other readings make clear that the resonances of these lines with political and cultural history are unquestionable. But the passage opens up the theme not only of history but of historicity as well; in effect, it proposes that history now takes place in a domain without origin or end, without ground or telos, and arises from an "effort, and expectation, and desire" that it places in the first-person plural and thus attributes in part to a collective subject. One might be tempted, then, to propose that this passage is a signal instance whereby, according to Thomas Pfau, "romanticism itself confronted the task of awakening to its own historicity during the massive upheavals brought about by Napoleon's drastic transformation of Europe's political, legal, and economic landscape between 1800 and 1815" – a historicity, a "perilous historical situatedness," that is at once new and constitutive of a Heideggerian modernity. Like other texts, this passage would then evoke the mood of radically vulnerable historicity, pointing to a condition that in the wake of rapid historical change is shared by modern societies as a whole.[33] Yet this reading would accept modernity's self-authorizing trope virtually at face value; in taking for granted that out of history might emerge historicity, it would make an unwarranted leap from one logical level to another, leaving out of view the broader rethinking of the very frame surrounding history that such a transformation would require.[34]

Only on this level does the import of the passage on the imagination become clear: it does not merely evoke a "modern" conception of history, nor does it only assist in the process of constructing such a concept, for as we have seen it everywhere indicates that what it foregrounds must arise out of a determinate cancellation of the concepts of origin and end, of divine solicitude for creation, and their reappearance in new, post-covenantal forms.[35] Furthermore, as we have just seen, it takes yet another step as it embraces this historicity, or what we might name more radically as the Real of history, the internal limit that consigns it to being endless and that installs a certain undead force within the activity of making history as its own alien, self-inundating principle. More theoretically astute than new historicism or even an attentiveness to Heideggerian historicity, the passage makes at least visible the *non*modern – and *non*secular – stakes of its emergence, and moreover it does so without losing sight of the sharply ethical resonances of what it captures.

Yet Wordsworth takes this ethical affirmation of the Real only so far. The placement of the Alpine episode in the overall structure of *The Prelude* reveals as much. To his credit, the poet foregrounds what Kant circumvents, making evident that the sublime, at its maximum clarity and strength, can only be an uncanny and traumatic experience. In his apostrophe to the imagination, he suggests that the ghostly force that haunts the gorge, that speaks in a certain madness from the rocks, crags, and stream, reappears (as I suggested above) in the "unfathered vapour" that crosses his onward path and disturbs the composition of his epic:

> Imagination! lifting up itself
> Before the eye and progress of my Song
> Like an unfathered vapour; here that Power,
> In all the might of its endowments, came
> Athwart me; I was lost as in a cloud,
> Halted, without a struggle to break through.
> And now recovering, to my Soul I say
> "I recognize thy glory." (6.525–32)

Here the poet recognizes the radical disorientation of the subjectivity that writes, even of the apparently composed and composing aspect of the poet himself. The poet recovers from that disorientation not so much through recovery proper as through articulating the crisis in a certain way, through depicting the experience of losing one's path as a mode of finding it; in that case, here he exemplifies, as I have argued elsewhere, the logic of errancy on which he has long based his poetics. But as a result, in subjectivizing the crisis, if anything he makes things even worse, transforming the episode from an interruption into a signal disorientation of the epic itself.

In doing so, the poet brings the epic within the orbit of Gothic practice. The undead subject who speaks in this passage sticks out, as it were, in relation to its background, taking on a form distinct from natural process as the poet addresses it in the apostrophe. Something here becomes *too* visible, *too* uncanny, too provocative to assimilate into the onward progress of narrative. In much the same way, Matthew Lewis's *The Monk* is invaded by a usurping, uncanny force: at one point the ghost of the Bleeding Nun appears every night to the astonished Raymond, who can imagine no way of delivering himself from her visitations. Her intrusions might have continued indefinitely, calling a halt to all further narrative progress, were it not for the appearance of the Grand Mogul, whose magical powers suspend them and open the way for Raymond to lay her body to rest.[36] In *The Prelude*, as in *The Monk*, the refusal of the supernatural leads not to a supremely empowered subject but rather to a haunting instance of the Real. In the epic, the uncanny visitation takes the form not of an actual ghost but of the ghostly, undead subject itself. But this time there is no Grand Mogul to arrive magically to make everything work out well; the ghost remains too visible, unburied, a haunting presence hovering over the rest of the poem.

The consequences for Wordsworth are evident in the lines I quoted at the beginning of this chapter. After the passage on the gorge, which follows the apostrophe to the imagination, the poet lingers over a night spent in agony at an inn, capturing well the sense of having to occupy a mind too large for its own good, too resonant and powerful for human endurance, too undead for a living mortality. By insisting on the traumatic effects of the sublime, the passage on the night in the inn strongly disputes any notion that one might transform the crisis of which it speaks into resolution. Furthermore, in an ensuing passage the poet describes a further night of disorientation by Lake Como (6.621–57), which also reveals the haunting underside of sublime elevation, after which he finds he cannot complete the episode properly but must apologize instead and simply break it off (6.658–80).

Thus it is no surprise that Wordsworth returns to this episode implicitly in the final book's passage on the ascent of Snowdon, where he attempts to transform errancy into arrival, delugic sublimity into a Noah-like survival, in effect attempting to subsume his ethical affirmation of a Real subjectivity into the sharply different project of the epic's final pages. The later passage's persistent, if cryptic, rewriting of the Alpine passage suggests that the poet has set himself the difficult task of expunging the ghost for good. Geoffrey Hartman, in his landmark study of the poet's work, grounded his argument in an analysis of the relation between these passages, contending that the interplay between them demonstrated how the "compositional sequence" of the Alpine and Snowdon passages overall "confirms Wordsworth's tendency to avoid an apocalyptic self-consciousness."[37] But the fact that he must rely not on an actual resolution of what the Alpine passage reveals but rather on a mere reversal of the latter's leading tropes suggests that he cannot avoid it and is attempting to counteract an episode that troubles him. Rather than finding avenues to overcome trauma through the actual burial of the ghost or an effective silencing of those excessively loud waters, he relies on his capacity for rearticulation, for figural dynamism, on which he drew in the Alpine passage itself. In short, he is caught within a series of volatile figures, inescapably bound to an "apocalyptic self-consciousness" that traumatizes him. Despite his best efforts, the poem ultimately interprets modernity as a mode not of self-authorization but of a radical homelessness, an absolute vulnerability both to alien natural processes and to an excessively vast and destructive property of mind. Thus the undead ethical subject that appears in the midst of the Alpine passage, like the episode itself, remains unassimilated within the poem. Despite Wordsworth's protest late in the poem against the consequences of his own insights in the Alpine passage, his epic ultimately acknowledges that the modern subject is, in every sense, the subject of disaster.[38]

The instability of the epic's apparent closure suggests that the poem cannot cohere around any stable claim, cannot point to any authorizing origin or end. In the absence of such a telos, the epic cannot contain the forces that frequently challenge the narrator with any number of hauntings all across its length. Incapable of warding off such intrusions or defusing their force, the narrator can only circle around them and articulate their disfiguring impact; like the forces that arise in the Alpine passage, they resist any effort to metabolize or thematize them. Again and again undead forces interrupt the narrative: one encounters them, for example, in the apparition that arises above the lake in the stolen boat passage of book one, the discharged soldier of book four, the drowned man of book five, the blind beggar of book seven, the evocation of the violence of the September Massacres in book nine, and the haunted scenes in the spots of time in book eleven. Readers have often been tempted to absorb such episodes into an account of the mind's sublimity and thus of its transcendental destination, but doing so requires one to set aside their uncanny attributes, their evocations of cruelty and violence, the sense of chance or accident that pervades them, and their dispersion across the narrator's domain of experience. They constitute, as it were, shards of a shattered and disfigured deity, remnants of what the poem seeks but cannot secure. In their scattered insistence, they also undermine the notion of the growth of the poet's mind – a sequence that, leading through the tale of their appearance, would culminate in a telos beyond them. Not only does this dispersion undercut the notion that this epic recounts a developmental narrative; as I suggested above, the epic's slide into first-person plural also suggests that this undoing applies as well to the notion of a developmental history, to a modernity that could unfold over a series of phases into something like maturity. On the contrary, these multiple intrusions do not allow one ever to move beyond them, as if one must remain caught within the threshold of the encounter itself. Out of that moment, nothing further can arise – precisely because even the apparently open history that follows speaks endlessly of its aimlessness, its undoing of telos, and thus of the uncanny, infinite process that explodes into view in this scene.

It is no surprise that Wordsworth attempts to contain the experience of the traumatic sublime – and by implication all of these uncanny visitations – within the rhetoric of book thirteen; nevertheless, his attempt to do so only draws further attention to the impasse it hopes to overcome, giving it a sharply ethical cast. On one level, this effort foregrounds the very fact that the Alpine encounter is traumatic, that it speaks of something unassimilable. The poem's difficulty with its incorporation of an undead subject into its own authorship bears the traces of a certain honesty. But on another, it raises a new kind of ethical question about the consequences for the subject of the disarray of prior ethical modes. As we have seen, for Kant ethics is a matter of conforming to the dictates of the moral law. Kant calls the aspiration to comply with that law "desire" and speaks of it at times in the terms of hope. Moreover, as we have seen, he argues that only an immortal soul might attain what it desires, perfect conformity to the law. Thus Kant specifies a certain infinity of desire, a certain endless, aspirational project. Yet he retains his focus on the moral law, setting aside the question of the affect of such endless desire. Wordsworth, as it were, takes up this theme and develops it further, for he attends not to the object of this desire but to the infinitely sustained aspiration itself, for a moment finding in its uncanny and apparently futile persistence the sign of what is most to be affirmed.

In stepping back from that affirmation, however, the poet ultimately makes more palpable the nature of the post-Kantian ethical challenge he has now posed for himself and others. *Should* one affirm this traumatic, sublime experience, and if so, how? Is it best to evade the implications of such an encounter, perhaps even reverse its import if possible, or to accept what it reveals as a signal part of one's "perilous historical situatedness," one's modernity? Is something revealed in that encounter that one must try to understand – or is what it might reveal too inhuman, too destructive, too threatening to a fidelity to the ordinary for one to acknowledge as an attribute of oneself?[39] In short, should one embrace what that radical disorientation reveals and fashion what Zupančič would call an ethics of the Real, affirming the latter in all its stunning import, thereby pursuing an ethical modernity?

These questions, while absolutely pressing for all those who inherit the problematic of modernity, leave in place the assumption that one can carry out an ethics that would affirm the Real in the first place. Doing so may not be possible for any finite subject, as Zupančič suggests.[40] Nevertheless, once these questions arise, they insist; they demand that one consider a response, even if one is impossible. Thus what Wordsworth encounters in *The Prelude* remains available to others; the question remains open, a provocation to all who follow.

4 *Trusting to the Billows*

Byron's Poetics of the Real

In his dramatic poem *Manfred* (1817) and several texts to follow, including *Childe Harold's Pilgrimage*, canto 4 (1818) and *Cain* (1821), Lord Byron takes up the ethical challenges of the cancellation of transcendence. Having already written of the prospect of the extinction of the sun – and thus of all earthly life – in "Darkness" (1816), capturing with great force the new awareness of the purely physical attributes of the natural world, in these poems he takes seriously the question of how to salvage a certain ethical integrity within a denuded universe. If human actions, and the world of which they are a part, are no longer grounded in any transcendental origin or end, it is not clear how the subject's endeavours might take on a certain ethical significance. No doubt that new awareness on some level makes one free of familiar impositions, but such freedom on its own does not bring with it any sense of inherent purpose. Thus rather than conferring the gift of liberty or an ideologically reassuring sense of moral autonomy, that awareness imposes on the free subject an enormous ethical challenge – an emptiness of purpose for which it is not evident how it may compensate.[1] In Byron's view one must be free merely to grapple with these questions; as someone who participated in ushering the term "liberal" into the modern political lexicon, he would repudiate many constraints on individual thought and action.[2] But it is also clear from *Manfred* – whose title evokes the notion of a "man freed" – that securing such a liberty is only a precondition for the much more challenging task of reconstructing an ethical life in the radical absence of any traditional orientation; in this regard, the play usefully anticipates the thought of the late Foucault.[3] In this dramatic poem and several texts to follow, Byron attempts to engage with the horror of an empty, infinite demand – one without reference to any overarching justification, without anchor in a transcendental telos – that had already begun to emerge in other forms in the work of Wollstonecraft, Godwin, and Wordsworth.

At first it might seem to go too far to claim that the awareness of disaster is a crucial motivating force over this period of Byron's career, for the scepticism that informs his overall stance commits him to a decided uncertainty on ultimate matters. As many critics have discussed, the poet repudiates any dogma of affirmation or denial both in his letters and poems, ultimately locating himself in the long tradition running from classical scepticism through its early modern exponents from Michel de Montaigne to William Drummond.[4] Such scepticism, evident in many of his important works, is especially pronounced in his poetic dramas, where, as Terence Allan Hoagwood points out, "[n]o transcendent voice is possible that would be able to make any answer absolute, and no means exist to make of any perspective or opinion (*doxa*) a transcendent truth."[5] The effects of such a stance are especially evident in *Manfred*: Stephen C. Behrendt proposes that it consists of "a 'dialogue' whose rhetorical model is that of the skeptical debate," in which "the two sides perform so well that each subverts (or entirely demolishes) the other."[6] Indeed, according to Emily A. Bernhard Jackson, it is quite possible to read the poem as bringing about a synthesis of "Hume with Berkeley, ultimately demonstrating that because all perception is the product of the self, it is subjective, uncertain, and hence and most significantly, malleable." Byron's exploration of these concerns is so rigorous in the poem, she argues, that it marks a transition from prior confusion "to *Manfred*'s philosophical certainty (even if that certainty is certainty of uncertainty)," in effect making his sceptical stand more visible than ever.[7]

The poet's insistence on the absence of any certain knowledge that might be found outside the subject locates him well within the broader cultural development in the Romantic era that places transcendental claims under erasure. But Byron's clearer stance in this regard arises alongside the development of an equally forceful sense that a catastrophic violence in the nonhuman domain bears directly on the fate of human institutions. The depictions of solar catastrophe in "Darkness," the undermining of theological and anthropocentric perspectives through an encounter with geological time in act 2 of *Cain*, and the reference to geological catastrophism in cantos 9 and 10 of *Don Juan* (1823), to take the most obvious examples, suggest that the consciousness of humanity's radical homelessness plays an increasingly central role in his thinking on a wide range of matters.[8] One must conclude that for Byron, the sense of that homelessness does not contradict, but rather confirms, what he attends to in his scepticism: here the absence of knowledge and the sense of disaster operate together as alternative figures of the same underlying condition, the undoing of any transcendental guarantee of humanity's flourishing.

Byron's sense of this erasure is one of the most acute in the period, going significantly further than most of his predecessors. Where Kant hopes to salvage an ethical telos even in the suspension of its alignment with a natural finality, arguing only that "we have a moral ground for also conceiving of a final end of creation for a world," "Darkness" suggests that a moral superstructure for human endeavour would collapse almost instantly in the face of a solar extinction brought about by natural causes.[9] As we have seen, Kant envisions the mortality of the universe in his scientific writings of the 1750s, a mortality that would necessarily include the extinction of the sun and of human life, but insists nevertheless that the cyclic disappearance and reappearance of the universe, as well as the infinite time span for this process, ultimately point to the transcendent greatness of God.[10] Byron, in contrast, focuses explicitly on the consequences for humankind of solar death, suggesting that in such an event, all bets are off: respect for holy things would yield to unholy purposes, political power would collapse, and mutual consideration would virtually disappear under the pressure of famine. In Kant's *Critique of Judgment*, the independence of natural processes from the demands of human morality make the teleological basis for a moral system merely a hopeful assumption, greatly diminishing the certainties previously inherent in ethical reflection. For Byron, the inhuman status of those processes is far more devastating, for it ultimately threatens the endurance of any supposed moral superstructure. Moreover, while some readers might wish to interpret the solar catastrophe in "Darkness" as an instance of the sublime, one that might move us precisely because of its cosmic violence against humanity, one could scarcely argue in a Kantian vein that this version of the sublime ultimately aligns with an apprehension of humanity's supersensible destination – precisely because that event extinguishes the basis for positing such a destination.

In adopting this approach to the question of solar death, Byron is quite original, initiating a fascination with human extinction that will play out in other late-Romantic texts, such as *The Last Man*. He primarily imagines in concrete terms the actual consequences of an event whose contours were broadly familiar. The notion of solar death was already explicit in eighteenth-century theories of the history of the universe; these theories, in turn, echoed the hypothesis of classical atomistic materialism in Lucretius's *De Rerum Natura*, which held that all aspects of the world, including the sun, would eventually pass away, and which reinforced the absence of any divine guidance or ultimate telos in its final depiction of the plague of Athens.[11] Within the context of classical and Enlightenment materialism, the poem draws as well on the eruption of Mount Tambora in 1815, which led to massive climatological disruptions around the globe, amplifying that event into the death of the sun and thus of all earthly life.[12] However, the fact that the poem brings the prospect of such events home to the conditions of ordinary life sharply challenges the terms of cultural discourse in the early nineteenth century, disturbing widespread assumptions even more than Enlightenment geology. Indeed, only recently has the death of the sun been registered outright in the philosophy of the West, as if at last to respond to the provocation already visible in Byron.[13]

Manfred inscribes this solar catastrophe anew, suggesting in its first scene that Manfred can call forth the spirits of the earth by the "tyrant-spell" of the "burning wreck of a demolish'd world, / A wandering hell in the eternal space" (1.1.43, 45–6). So summoned forth, the very spirit that controls the star "which rules [Manfred's] destiny" now rules over a "wandering mass of shapeless flame, / A pathless comet, and a curse, / The menace of the universe," a star that is now "[a] bright deformity on high, / The monster of the upper sky!" (1.1.110, 117–19, 122–3).[14] In these lines the poem radicalizes an element present within the etymology of the term "disaster"; that term is derived, via the French *désastré*, from the Italian *dis-astro*, which, as Marie-Hélène Huet argues, "designated the state of having been disowned by the stars that ensure a safe passage through life. The word is thus directly related to disorders of uncommon magnitude: the destruction, despair and chaos resulting from the distant power of cosmic agencies."[15] Yet Manfred is not disowned by a star but is ruled precisely by a shapeless, monstrous deformity, a "burning wreck of a demolish'd world." He is governed by something more ruinous than disaster, for rather than having been *disowned* by stars that presumably still ensure the safe passage of others, he is *owned* by a deformed and monstrous star that eradicates any sense of safe passage for himself or for others. In this transposition from the loss of a transcendental guarantee into the presence of extinction, the poem not only brings to bear the insights of "Darkness" but also identifies them as elements of its version of the internal limit, a horrific eruption within what might otherwise seem to be the finite subject Manfred.

Confronting these pressures with special attention in *Manfred*, Byron sets in motion an investigation that will eventually take him across several poems, setting himself the task of working out the consequences of such a disaster for the ethical subject. In this text, the subject encounters its own extinction as the mark of what negates its transcendental origin or end, the sign of what it cannot overcome or even truly conceive but must nevertheless accept as an attribute of its ultimate condition. This imposition of disaster cannot contribute to any process that would overcome it in favour of a positive human destiny, but must rather provoke the attempt to construct an entirely different scenario, an ethics that can take upon itself the measure of the Real. Because *Manfred* mediates these concerns in a dramatic poem that draws on resonances of the Gothic outcast, the Alpine sublime, and the Faustian pact, it takes the risk of implying that it is exploring the implications of those conventions rather than its own ethical problematic. Despite such appearances, however, the play resolutely reframes each of these borrowings, cutting through their premises to expose other possibilities altogether. In doing so, it attends at length to that infinite aspect of the subject that traumatized Wordsworth so thoroughly in *The Prelude* and dares to work through that intolerable, unassimilable aspect of the subject from which the earlier poet shied away. Pursuing its investigation to the bitter end, the play ultimately arrives at a formulation of the ultimate act in the Real – the act whereby the subject brings down a fatal judgment against itself. *Manfred* thus constitutes the main staging ground for Byron's explorations of this book's themes, providing him the basis for the ethical reflections that appear in several poems to follow; one simply would not be able to understand the stakes of that overall trajectory without deciphering *Manfred*'s strategies and concerns.

Nevertheless, because that play resolves its concerns with Manfred's death, which takes place in a mode of radical singularity, conceived outside of its impact on social relations, it leaves unresolved the question of how its final act may be understood in any wider context, in any properly social, political, or historical terrain. To complete his exploration of the overall problematic, Byron must incorporate the breakthrough in *Manfred* in a more historically and socially engaged poetics. One might think that the central exhibit in this regard is his second metaphysical drama, *Cain*, in which he once again takes up the themes of earthly life and extinction, the burden of singular guilt, and the refusal to defer either to God or to his opponent. But in that play, rather than extending the investigations of *Manfred*, the poet approaches them from a sharply different perspective, considering ethics from the position of a subject who discovers that there is need of such a thing – that there are such things as death and murder – and thereby also a sense of guilt that imposes itself on him. Such a perspective, however fresh, does not go so far as the final stanzas of *Childe Harold's Pilgrimage*, canto 4, in which the narrator, plunging beyond a landscape of ruins into the sea, that scene of perpetual shipwreck, seizes its billows as he writes – and thus incorporates what wrecks the human aspiration to ascendancy into his very stance as a poet. In that move, Byron enacts an instance of Lacanian subjective destitution, not through the infinite subject's annihilation of its own quotidian form, as in *Manfred*, but by incorporating what annihilates *all* human endeavour into the poetic performance of human nullity. In these stanzas, then, he radicalizes the gesture that concludes the poetic drama, converting an ethics of singularity into a poetics of collective disaster.

The fact that *Manfred* pushes beyond the premises of those literary scenarios on which it draws is already clear in its use of the Alpine setting, a landscape that in *Mont Blanc* (1816) symbolizes inhuman geological processes (earthquake, flood, hurricane, avalanche) from which the "race / Of man, flies far in dread" and that will soon, in *Frankenstein* (1818), serve as the appropriate setting for the speech of the monster.[16] It serves as the earthly counterpart of the wrecked star, a scene defined by horrific processes hostile to human flourishing. As Stephen Cheeke suggests, the Alps in the poem stand "in their enormity as particularly large reminders of the absence of any non-material spirit inhering in the physical world"; they are thus emblems of a transcendence drained of spirit, an evacuated version of the infinite.[17] Manfred's attempt to inhabit such a space no doubt indicates his overweening ambition, his wish to overleap the human condition and to carry out a more-than-aristocratic, singular project. Evidently the poem wishes to suggest that confronting the significance of disaster (for lack of a better term) constitutes a transgressive act that must take on aspects of the horror or monstrosity it encounters: Manfred's enterprise takes him beyond what any subject can endure, into hyperbolic heights that can only evoke or perhaps lead to their corresponding depths (a fact made evident in the scene of near suicide). It is therefore quite telling that to enable this project the poem must locate Manfred within the very landscape that apparently negates teleological satisfactions, putting in their stead a power characterized at once by its emptiness and its catastrophic effects. Only in such a space, the poem suggests, could its protagonist confront what it might mean for him to be under the sway of a "monster of the upper sky."

Moreover, rather than providing Manfred with a moment of sublimity, as in Wordsworth or Percy Bysshe Shelley, this landscape captures in external form an aspect of what is already present within him, a sense of an unbearable condition he cannot surpass. In a strict homology with the temporality outlined above, the landscape confronts him not with the undoing of an immortality to come but with a shattered and useless immortality that imposes itself in the present. How could a poem taking the measure of geological, astronomical, and cultural disaster home in on *this* feature as the primary sign of an ethical impasse? If, as Lyotard and Ray Brassier propose, the death of the sun has in some sense already taken place, echoing Byron's treatment of the theme, then a certain exploded absolute has also intruded upon the apparent temporality of the present, giving it the full weight of the negated telos.[18] Such an invasion ultimately confirms Copjec's argument that the cancellation of transcendence does not erase it entirely but inscribes a certain infinity within finitude – invading the latter with a power too large for it to bear. In *Manfred*, immortality is not the sign of human sovereignty over death or the promise of an eternity in either heaven or hell; on the contrary, with the obliteration of transcendence, immortality becomes at once empty and disastrous, spiritually indecipherable and utterly traumatic. On the one hand, the sign of cosmic horror enables Manfred to see that he need not submit to any external force, even the desolate scene surrounding him, for its overarching significance has been displaced into his own heart; as a result, he has known instead the "fulness of humiliation, for / I sunk before my vain despair, and knelt / To my own desolation" (2.4.40–2). On the other, the presence of that interior desolation is ruinous for him – so from the start of the poem he seeks relief from immortality in oblivion (1.1.144).

The poem's reading of immortality as traumatic might seem strange for readers accustomed to the opposition between a belief in immortality and a modern insistence on mortality, between the sacred and the secular. Thus the play's nonsecular intervention in this respect warrants careful examination. A full encounter with the implications of immortality, after all, is not necessarily reassuring. Three decades later, in perhaps the best statement of the traumatic impact of the prospect of immortality within the context of faith, Søren Kierkegaard would argue that it is a matter not of rational debate, of theological proof, but rather of an imperious imposition: "Immortality is the Judgement or the separation between the just and the unjust"; it is "not a continuation," not the fulfilment of "an idle, effeminate ... wish for a life after death," but an eternal "separation between the just and the unjust."[19] It is the sign, in short, not of an infinitely extended temporality but the appearance within time of *another* temporality, an infinite demand for justice – in which case, one might well argue, the day of judgment, rather than being postponed until the end of history, takes place forever in the present moment. Such a treatment of the theme, avant-garde in relation to the more reassuring version of immortality available within early modern orthodoxy, in some ways already prepares the way for, or perhaps recalls, aspects of transformations in the concept under the pressure of modernity. Thus it is no surprise that the potentially traumatic effects of this argument are only heightened in the earlier, even more relevant rendition in Kant's second critique, where immortality loses its reference to divine judgment and speaks instead of an empty, infinite excess over biological or temporal existence, an excess that appears in one's apprehension of the moral law. In Kant's argument, this excess is associated with a human freedom which liberates the subject from the determinations of sense at the cost of imposing on it a horrific, implacable demand. *Manfred* heightens this effect still further when its protagonist endures such an imposition as an instance of disastrous transcendence, evident both in the landscape surrounding him and in the "desolation" of his own heart. It is as if this poem at last makes visible the senseless violence of the moral law in the "burning wreck of a demolish'd world" or in its counterpart in the Alpine landscape.

The poem reinforces these aspects of Manfred's immortality in the anonymous curse voiced in its first scene. This voice lays out with exemplary precision the consequences that must follow when a finite subject is invaded by the infinite, making clear that immortality is at once alien and absolutely intimate to the apparently free subject. "There are thoughts thou canst not banish; / By a power to thee unknown, / Thou canst never be alone," it says, suggesting that the very form of solitary thought now bears the impress of what exceeds it, as if it must henceforth be haunted by its unknown power (1.1.205–7). This voice condemns him as well "to this trial; / Nor to slumber, nor to die," binding to him the "clankless chain" of his deathlessness, cursing him with an immortality beyond human endurance (1.1.253–4, 259). In a further twist, this same voice a few lines earlier claims that it has distilled from Manfred's tears and blood the "strongest" "poison known" (1.1.241, 240); the conjunction of these passages suggests that this poison of heart and this unbearable deathlessness are two aspects of the same fate, a *disastrous* immortality.[20] Such a status might seem to place Manfred in "the brotherhood of Cain" (1.1.249), one who, while condemned, nevertheless sustains the privilege of divine protection, a possibility reinforced on occasion when Manfred attempts to perform the status of an accursed, inhuman solitary, one whose spirit "walk'd not with the souls of men, / Nor look'd upon the earth with human eyes," who "had no sympathy with breathing flesh" and "breath[ed] / The difficult air of the iced mountain's top" (2.2.51–2, 57, 62–3). Yet the poem does not treat him from an external, social perspective, as the myth of Cain would require, but rather from an internal one, from the perspective of his own thought, thereby tacitly making him representative of a potentially shared condition, the accursed state of modern subjectivity. The play's location of Manfred at the height of the Alps, at the utter pitch of aristocratic elevation, and under the sign of immortality, consigns him not to a desperate elitism but to a state he shares with every modern subject, suggesting that such a subject finds itself in a hyperbolic condition, far beyond its ordinary social references and devastated by forces it cannot endure. The passage reinforces the interior perspective on these matters by giving the curse to an anonymous voice – one that seems to speak for that excessive dimension of Manfred's own subjectivity, as if his immortality, in its own voice, imposes itself as a curse upon him.[21]

In its sheer implacability, immortality itself constitutes a sort of curse; only a slight extrapolation from Kierkegaard's account would already suggest as much. But in *Manfred* the ever-presence of infinite judgment is a curse as well because it strips away every possible justification from his previous evil deeds. As the protagonist declares early in the next scene, "I have ceased / To justify my deeds unto myself – / The last infirmity of evil" (1.2.27–9). Under the pressure of absolute judgment, the motives, contexts, and retrospective rationalizations for his actions fall away, leaving them utterly exposed, so that for him, in the absence of anything to protect him from the Real of his own ethical condition, it is "fatality to live; / If it be life to wear within myself / This barrenness of spirit, and to be / My own soul's sepulchre" (1.2.24–7). This state of deathless barrenness, this endurance in the Real, comes about in part because without any protection against the infinite demand, each of his past actions takes on an immortal significance. In his exchange with the chamois-hunter in the following scene, Manfred declares, "Think'st thou existence doth depend on time? / It doth; but actions are our epochs: mine / Have made my days and nights imperishable" (2.1.51–3). If, as Kierkegaard proposes, immortality is judgment, and in some sense that judgment is taking place here and now, then it might well take place in the very form of the subject's memory of his deeds, in his awareness of the deathless significance of his past actions. In that case, as Manfred says to the abbot late in the poem, "there is no future pang / Can deal that justice on the self-condemn'd / He deals on his own soul" (3.1.76–8); if judgment is now an act carried out by the subject itself, the future day of judgment falls away – in the face of a perennial self-condemnation.

The dramatic poem's hint that, although existence depends on time, in some respects it exceeds the determinations of time accords well with Kant's argument in the second critique, where the philosopher argues that even if all one's actions are apparently determined by circumstance, from the viewpoint of "an intellectual intuition … the entire chain of appearances, with reference to that which concerns only the moral law, depends upon the spontaneity of the subject as a thing in itself, for the determination of which no physical explanation can be given."[22] No chain of physical circumstances can provide an excuse for an immoral act. But by the same token, no act eventually disappears into the array of circumstances from which it arose; it remains within the immortal subject as an imperishable fact. Thus it is an error to regard *Manfred* as a play everywhere displaying narcissistic self-regard; on the contrary, it attends to how the subject's moral faculty can render judgment on its temporally situated deeds and points to the radical self-division between its free judgment and the entire domain of its pathological acts. But such a relief from an apparent narcissism is not necessarily good news; in fact it brings to bear what is most intolerable about a Kantian attempt at secularization, for it highlights the utter absence within Kant – or Byron – of divine mercy, of any alterity in relation to whom the subject might work through the implication of past deeds and receive forgiveness. The only relief from guilt Manfred can imagine is oblivion in death; as long as he can remember his own deeds, he is self-condemned.[23]

The impress of these demands on his subjectivity is so strong that ultimately the significance of the landscape – or indeed of the "star condemn'd" – begins to fall away. As Cheeke argues, the Alps in this poem disappear "into what we might call 'Alpineism'[;] that is, they are not primarily a setting, nor even a metaphor," but rather represent "a mind rising above its place and time."[24] The momentum of this logic culminates in the final scene, where the poem invokes and revises the assertion of autonomy by Milton's Satan:

> The mind which is immortal makes itself
> Requital for its good or evil thoughts –
> Is its own origin of ill and end –
> And its own place and time – its innate sense,
> When stripp'd of this mortality, derives
> No colour from the fleeting things without,
> But is absorb'd in sufferance or in joy,
> Born from the knowledge of its own desert. (3.4.129–36)

Here the mind's capacity to judge itself quite apart from the determinations of space and time – a capacity writ large in Kant's second critique – makes it the scene of "its own origin of ill and end," its teleology, and accordingly of its own requital, its judgment. That capacity relieves Manfred of any satanic stance that the allusion might suggest, for unlike Satan, Manfred need not define himself over against God;

he repudiates *all* supernatural powers, including that of Arimanes, the poem's exotic stand-in for Satan. But while that capacity enables the subject to dispense with an external or eventual judgment, it forces the subject to accept what arises "from the knowledge of its own desert" – of what it deserves, to be sure, but also of what is its *desert*, its radically placeless and denuded state. To live without any external agency of judgment, this passage suggests, is to live in a desert – not one imposed by an accursed star, nor even by the Alpine scene, but by its own immortal yet featureless attributes. While this remains a declaration of independence from external authority, it also points to the utter subordination of the free subject to a power of moral judgment that remains at once intimate and alien.

The fact that the dramatic poem leads its protagonist to this stunning statement of moral independence should give one pause, especially insofar as it also seems to insist on its uncertainty on ultimate matters. Although the poem consistently articulates a scepticism about the availability of any external source of certain knowledge, it does not suspend the demand that Manfred arrive at an ethical judgment of his actions. The disappearance of such external authority, it seems, only sharpens the insistence that Manfred himself must pass judgment on his deeds. The severe uncertainty in one domain leads to an implacable demand in another. Such a shift from a sceptical understanding of subjectivity to an imperious, Kantian demand suggests that the latter arises from and responds to the former, grounding itself not on any disputable notion, such as the consistency of the empirical subject (a favourite topos of sceptical treatment), but on the transcendental necessity of judgment itself. The poem retraces this move within the development of its protagonist, describing how he gradually becomes aware that his lack of knowledge must give way not to any new doctrine but rather to the sheer demand for judgment in its own right, a judgment that in the view of the poem, as in that of the critical philosophy, he must render himself.

But this shift into the terrain of independent judgment is not the entire work of the poem. Insofar as it already begins with the premise of a disastrous immortality, *Manfred* rereads that historical sequence critically, foregrounding the inadequacy both of scepticism and of Kant's formulation of his ethical theory. The poem makes clear that since its protagonist already endures that immortality from the start, in attempting to find solutions to his dilemma in his encounters with various spirits he is ultimately attempting to circumvent or avoid his ethical dilemma. This interplay with spirits constitutes most of the action of the dramatic poem, suggesting that despite his fierce resistance to subordination, he is still incapable of assuming the full consequences of his accursed state. Moreover, insofar as the play posits that Manfred is already aware of his immortality, it sets him the task of discerning how to affirm it. In effect, then, it radicalizes its Kantian resonances, for its drama arises from a *second-order, post-Kantian* task of asking *what the free subject must do with this state*, how it must *respond* to the uncanny fact of its immortality and the consequent imperishability of its deeds. It proposes that it is not enough for the subject to become aware of its subordination to the moral law and all it entails; it must also work through the *consequences* of that inner subordination, that awareness of its catastrophic state. And since that state is on some level intolerable to the subject, the ethical challenge does nothing less than require the subject to carry out a virtually impossible act, that is, willingly to assume a burden that greatly exceeds its capacity.

As I am suggesting, then, much of the play shows how Manfred attempts to evade that seemingly impossible task, even as he gradually becomes aware that no other option is available to him. From the first scene as he invokes the aid of spirits through the "tyrant-spell" of "a star condemn'd" (1.1.43, 44), he relies not on any traditional supernatural power but rather its evacuation, taking a stance over against any form of submission. Manfred's success in summoning spirits of the earth through this spell suggests that it has a certain efficacy over natural forms. But as one might expect, insofar as this spell invokes a stellar instance of natural disaster, it can bring forth only personifications of natural process – avalanche, ocean, earthquake, hurricane – whose sway over earthly matters, while physically supreme, must remain destructive. Such forces cannot give Manfred what he seeks, for they cannot assist one whose challenge is to decipher the ethical significance of what they represent. *Manfred* reinforces this development in its second scene, where the protagonist exclaims that the beauty of the Alps, however great, cannot inspire love in him (1.2.9); he seeks something that lies beyond anything found in natural forms. Here the poem takes a definitive step beyond the aesthetics of the sublime, for it suggests that someone like Manfred, who is already under the sway of the supersensible in his explicit knowledge of his disastrous immortality, has already worked through what the sublime has to offer him and now enters what one might call a post-sublime condition, a solitude that has already incorporated sublimity and thus remains beyond its reach. Everything here works as if Manfred inherits the condition of the narrator who, in books six and twelve of *The Prelude*, experiences and imposes the devastations of a disastrous sublime and now must consider how to endure his traumatic and traumatizing condition.

Henceforth Manfred invokes the aid of spirits primarily to receive absolution from the Phantom of Astarte, from the person he wronged; his quest, in short, is not for a forgiveness that supernatural powers can give but to use their aid to receive something only another human being can provide. This insistence on the greater validity of human relationship, however, requires him to overcome the barrier between the living and the dead. Such an endeavour can scarcely succeed within the premises of the poem, not least because the Phantom of Astarte, like Manfred, is structurally independent of what any spirits may wish to require of her. The play allows Manfred to glimpse what may be the form of Astarte near the end of its first scene, going far to motivate the rest of its action; moreover, by staging the scene in which she calls his name and predicts his demise on the morrow, it incites the protagonist's final movement towards ethical resolution. In these instances, by calling her forth the spirits have at least a minimal agency in prodding Manfred towards his final act. But since they otherwise deny him what he seeks, even as they perpetually demand that he subordinate himself to their power, their presence primarily constitutes a temptation for Manfred to accept their mastery over him.[25] Yet the play suggests that such mastery is without merit, for these forces cannot give him oblivion or force the Phantom of Astarte to forgive him. Their aid is useless to him, their claims to ascendancy fraudulent. The entire apparatus of forbidden knowledge, it turns out, is irrelevant to Manfred's ethical project, not simply because of the scepticism that sees through all supernatural claims but more fundamentally because the infinity of the moral law now operates within him and thus no longer derives from any external authority. In this respect, *Manfred* sets itself apart from Goethe's initial *Faust* (1808), suggesting that the latter play, retaining far too much of the legend's premodern premises, at least in part evades the central ethical questions it raises. In contrast to Goethe's protagonist, and thanks to the consistent failure of the spirits to provide him what he seeks, Manfred gradually begins to understand that he can find a resolution to his accursed condition only through a further stage in his own ethical development, quite apart from what any external agency – including the Phantom of Astarte – might give him.

To comprehend the task that Manfred must pursue, one could scarcely do better than to consider recent readings of the Kantian moral law in the Lacanian tradition, readings that foreground the radical consequences of Kant's ethical theory. In her study *Ethics of the Real*, Zupančič points out that Kant describes "diabolical evil" "in exactly the same words he used to describe an ethical act," for it too "is a purely *formal* act," one that "complies with the form solely for the sake of form" and "exclusively for the sake of duty," obeying not "a sensible impulse" but rather a maxim and arising not from natural causes but from an *"act of freedom."*[26] Although Kant valiantly resists this implication, it is impossible to distinguish between a radically good or evil act within his system because in each case one acts according to duty alone, a duty that derives from no external agency. To take Kant seriously, one must go beyond him. As Zupančič argues, if we resist the maxim "Act in such a way that the *Führer*, if he knew about your action, would approve of it," then we must also resist the axiom "Act in such a way that God, if He knew about your action, would approve of it"; one follows duty and duty alone only if one abandons any external justification for what it demands. It follows that "the very structure of the act is foreign to the register constituted by the couplet good/bad."[27] Thus in *Dangerous Liaisons*, only Madame de Merteuil, not Valmont, "remains loyal to her duty until the very end," because "she refuses to give up on her desire"; the same is true of Moliere's Don Juan, in response to whose "steadfast refusal ... to give up on his enigmatic desire, does Heaven become powerless and fall from its position as Master."[28]

Manfred departs from these literary precedents; its protagonist is not forced to undergo the highly symbolic shame of smallpox imposed on Merteuil, nor is he engulfed, like Don Juan, by what Zupančič reads as the comic spectacle of fire and thunder.[29] One might infer that Byron takes the theme of diabolical evil a further step, allowing his protagonist to escape such impositions and thus stripping away the trappings of punishment by external forces. Yet the poem complicates any simplistic account of that departure from precedent by constructing a protagonist who does not seduce others out of a certain implacable commitment to evil, for instead, he falls in love with Astarte, who dies of what she sees in his heart. The poem focuses not on seduction but on another scenario altogether, once again departing from its antecedents into more adventurous terrain.

In that case, the play asks us to ponder how its central crime evokes aspects of that tradition while departing from it. What is it about Manfred's relation to Astarte that is worthy of the literary treatments of diabolical evil even though it lacks any reference to the deception or manipulation of others? For Byron the central act arises from love, not seduction – from a great intimacy rather than from the subjection of another. But in that case *Manfred* comes closer to modern ethical norms than its predecessors, suggesting that even in love subsists an element of diabolical evil. How could this be so? One notices right away that this version of love brings Manfred and Astarte into too great an intimacy; the poem hints at a form of incest that, in the view of Frederick Garber, "reduces to its smallest reach the distance one needs to go to get outside the self."[30] Indeed, this relation between Manfred and his Shelleyan epipsyche is so intimate that it virtually coincides with the self-relating evident in Kantian ethics – as if the love relation exposes something still encrypted within the latter. Here *Manfred* takes up a theme writ large in Shelley's *Alastor*, whose Poet, having dreamt of a highly idealized veiled maid, gives up all other objects in the world of sense to pursue her prototype into the realm of death. One might say that Shelley's Poet enacts a Lacanian ethics of psychoanalysis, even at the cost of death – and thus remains faithful to his own version of desire. Manfred seems to depart from this pattern, for the reader must infer that he apparently consummates his desire for this idealized counterpart, bringing about within this life what the Poet seeks in death. This consummation, however, constitutes a form of erotic disaster: evidently, for him to join with a female figure who so directly embodies the better aspects of himself is to expose the Real of himself to another. If, as the poem suggests, Manfred's repudiation of any external morality allows him to enter this relationship in the first place, and if in consequence his subjectivity already incorporates the erasure of transcendence, installing a "desert" in his heart, then it is impossible for him to become intimate with a counterpart of himself without revealing that desert (the Real of his subjectivity) to her and devastating this better version of himself.

On one level, then, *Manfred* demystifies the Kantian notion of moral autonomy, revealing in this erotic scenario that an absolute intimacy of the subject with its own desire – whether out of duty, love, or both – can only be catastrophic. Manfred operates under the sign of a deformed and monstrous star in part because his condition has been shaped by a mutilated A*star*te, here again an external symbol of his internal condition. In effect, the poem suggests, one who gazes on his own heart – or attempts to remain faithful to his own desire – can put into action only the obliteration of transcendence that produced his ethical independence in the first place. Once literature expunges from itself the relation of the ethical agent to the trappings of external supernatural agencies, as it does in *Manfred*, then one thing becomes clear: to remain faithful to one's desire can lead to no other result than a confrontation with one's disastrous subjectivity, and thus not to independence but to an encounter with an intolerable subjective singularity. To pursue an ethics of the Real, in short, forces one to encounter the devastating, annihilating Real of one's own desire.

This scenario remains faithful to aspects of the tradition that the poem invokes: the refusal both of Shelley's Poet and of Manfred to desire someone unlike himself, to accept the otherness of the erotic counterpart, signifies a wish to overleap the constraints of intersubjectivity and therefore to seek an erotic satisfaction foreclosed from the relations of finitude.[31] One must conclude that for Manfred to realize his desire for Astarte is impossible, just as it is impossible for the Poet to consummate his love for the veiled maid. The scandal of *Manfred* is not merely that it gestures towards incest but that it hints at the prospect of a perfect satisfaction of desire; it is as if Manfred experiences a kind of jouissance foreclosed by the relations of intersubjectivity. But for that very reason, here as in *St Leon*, the realization of the impossible makes evident that it must also remain forbidden: the achievement of such a satisfaction does not confirm, but devastates, the subject.[32] That satisfaction bears Astarte away, leaving behind a Manfred who has in some sense endured his own death (as the protagonist explains to the abbot in a late scene: 3.1.138–53) and thus who now experiences a mode of desire no longer oriented to anything visible in the material world.

The poem's simultaneous evocation of the impossible erotics of *Alastor* and of the forbidden knowledge of *Faust* suggests that it finds in these divergent scenarios instances of the same overall pattern, an attempt to achieve what must remain structurally foreclosed. For that very reason, however, the text steps beyond the biographical context that many of its initial readers, and indeed many others, have attempted to find in it. Although the biographical Byron committed incest with his half-sister Augusta – and enjoyed sodomitical relations with young Greek men, in a further level of forbidden satisfaction encrypted in the poem, as in related Gothic tales and in Byron's own earlier texts – such literal satisfactions, however transgressive, hardly allowed Byron to enjoy perfect fusion with his erotic partners, for they necessarily remained within the domain of intersubjectivity that does not apply in this tale.[33] Insofar as Byron gestures towards his biographical actions in the poem, he does so to invoke a satisfaction missing from his actual erotic relations, but for that reason he dares to isolate an ethical question more brutal than biographical experience alone would impose: How might one take responsibility for the jouissance one desires? How might one take upon oneself the burden of what nevertheless remains foreclosed from the domain of actual experience? How might one, in short, take responsibility for the Real of one's desire?

In taking up this question, *Manfred* also enlarges its deconstruction of Kantian moral autonomy. Insofar as the poem suggests that the protagonist realizes an impossible jouissance and thus must face the Real of his desire, it also proposes that he should remain faithful to a radical ethical singularity – and *must also take responsibility for the Real of ethical singularity itself*. In this regard, the poem follows through on the second-order ethical task mentioned above, demanding that the subject who has remained faithful to its desire take responsibility for the consequences of such fidelity. To its credit, the poem voices this demand by treating the scenario of Manfred's relation to Astarte merely as a prologue to its central dramatic action. Its core concern, after all, is how the protagonist, faced with the devastating consequences of his moral and erotic singularity, can do more than merely suffer the tormenting memory of his forbidden deed. The ethical challenge of the poem, in short, is retrospective: How can Manfred affirm his prior actions – or, as I asked a moment ago, how might he take upon himself the full consequences of the Real of his desire?

Perhaps only now can one glimpse the significance of Manfred's attempts to find an intersubjective refuge from the torments of that memory. In a similar position, Caleb Williams, having repudiated all social relations in the name of a structurally forbidden knowledge of his society's total injustice, becomes mad, incapable any longer of sustaining his singular position. As we have seen, in the novel's second, revised ending, Caleb withdraws his total condemnation of the social order and recognizes the cost of his accusation, affirming his relation with Falkland and consequently recovering a social identity and an effective mode of speech. *Manfred*, on the contrary, explores the possibility that the singular subject might sustain its position over against the entire social order in a kind of sovereign solitude, thereby insisting on the validity of a total negation, even if doing so must consign the protagonist to the structurally forbidden position of the Real. In the first ending of *Caleb Williams*, Godwin in effect condemned his protagonist to madness while allowing his readers to discern the fraudulence of the society that drove him to that impasse, separating the protagonist from the insight which his experience permits another; *Manfred*, however, disallows such a split, insisting on the possibility that its protagonist, like its reader, might sustain a total negation despite all odds. Thus Byron ends up adhering more closely than Godwin to a position of strict moral singularity, locating his protagonist in the purely structural, empty place of an ethical infinity, holding open the possibility of an absolute denunciation of his society from which Godwin retreats. Yet the counterexample of *Caleb Williams* makes remarkably clear that such a position is almost impossible to sustain; the longing to escape that radical solitude, that madness, through an appeal to intersubjectivity imposes itself as a near necessity.

How, then, must we read the ending of this poem? What, if anything, does Manfred achieve in his final act? In the final scene, addressing the spirits who wish to gain mastery over him in a moment of what

Martyn Corbett calls "tremendous self-assertion," he repudiates their power: "Back to thy hell! / Thou hast no power upon me, *that* I feel; / Thou never shalt possess me, *that* I know" (3.4.124–6).[34] He can make these stunning declarations, of course, on the basis of what he claims in the lines that follow – that the "mind which is immortal makes itself / Requital for its good or evil thoughts" (3.4.129–30). The gods are powerless now because Manfred claims the capacity to assume responsibility for his actions in his own right. But how can he do so? Through what agency can he in fact take that burden upon himself?

The play asks us to read Manfred's final action – his death – as its ultimate resolution. But in doing so, it poses a major challenge to its interpreters. After all, ever since its first scene Manfred has sought oblivion as a means of escape from his knowledge in the Real; such a death might seem to provide him precisely with that oblivion. Yet over the course of the poem, the significance of that death has transformed entirely. In his final extended statement, from which I have been quoting, Manfred goes on to declare to the spirits, "*Thou* didst not tempt me, and thou couldst not tempt me; / I have not been thy dupe, nor am thy prey – / But was my own destroyer, and will be / My own hereafter" (3.4.137–40). He takes total responsibility for his actions; rather than seeking oblivion, he affirms the full dimensions of his deeds, refusing to attribute them to any other agent or to take refuge from their consequences under the shelter of any other force. Far from evading the consequences of his desire here, Manfred declares that he destroyed himself in his deeds, just as he will destroy himself hereafter – that is, a few lines later in his death.

Here I allude to an aspect of the poem's ending that receives remarkably little comment. Manfred suffers from no disease; he is still younger, for example, than the chamois-hunter (2.1.49–50), and no external agent deprives him of life. Yet he dies all the same. That death, in short, is not a natural event; it is caused by nothing in the realm of sense. It realizes what is infinite in Manfred, the Real of his singularity. Much like his relation with Astarte, it brings about something structurally forbidden to those who inhabit the realm of sense. In effect, then, the poem indicates in that final extended speech that if Manfred could realize what is erotically forbidden – and could thus be "[his] own destroyer" – then he can also bring about another impossible event, a further destruction caused by nothing other than a certain infinite capacity within him.

How can a subject tormented by his immortality end up bringing about his own death? Does that death not suggest that he evades the more terrible and heroic burden of assuming his guilt while remaining alive? But the poem suggests that in causing his own death, Manfred enacts a final and total repudiation of all external agencies, declaring once and for all that he is a self-determined ethical agent; he realizes his infinite singularity, his immortality, precisely through the death itself, through an event caused by nothing in the body or the natural world. As we have seen, Kant suggested that no subject could realize a perfect conformity to the moral law within a mortal lifespan, arguing on that basis for the immortality of the soul. Manfred, however, does complete that perfect conformity – ironically, through the singular act of his own death. It is as if he brings about what he could realize throughout his entire afterlife in a single moment, whereby he repudiates every alternative conception of the afterlife. After all, in every other tale of this sort, the afterlife arrives precisely through the protagonist's submission to devils who would carry him away; the traditional figures of Faust and Don Juan both succumb at the moment of death to the agency of the devil. Manfred's self-willed demise thus spurns the traditional denouement, repudiating the conditions the latter would impose on his ethical singularity. Moreover, the poem imposes this stark punishment while insisting that it is *worse* than traditional impositions: "[T]here is no future pang / Can deal that justice on the self-condemn'd / He deals on his own soul" (3.1.76–8), for the torments imposed by others can never cut so deep as a remorse one recognizes and enforces on one's own terms.

One might ponder whether Manfred knows that his death relieves him of any further subjection to supernatural agencies. The resolute scepticism of the poem on this point might be taken to hint that he cannot know for sure what will transpire after his death. But much as the play aligns a certain scepticism with the sign of an extinguished, monstrous star, and thus with the cancelled telos of natural disaster, and much as it indicates that he can destroy himself through enacting an impossible, disastrous jouissance with Astarte, it insists that he can bring about a final, singular event in his death as well. In that case, the final deed completes the disastrous ethics at the poem's heart, finally realizing a fate imposed not by the star but by Manfred himself.

Insofar as this final act replicates the impossible deed of his union with Astarte, it too is an instance of the impossible – an act that presumably lies beyond what any finite subject can bring about. As we have seen, that event takes place because of the assertion of what is immortal and infinite within Manfred, the immortality that can invade, and interrupt, the logic of his mortality – and thus of his more ordinary, mortal self. One could conclude with Zupančič that the absolute ethical act can take place only when it is realized over the objections of the subject, in what she calls a "subjectivation without subject." But much as she argues, following Lacan, that "on a certain level every subject, average as he may be, wants his destruction, *whether he wants it or not*," and therefore wishes to commit an annihilating, ethical act despite his better interest, we may conclude that Manfred enacts precisely what any subject desires – even against his will.[35] He realizes an aspect of himself that vastly exceeds his finite wishes, bringing about – as we have seen – the realization of his immortality through the enactment of his death.

If this analysis holds, then one of the most telling gestures in the poem takes place in the protagonist's final line, when Manfred tells the abbot, "Old man! 'tis not so difficult to die" (3.4.151). Byron's publisher John Murray omitted this line from the poem on its initial publication, prompting the poet to declare, "You have destroyed the whole effect & moral of the poem by omitting the last line of Manfred's speaking."[36] Byron's response indicates that this line is by no means trivial or anti-climactic, a release from the high intensity of the poem; on the contrary, that line is the poem's culmination, for it declares that to take the final step of ethical subjectivation is not in the end all that difficult: once one finally abandons any alibi for one's acts and any search for higher knowledge about one's fate, it is not so difficult to choose the course of one's life – and all its deeds – as if from the perspective of eternity. In effect, he suggests, one can choose to affirm one's entire life in advance, declaring absolute independence from any judgment rendered from elsewhere by taking the entire responsibility for the Real of desire upon oneself through the infinite imposition of one's own death, and in the same gesture transform that death from a mere fact of mortality into an ethical achievement, the realization of one's ethical project. Only through that act, the poem implies, can one truly expunge one's dependence on external agencies to render judgment and thereby fully embrace the disaster at the heart of the free subject.

Insofar as the dramatic poem brings about Manfred's death through no obvious physical cause, it also dismantles the scenario we have seen in previous chapters whereby the ethical subject chooses death in order to refuse compliance with the demands of an unjust sovereign. In the culminating moment, Manfred declares his independence from all external forces not by undergoing a hanging at the gallows – or an eternity of torment in hell – but through an act that undoes the scenario itself. He neither appeals to a God of justice nor scorns an emblem of injustice, turning aside from all such agencies to bring about justice upon himself. In this gesture, the play broaches an ethical insight very close to that which will inspire Shelley's *Prometheus Unbound*, a poem written in part as a response to *Manfred*. In celebrating Prometheus's decision to withdraw his curse against his tormentor, Jupiter, Shelley's poem suggests that an ethics akin to Kant's – one that still invokes the notion of an opposition to evil – keeps that evil alive as its precondition and thus indirectly collaborates with what it resists. While *Prometheus Unbound* unquestionably sets out to do much more, and indeed to dispute much of what is on offer in *Manfred*, one must nevertheless note that Byron's poem precedes Shelley's in cutting through the dominant ethical impasse. Some might be tempted to argue that it can do so precisely because it relieves Manfred of the difficulties of intersubjectivity. But the play offers Manfred no such relief, for even in the absence of human interlocutors, Manfred could establish relations of dependence on or defiance of supernatural agents. He wins his way beyond both dependence or defiance only by repudiating both at great cost and under the most intense pressure.

Manfred's refusal even of this form of dependence bears not only on the ethical considerations of that moment but on ours as well. His stance proleptically responds to that of Lee Edelman, who in *No Future* proposes that queer subjects accept the hostile accusations of homophobes and actively assume the status of the Real, thereby expressing an utter repudiation of a reproductive heterosexuality and its ideological pretexts, the child and the future.[37] Such a position captures much about *Manfred*: it too takes the risk of affirming a prohibited eroticism, abandoning virtually every normative value in the process. But Edelman's stance also falls short of what *Manfred* would regard as a genuine act in the Real, which responds to the entirety of one's life in the past, present, *and future* and thus cannot fall prey to the refutation that must take place when the future necessarily comes, however severely one may refuse it. Moreover, because Edelman's stance relies on the defiance of social norms, it depends on injustice for its precondition and remains indirectly complicit in the society it attempts to undermine. *Manfred* reveals a sharper alternative: it cuts through false impositions not through defiance but by imposing the entire burden of one's acts on oneself, not by playing the role of an outcast but by committing an act without reference to the conditions that others might wish to impose. The play's refusal of the Kantian reliance on the sovereign bears as well on a queer ethics of our moment, showing that even now it is capable of cutting through our own apparently avant-garde sense of ethical radicalism.

Nevertheless, the fact that Manfred can resolve his dilemma in this way reinforces that the deed he must confront is his own. The resolution on view here cannot apply – at least not directly – to the story told in *Caleb Williams*, in which Caleb comes to know what he considers to be the Real of Falkland's life; nor to that told in *St Leon*, where the protagonist takes on an impossible physical state and exercises a foreclosed social power thanks to his applying a forbidden knowledge; nor to that in *Frankenstein*, where Victor's knowledge in the Real produces the body of the monster, who comes alive and is henceforth an independent ethical agent. In such stories, an impossible knowledge creates a situation of intense rivalry, a struggle for mastery, which in principle must conclude either with the renunciation of any illusion that there is such a thing as knowledge in the Real or with the Real's full realization in disaster for all parties. *Manfred* escapes these scenarios by focusing on a protagonist who confronts the purely ethical Real of his *own* life, setting aside the array of complications that arise from an intersubjective struggle.

In this regard, however, it reconceives of its problematic in still another way. In the novels just mentioned, the ethical protagonist is often separated from the full consequences of his deeds, enabling the tale to split the act from the horror of its memory. A similar scenario unfolds in a later drama, *The Cenci*, in which Shelley focuses on the ethical dilemmas facing Beatrice, who must decide whether to respond with violence to the horrific depredations of her father. Once again, no matter how compelling the play's ethical explorations may be, they nevertheless divide the father's evil from the horror of contemplating it, allowing everyone to project a sense of pure evil onto him and thereby to protect Beatrice from too hostile a judgment of her acts. In contrast, *Manfred* depicts a protagonist who is similarly implicated in acts that involve incest and the shedding of blood, but it remains resolutely focused on the inner state of the criminal himself without projecting his act even slightly onto another.

As these various comparisons make clear, *Manfred* stands out in its own era – and beyond – for its refusal to disperse ethical questions across intersubjective scenarios, complications, and difficulties. Its resolute focus has the virtue of illuminating what consequences ensue from an unmediated ethics of the Real, what transpires from the subject's direct confrontation with itself. In many ways, then, it is a hyper-modern text, an exemplary reflection on what must follow from a rigorous consideration of the internal limit.

Yet this stance has its costs. In its final scene, as I suggested above, *Manfred* ultimately consigns its protagonist to the category of the Real. It gives him a truly counterfactual position, one it conceives in figurative and tacitly philosophical terms, not with a status available to the conscious subject or the social and political agent. It does so in part to isolate ethical singularity as such, providing no reassurance, no compromises with the games of identity, no avenues for intersubjective affirmation – opting instead for the stakes of an infinite judgment. Thus in part it replies to the ethical insight of *St Leon*, which holds that an ethics of the Real ultimately places the subject in a position from which he cannot successfully change the world as it is, for his doing so leads either to economic disaster or to a struggle to dominate his magical powers. Godwin, like Edelman, assumes that to enact an ethics of the Real is to be consigned to the *social* equivalent of the Real – to a position lived out biographically, in quotidian reality, as an absolute pariah. *Manfred*, in contrast, suggests that the act in the Real takes place in an absolutely interior domain, on the level of the subject's disposition to itself – in a space of ethical or psychoanalytic insight logically prior to its effects in social and biographical reality. It gives the subject an unhesitating ethical authority, but one that pretends to no definitive knowledge of things as they are, no mastery of the social order, and indeed no necessary commitment to bringing about any greater good.

On one level, then, Byron's dramatic poem points to the limitations of Manfred's ethical achievement: it underlines the irony of that ethical authority by giving it to one who in its final scene vanishes into death. A singular ethical gesture that takes place outside of any complicating social context evidently produces an act with virtually no consequences outside itself. An act that fully assumes the burdens of a disastrous subjectivity, that takes upon itself the violence specifically of the *conditions* that necessarily impinge on history, seems to disappear from the positive scene of that history, scarcely altering the domain where pathological subjects conduct their affairs or where the antagonists of a finite politics hold sway. Such a result is embedded in the play's counterfactual premises: when even the erotic relations of the protagonist are scarcely intersubjective, the import of his final ethical gesture must remain equally so. Manfred's achievement seems at once infinite and empty – at once extraordinarily significant and insignificant, exemplary and hollow.

Yet the fact that the play works out these themes in a counterfactual vein, giving Manfred a crime and a resolution not available to any finite subject, suggests that its tale serves as a metaphor for another, more subtle contention. Just as one must translate the counterfactual narratives of *St Leon* or *Frankenstein* into other terms to grasp their import, one must do the same with *Manfred*, recognizing that it does not stage a merely asocial tale but rather deploys a nonrealistic narrative to capture the logic of a subjectivity that obtains even outside those terms. Through this means, the play shows how a subject, in taking responsibility for its jouissance – and for the disastrous materiality that subtends the history in which it participates – is defined no longer by them but rather by its own retrospective act, its own capacity to strike against the sway of the quotidian subject and henceforth live on other premises. While this act is virtual, taking place in a nonphenomenal domain, and thus seems to have little effect, the poem's philosophical stakes hint that on the contrary it has the immense effect of reconceiving of the subject's conditions of possibility, transforming an imposed condition into one it has taken upon itself. Manfred's impossible death therefore stands in for an act whereby the subject overcomes the trauma of its disastrous situatedness, abandons any nostalgia for a prior condition or search for a redemptive alternative, and transforms even a sceptical uncertainty about its condition – all through an act of radical dispossession. In that act, it destroys the inherited notion of the subject still anchored to origins and ends, self-evident values or finalities, grounds or destinies, inherited loyalties or attachments, in favour of one grounded in nothing besides this act itself. In short, by bringing the act of destroying transcendence into the subject itself, it brings about a second- or third-order counterpart of the event that defines modernity, creating a subject now explicitly defined by the internal limit and producing what we can now see as a quintessentially modern or even hyper-modern subject, one capable of living in a world defined by a ruined star.

Such a subject, of course, continues to live within social relations and on the field of history. But it does so without being compelled to understand those relations within the terms they supply. Because it has affirmed itself in the Real, it knows that it need not regard itself as fully determined by social or historical conditions. By defining itself in this way, the subject finds in itself the internal limit of power, "the minimal gap that divides power from itself"; as a result, Copjec argues, the subject "is able to free [itself] from submission to the forceful pull of [its] own determined and determinate identity."[38] To arrive at that stance, of course, it must not only enact a version of Manfred's final gesture but also go beyond it, *returning to finitude* and embracing it as the field apart from which its own infinitude must remain empty, useless, and forgotten. Only with such a further step – only with a dialectical turn from immortality back to mortality – can its ethical realization have any historical purchase at all.

Thus *Manfred* itself is incomplete on its own terms; without the poems to follow, where the poet can put its insights to work in ways the play does not anticipate, it would remain autotelic, stuck in a space even more private and elusive than is typical for a closet drama. The fact that a reader of the play must turn to later texts to conceive of its implications suggests that rather than providing a final statement of its concerns, *Manfred* sets into motion a longer sequence, outlining with exemplary care the contours of a problem that the poet can complete only in further texts. Its place within that sequence suggests, in turn, that remaining within an entirely autotelic register falsifies the subject, reducing it to a problem that has a purely formal resolution. Thus only the act of putting that resolution to work within the domain of finitude makes visible its effect for actual subjects, finally clarifying what sort of difference *Manfred* can make on the field of history.

One might initially assume that Byron extends *Manfred* in this way through his second metaphysical poetic drama, *Cain* (1821), for in this play, he takes up a range of themes embedded in the earlier play but not explored at such length there, engaging in much greater detail with the history of life, its consequences for one's relation to biblical teaching, and fundamental conceptions of death and guilt. The play certainly lays down a marker in its period for exploring how modern scientific knowledge ushers in a condition based on the erasure of the rainbow covenant, joining with several other Romantic-era texts I discussed in chapter 3. Yet it approaches this question in an unusual way: relying on a pre-covenantal biblical tale, it considers the contours of ethics from a position *before* ethics, from a state unaware of what its demands entail. Where *Manfred* followed the development of a protagonist facing the consequences of his earlier deeds, *Cain* traces the history of a character confronting earthly – and ethical – disaster for the first time, discovering through these experiences the sheer necessity of having an ethics in the first place. Without a prior understanding of death – and hence of the possibility of murder – the subject simply cannot sense the full weight of responsibility in the face of others. The play thus evokes the shape of a potential ethics from a perspective that, however intractable, remains stunningly naive, unaware of its own implications almost to the bitter end. Such a strategy, however, implies that the modern subject, like Cain, must think ethics from scratch, taking seriously how the awareness of deep time may displace received understandings of God and Lucifer, the initial stories of Genesis, and indeed the crime of Cain. Rather than pushing towards ethical resolution, as does *Manfred*, *Cain* removes prior, familiar resolutions, erasing old barriers to ethical reflection and clearing the space for a far more capacious debate. Within this context, the play reprises key themes in *Manfred*: refusing to submit to God, Cain also resists submission to Lucifer, maintaining all along the stance of potential independence, so that when he does discover death and murder, he accepts responsibility not out of obedience to God but through an astonished, internal self-condemnation. In opening the way to fresh reflection on the basis of a new awareness of life's history and an insistence on ethical independence, then, *Cain* goes far towards offering up a new style of engagement with its themes.

Yet the poetic drama suffers from a number of constraints. Even while sustaining this novel investigation, the play follows the biblical story with sufficient fidelity to replicate familiar categories. For one thing, it depicts a protagonist whose refusal to comply with divine commands casts him in the role of defiance, however complex his stance may actually be; moreover, by showing in its final pages that Cain will be subject to God's condemnation, it makes his independence subject to an external authority, as a result ironically undercutting that very independence. By complying with the biblical tale, Byron perforce returns to categories beyond which his achievement in *Manfred* had already taken him.

It is better to turn back from the later play towards the poem that followed immediately on the publication of *Manfred*: *Childe Harold's Pilgrimage*, canto 4, which was written over the course of the next year (1817–18). While the partial breakthrough in *Manfred* does not immediately suspend *Childe Harold's Pilgrimage*, suggesting that Byron must work through its implications within, rather than against, the terms of the latter poem, it does inspire the poet to bring the latter to an end – and to do so in part by transforming the stance of the narrator, whose persona, affect, and orientation are central to that poetic effort overall. Most of canto 4 foregrounds themes and concerns it shares with *Manfred*: here the ruins of Italy inspire the narrator to ponder the equally ruined status of a mind that, like the tannen, groundlessly endures the shocks of Alpine heights (stanza 20), that in its solitude must strive either with God or with demons (stanzas 33, 34), that witnesses in Rome "Wrecks of another world, whose ashes still are warm" (stanza 46, line 414), that calls upon itself an ancient and unavoidable nemesis (stanzas 132, 133), and that muses on something within it "which shall tire / Torture and Time" (stanza 137, lines 1228–9).[39] These reflections revolve around an extended sequence on how the mind, "diseased" by "its own beauty," casts a "fatal spell" upon itself, endlessly pursuing its phantoms, revealing that it cannot belong to the "harmony of things" and that in consequence its "last and only place / Of refuge" is its "right of thought" (stanzas 122–7, lines 1090, 1104, 1227, 1137–8). This canto displays once again a mind traumatized by its own immortality, its own infinite judgment – one that, confronting its phantoms, eventually sees through them to itself as its "last and only" place. In encounters with one monument after another, one historical episode after the last, the poem suggests that historical action aims for something it perpetually misses, not merely falling short but revealing to the historical subject a fault in the very fabric of action itself, in that gap between finitude and infinity – or more radically in desire itself, which it conceives as a fatal disease. The field of history, then, becomes an array of triggers for such meditations, sites to inspire endless new attempts to evoke the wrecked situation of the modern subject. What *Manfred* thematizes in one way, canto 4 does in another: suffering a ruined immortality, crushed by his own delusions, and beholding the ashes of the world, this narrator brings a tortured sensibility onto the field of European history, finding there perpetual reminders of a state he shares.

While Byron cannot restage the resolution of *Manfred* within the terms of this genre, the play's final gesture nevertheless incites him to conceive how it might permit him to reframe the premises of *Childe Harold's Pilgrimage* as well. In the late, key stanzas of that poem, the narrator, plunging into the sea, comments on how it despises humankind's "vile strength … For earth's destruction," suggesting that having moved beyond land, on which the signs of that strength are visible in an endless display of ruined monuments, he has at last entered a new and different space (1614–15). But since the sea, too, is a domain of ruins – since it contains countless shipwrecks, the remains of "oak leviathans," each claiming the "vain title" of "arbiter of war," which so often "melt into [its] yeast of waves" (1624, 1626, 1628) – its distinctive status comes not because it is a scene without ruins but because it buries them in its depths, reducing them to anonymity and oblivion under its greater sway. The sea is thus another metaphor for the sheer process that potentially eviscerates every human achievement; like solar death or the Alps, it stands in for the principle of disastrous materiality that subtends all history.

Yet within this scene something remains. According to the narrator, who in this passage addresses the ocean, it erases signs of any distinctive achievement, burying them in its anonymous movement, leaving no "shadow of man's ravage, save his own," when he "sinks into thy depths with bubbling groan, / Without a grave, unknell'd, uncoffin'd, and unknown" (1608, 1610–11). These bubbles – the sole marker of "man's" exposure to disaster in an object that, while coherent, surrounds nothing but air – constitute a precise version of the internal limit; moreover, they soon take on another significance when the narrator reveals that his "joy" was "on thy breast to be / Borne, like thy bubbles, onward," for the sea's "breakers" were to him "a delight," a "pleasing fear, / For I was as it were a child of thee, / And trusted to thy billows far and near, / And laid my hand upon thy mane – as I do here" (1649–56). If those bubbles signify the destruction of human achievements now embedded within the notion of history, the narrator's seizing them transforms them into a sign of his capacity to take upon himself the consequences of that exposure. Where *Manfred* conceives of such an act in terms of a private ethical gesture in response to one's prior deeds, these stanzas contemplate instead a capacity to take upon oneself the implications of a shared condition, the eventual destruction of any human endeavour, and to absorb that condition into one's mode of address to the literary public. Rather than enacting this gesture through the annihilation of the individual subject, these stanzas incorporate what destroys historical aspiration into the poetic persona. The self-enclosed event that concludes *Manfred*, then, here becomes a sweeping gesture, an act that installs the Byronic poet as the performer of the Real in a post-covenantal culture. Yet the supreme confidence Manfred brings to his final act emerges here as well: the poet carries out this gesture as he trusts the billows, hinting that the sea, despite its destructive power, is a medium strong enough to bear him up, to reward his confidence, and thus to authorize a newly evacuated mode of writing. One can trust oneself, it seems, to the very medium of disaster.

It is worth pausing as well over the fact that these stanzas return us to the theme of shipwreck with which we began in chapter 1, this time in a new key. Here the poem marks out the difference between the contingency of a given natural disaster (as in *Mary: A Fiction*) and the much vaster process of a disastrous materiality intrinsic to finitude, between a given shipwreck and the scene of *perpetual* shipwreck. Moreover, rather than interpreting the scene of disaster in relation to an ultimate destination that remains out of view, the poet converts the apocalypse to come into the negativity of a disastrous persona in the poem itself. In doing so, it also alters the resolution of *Manfred*: rather than bringing the force of a disastrous immortality to bear on the quotidian subject, here an obliterated telos befalls the scene of history, eviscerating the solid ground of historical action, converting it into the sea of mere historicity, the flow of events without substance and without end – a flow captured well in those bubbles and the persona who converts their state into his own. Henceforth, the narrator – and the Byronic poet more generally – can fully identify with this newly substance-less state, this fate of floating without ground and moving onward without destination in the field of that process without subject, that movement of endless oblivion, that space of perpetual disaster.

This mobilization of the Real within Byron's poetics may well mark the striking shift in affect, tone, and persona from the early to the late career.[40] The Oriental tales, for example, as well as nearly the whole of *Childe Harold's Pilgrimage*, thematize the Real as intractable trauma, as the site for a wound that no genre and no poetic stance can fully process. If anything, *Manfred* takes that tone to its height, creating an affect that for some readers is almost unbearable in its melancholic performativity. The conclusion of the play cuts through that affect, opening up the space for something else that it does not attempt to specify. When the poet radicalizes this shift in canto 4, incorporating the ethics of singularity into a poetics of disastrous historicity, he opens the way for what soon becomes the comic irreverence of *Don Juan* (initial cantos, 1819), mobilizing the Real not as trauma but as a principle that ungrounds all conventions and destabilizes even genre, notoriously allowing himself as a result to mock heroism, epic, fame, and many other traditional signs of value in the process. The later poem serves well as a further development in this sequence in part because it focuses on a character who, much like the Faust whose legend lies behind *Manfred*, must presumably be carted away at the end by the devil. Resting on the prior achievement of *Manfred*, however, *Don Juan* (more radical than *Cain*) suspends any such denouement, any reference to external punishment; moreover, by incorporating the shift to a poetics of disaster enacted in the final pages of *Childe Harold's Pilgrimage*, canto 4, it deploys a socially engaged, vastly urbane version of that poetics, enabling its narrator to articulate with unsurpassed sophistication a state of relaxed scandalousness, combining a piercing refusal of hypocrisy with a joyous and digressive scepticism.[41] Here at last the breakthroughs of the prior poems come to rest in a persona utterly at ease with the loss of all hope and any certain destination, one who trusts himself to the billows of a pointless historicity.

From "Darkness" through *Don Juan*, then, Byron enacts an increasingly mature understanding of the consequences of disastrous materiality, moving through several phases as he clears the space for an ethics of the Real and then, by incorporating that breakthrough into his poetic persona itself – the sign of a radical fault in the field of history – makes it possible for him to deploy it in his extensive, potentially unlimited evisceration of his world. From a perspective sympathetic to modernity, Byron's effort is well-nigh incomparable, for he dares to go further into a potentially traumatic realization from which others shy away; he enters a problematic whose contours only gradually become visible to him, eventually trusting himself to the sheer movement of historicity and thus becoming a signal interpreter of modernity for his time. But from a perspective not already committed to modernity, this sequence can be said to make a certain violence even more severe, for through it the subject undergoes an act of auto-devastation, incorporating into itself the force that annihilates all human endeavour. In becoming modern, it seems, one must become a fully disastrous subject – one who instantiates that force which perpetually devastates human history from within.

5 Tarrying with Disaster

Ethical Destitution in Shelley's "The Triumph of Life"

Percy Bysshe Shelley occupies a singular position within the thematic of a Romantic poetics of disastrous subjectivity. Like Mary Shelley, he inherits the radical critique of British society evident in the work of Mary Wollstonecraft and William Godwin, building aspects of that critique into his work from the beginning of his career. A student of late-Enlightenment investigations into the history of the earth and the sciences of life, like several of his predecessors, including Kant and Wordsworth, he dovetailed the concept of an endless series of natural disasters intrinsic to earth's geological history with his concerns as a philosophical radical and with the aesthetics of the sublime, bringing aspects of them all into his overarching poetic practice. Perpetually attentive to the ethical stakes of the traditions he inherited and revised, in tandem with Lord Byron he took seriously the project of creating an ethical stance worthy of his revisions of prior modes of thought. Because he is ambitious at once in his political, philosophical, scientific, and ethical concerns and committed to fashioning an intellectually and aesthetically capacious position, his work provides an unusually sophisticated version of what is at stake in the period's explorations of disastrous subjectivity.

That sophistication deepens as his career progresses, reaching a point of remarkable intensity in the poet's final, incomplete masterwork, "The Triumph of Life" (1822). Readers have long regarded it as among the most ambitious and difficult of all Romantic writings, a text that seems to anticipate and complicate aspects of psychoanalytic and deconstructive thought in its poetics of searing negativity. In the present context it is not difficult to reinforce this sense of the poem by emphasizing how directly it incorporates into its very texture the notion of a disaster taking place not only in the distance, at the peak of Mont Blanc, but also in the very preconditions of human experience and indeed in certain attributes of subjectivity itself.

But the poem does not rest easily within such an appropriation. Although it articulates a stunningly conceived poetics of self-destructive figuration, it does so in terms that perpetually invoke an alternative possibility; through the situation of its narrator, its genre, a range of allusions and gestures, and its invocations of philosophical and poetic traditions, it consistently invokes an ethical possibility beyond its central scenario. Drawing on the intellectual system to which Shelley adhered throughout his career, a theistic atomism which emphasizes both a material contingency and a transcendental power of which human beings can have no certain knowledge, the poem evokes both a radical negativity, allegorized in the figure of Life, and a fidelity to the good. The poem thus takes the measure both of a rigorous sense of a disaster immanent to human life and of an orientation, extending from ancient virtue ethics through its present, towards a final cause. Consistently bringing this ethical orientation into play, the poem displaces the authority of Life's triumph to focus on the difficult question of how to respond to what that triumph reveals.

In doing so, "The Triumph of Life" ultimately brings into view the failure of every ethical response it considers, showing that the attempt to seek knowledge regarding what exceeds Life must fail and that the attempt to articulate or realize a higher principle in terms available to human beings must at least partly falsify it. Furthermore, it proposes that even sacred action to overcome Life's triumph – whether in the form of divine violence or radical self-sacrifice – either replicates violence or leaves its power intact. Even the attempt to realize the good undercuts that good; even divine action falls prey to contradiction. In its furthest reaches, the poem hints that even the premises of premodern ethical traditions must collapse, that the very effort to realize the good (by human *or divine* agents) must fall prey to the gap between an infinite justice and the conditions of finitude. While other texts of its period speak of this gap, only this poem begins with such an insight and sets out to articulate its consequences. It is thus a unique statement, perhaps the only one of its kind in the entire tradition of ethical reflection, mapping out a stance that may have no parallel before or since. It ultimately speaks of a stunning ethical destitution – one so radical that it surpasses any possibility that the subject might assume its burden through still another gesture, might incorporate it into still another rendition of subjectivity. Instead, the poem suggests that the subject is left without recourse, caught in relation to a finitude and infinitude that both fail, and must perforce endure indefinitely in its destitute state, tarrying with a perpetually renewed disaster.

Many of the key premises of "The Triumph of Life" are already visible in *Mont Blanc* (1816). One might initially set out to read the earlier poem's concept of Power within the terms of disastrous transcendence, for it might seem to derive from a force that, cancelling an origin or end to history, operates through material processes hostile to human concerns. Part 4 of that poem suggests that "Frost and the Sun in scorn of mortal power" have heaped high on that mountain "many a tower / And wall impregnable of beaming ice," which glacially pours forth "a flood of ruin" that has "overthrown / The limits of the dead and living world" and from which "[t]he race / Of man flies far in dread" (103, 105–6, 108, 112–13, 117–18).[1] Through their very destructiveness, "these primaeval mountains / Teach the adverting mind" (99–100), hinting that the glacier's violence against human dwelling reveals an absolute capacity we must admire, thereby producing a poetic analogue of the Kantian sublime in which the pain endured by the presentation of the senses points us towards a supersensible Reason. The poem seems to reinforce such a reading in part 3, which contemplates the "frozen floods" and "unfathomable deeps" of the mountain's peak and asks, "Is this the scene / Where the old Earthquake-daemon taught her young / Ruin? Were these their toys? or did a sea / Of fire, envelope once this silent snow?" (64, 71–4). Such questions apparently hint that Power is the form transcendence takes in the wake of modern geological knowledge, a figure for the force of natural disaster that perpetually threatens to disrupt the preconditions of life.

Yet the poem's reply to its question immediately opens up an alternative prospect: "None can reply – all seems eternal now" (75). Power lies in eternity, beyond the domain of human cognition, beyond even the form of understanding that operates in early nineteenth-century natural philosophy. *Mont Blanc* makes this suggestion not to undermine confidence in the scientific hypotheses emerging in previous decades but to distinguish their import from a more fundamental, constitutive limit of human cognition, a limit that for Shelley has always been, and always will be, unsurpassable. In effect, then, it adapts geological disaster's capacity to undermine a naive anthropocentrism to register a distinct, and more telling, scepticism regarding the mind's ability to reach certainty regarding the lineaments of transcendence.

The poem thus gestures to a complex philosophical position articulated more explicitly in Shelley's prose. Such a scepticism is central to what the poet calls "the intellectual system" to which he held throughout his life ("On Life" 507) – a modesty regarding ultimate claims which does not permit faith in a creative God, only a "hypothesis of a pervading Spirit co-eternal with the universe."[2] One might think that for an heir of the classical atomism in the Epicurean tradition such as Shelley, even this minor concession to theism might go too far, but as Michael

A. Vicario argues, his position derives from early modern revisions of classical teachings (in the work of such authors as Pierre Gassendi and Ralph Cudworth) that place atomism in the context of a "necessary, and for the Epicureans permanently unapparent ontological domain." In Shelley's work, such a theistic atomism holds that "[a]bstract thought … necessarily withdraws from tactile distinctions" to "suspend the immanent material categories in the interest of future ethical possibility."[3] This blend of atomism and ethical idealism comes to the fore in "A Defence of Poetry," in which Shelley, accepting Sir William Drummond's sceptical epistemology, also extends his insistence on the human orientation to a final cause: "All things exist as they are perceived: at least to the percipient … But poetry defeats the curse which binds us to be subjected to the accident of surrounding impressions … It makes us the inhabitants of a world to which the familiar world is a chaos" (533).[4] It appears as well in the poet's insistence that "man … disclaim[s] alliance with transience and decay, incapable of imagining to himself annihilation, existing but in the future and the past, being, not what he is, but what he has been, and shall be. Whatever may be his true and final destination, there is a spirit within him at enmity with change and extinction, [or, in an alternative formulation in this draft, with] nothingness and dissolution" ("On Life," 506).[5] As these passages demonstrate, in Shelley's rendition of "the intellectual system," humanity, caught within a materially and epistemologically delimited domain, looks beyond it towards a final cause whose precise contours it cannot know and whose emergence no transcendental agency can guarantee. In the terms of *Mont Blanc*, humanity is poised between the complex interactions of perception and what operates in sleep, dream, or death – between contingency and spirit, mutability and finality. If on the one hand the mind participates in an "unremitting interchange / With the clear universe of things around" (39–40), it responds to the "[s]ilence and solitude" that appears in the domain of such "things" with its own "imaginings" (144, 143), discerning in the gaps within the phenomenal field the prospect of something unknown that lies beyond it.

This shift towards a sceptical, rather than disastrous, notion of transcendence has important implications across a series of registers. Near the end of part 3, immediately after declaring that "None can reply," *Mont Blanc* suggests that the notion of Power can sharply disrupt familiar theological certainties: "The wilderness has a mysterious tongue / Which teaches awful doubt, or faith so mild, / So solemn, so serene, that man may be / But for such faith with nature reconciled" (76–9). Here the awful doubt that undercuts religious interpretations of transcendence is at the same time a mild faith that prevents one from embracing a merely phenomenal reality. One might think that this passage is exemplary in its modernity, at once emptying transcendence while retaining it and thus constructing what one could call, borrowing from Lefort, the empty place of theological Power – a version of the Real that militates alike against traditional transcendence and any notion of a self-consistent, grounded nature. But in treating doubt as "awful," as a species of awe, and aligning it with faith, the poem invokes the minimal theism it sees as consistent with its epistemological scepticism, expressing confidence in an ontological domain structurally distinct from the operations of finitude.[6]

In doing so, it opens up certain ethical and political possibilities as well, for in the next lines it suggests that the mountain has a voice "to repeal / Large codes of fraud and woe" (80–1). These lines might seem to gesture towards the Lefortian empty place of political power, to imply that this voice undercuts historically contingent political and legal arrangements grounded in a false certainty regarding transcendence and thus opens up a space that enables the ideological contests of the modern political scene. Indeed, in "On Life" Shelley might seem to confirm such a reading, especially when he argues, in a reformist vein, that when "the intellectual system ... destroys error, and the roots of error," it "leaves, what it is too often the duty of the reformer in political and ethical questions to leave, a vacancy" (507) – precisely that which appears when "None can reply," when the absolute limits on human cognition impose themselves, as well as the vacancy that appears in the final word of the poem (*Mont Blanc*, 144).[7] But such a passage ultimately insists that scepticism produces such a vacancy not only to open up the space for the movement of reform, and thus for the ideological contests taking place in the modern public sphere in which such a movement must participate, but also to carry forward an ethical and political labour which, in "destroy[ing] error, and the roots of error," enables a more effective attempt to realize humanity's final cause. It focuses less on the task of creating a transformative ideological consensus than on the ethical labour of recognizing the limits of one's present convictions, of stripping away false certainties.[8] Such a labour, extending back to classical antiquity, greatly exceeds the context of early nineteenth-century political reform or even of the modern democratic politics of concern to Lefort. Indeed, when the poem locates the demand for that virtuous undertaking in the voice of the mountain, in a Power that according to Shelley has called for the repeal of fraud and woe since its conception in antiquity – a repeal already envisioned in the attack on superstition Lucretius mounts throughout *De Rerum Natura* – the poem effectively aligns itself with an imperative voiced throughout the entire history of the West, one not at all dependent on the Enlightenment, though doubly urgent in its wake.[9]

Thus while the poem is consistent with the advocacy of reform Shelley espouses throughout his career, it locates it within the terms not of a liberal or revolutionary politics but of an intellectual system that, in the poet's words, offers "no new truth," no significant departure from a theistic atomism he inherits from a tradition extending over many centuries – a tradition consisting of "a *moral and* intellectual system" holding to "the sacred and eternal truths" that Christianity inherited from "the esoteric doctrines of the poetry and wisdom of antiquity" ("On Life," 507; "A Defence of Poetry," 525; emphasis added).[10] In *Mont Blanc* one encounters not an exemplary statement of modernity but rather a stance that attempts to revive an ethical orientation it claims to inherit from the collective work of millennia and that aims to realize, over many coming generations, an incrementally evolving notion of the common good, even if bounded by the constraints imposed on human understanding and by the determinations of contingency. Such a telos, one might add, is not already embedded in the creation as a predisposition within all things; that scenario would directly contradict atomistic materialism. Instead, in this poem the telos is a final cause, a goal to which the ethical subject may aspire.

The stance visible in *Mont Blanc* thus constitutes a formidable departure from the premises on which many other authors of the period rely, premises I have so far outlined in this book. Shelley accepts the findings of geological and astronomical science but still orients himself to an ultimate good, even if he does not know precisely what it may be (compare "On Life": "*Whatever may be* his true and final destination" [506]; emphasis added). Moreover, insofar as he holds that the Epicurean tradition similarly brought together atomistic physics and an ethics of virtue, participating in the formation of the ethical tradition extending to his own day, in effect he locates his own stance within a mode of thought that would not be disrupted by that scientific knowledge. He holds, then, to a tradition that can absorb the awareness of natural disaster within a framework still oriented to a final cause, easily undoing the usual narratives of secularization. Thus his stance differs sharply from that of Byron, for whom the eventual extinction of the sun poses an ethical dilemma; for Shelley, such an event cannot alter humanity's ethical labour to bring about its collective good. As a result, Shelley feels no pressure to construct an ethics that can mediate a new awareness of geological or astronomical disaster – that is, what took the form for Byron of an ethics of the Real; he focuses instead on the demand to realize a transcendental good within a materiality so defined, to put an ethics of virtue to work within the constraints of history.

Such an effort, broadly speaking, defines Shelley's writing over the years after the composition of *Mont Blanc*, leading him to invent a wide range of telling scenarios that at once envision the prospect of overleaping human finitude and expose the impossibility of such an achievement. But in "The Triumph of Life," Shelley radicalizes his long-standing poetic practice, daring to depict mutability and human finitude as a virtually unsurpassable force whose triumph is well-nigh incontestable.

The poem's continuities with *Mont Blanc* are strong; on its initial level, "The Triumph" similarly acknowledges geological or astronomical catastrophe, incorporating recent scientific hypotheses regarding the preconditions for human life into its basic premises. As P.M.S. Dawson points out, when the narrator speaks of "All those whose fame or infamy must grow / Till the great winter lay the form and name / Of their green earth with them forever low" (125–7), it invokes what Shelley in 1816, in response to his seeing the glaciers of Mont Blanc, described as "Buffons [*sic*] sublime but gloomy theory, that this earth which we inhabit will at some future period be changed into a mass of frost."[11] In that summer, the glaciers near the mountain, under the pressure of a global cooling caused by the eruption of Mount Tambora in 1815, were expanding through nearby valleys in such a way that the poet took the prospect of a greatly expanded landscape of ice as a figure for the eventual fate of the earth.[12] The concept of a global – or cosmic – cold death arises elsewhere in Romantic-era writing as well: in *Zoonomia* Erasmus Darwin argues that the second law of thermodynamics, taken far enough, gives us a universe "[w]ithout heat and motion" in which matter would inevitably "freeze or coalesce into one solid mass," and the astronomer William Herschel at one point argues that the "stars of the milky way … will be gradually compressed through successive stages of accumulation," suggesting that the form of the current universe "cannot last forever."[13] Building on the understanding of the laws of physics in the wake of Newton, especially the laws of gravity and of thermodynamics, these natural philosophers concluded that something like a "great winter" would indeed befall the universe.

But the poem expands upon that notion of catastrophe, suggesting that a radically disorienting force operates not only in the remote future but also within ordinary mortal life. Whereas *Mont Blanc* brings into play aspects of an inhuman geological history, "The Triumph of Life" transposes such a catastrophe into features intrinsic to human experience. Rather than meditating over the consequences of disasters that may take place in the geological or astronomical domain, it folds the import of such distant events into the movement of finitude, finding the equivalent of earthquake and ruin in the churning of the wheels of Life over the dancers in its tempest. It incorporates the earlier poem's depiction of forces "in scorn of mortal power" into its renditions of a disastrous mortality: Life's "icy cold" glare (78) brings into view the inhuman force of the mountain's frigid wasteland; its indifferent trampling of human lives replicates and extends the glacier's destructive invasion; its perpetual tempest transposes the geological processes on the mountaintop into the destructive temporality that forever generates and devastates human life; and its shapeless shape brings aspects of the incomprehensible, sublime force beyond the human domain into the unreadable violence that operates within that domain itself. Thus "The Triumph" attempts to radicalize the earlier poem's figurations: whereas geological disaster takes place on a vast scale of time, it now also appears within the span of the "mortal day" of humanity as a whole and indeed within the lifespan of the individual human being (229).

Furthermore, much as *Mont Blanc* affiliated geological disaster with an unknowable Power that lies beyond it, so also does "The Triumph" conceive of this ever-present, immanent disaster in relation to a stunningly displaced and refigured version of traditional theophany. As Harold Bloom points out, the chariot of Life alludes to the *merkabah* of Ezekiel, which inspires in turn the chariots appearing in the book of Revelation, Dante, and Milton: the fiery brightness emanating from the car, the "thick lightnings" that surround the "Shapes which drew it," and the charioteer's four faces, among other details (96, 99), show that through this imagistic cluster the poem directly revises biblical and canonically poetic figures for transcendence.[14] This travesty of the *merkabah* creates an image of an apparently unsurpassable power of devastation inimical to human flourishing, one that at the same time seemingly erases every trace of transcendence. The poem thus invites us to consider this image as an exemplary sign of a cancelled transcendence – that is, as a poetic rendition of the internal limit of the Real.

The poem extends these already powerful violations in its revised conception of the genre of triumph itself. Like Petrarch's *Trionfi*, it derives its terza rima as well as its formal procedures from Dante's *Divine Comedy*, featuring a narrator who, under the tutelage of a guide, enters a specific scene, encounters an exemplary figure, and listens to his tale in order to respond, suggesting that it, like each of Petrarch's *trionfi*, is "modelled on the pattern of events structuring" a single canto of Dante – except that in the case of Shelley's poem, the guide and example are the same and the consequent ethical teaching obscure.[15] Moreover, by establishing its genre in relation to the *Trionfi*, in which

Love's triumph over human beings is eclipsed by Chastity, then by Death, Fame, Time, and Eternity in turn, and by "conflat[ing] the successive triumphs of Petrarch's series into one vision," the poem "succeeds in reconstituting the several triumphs of Petrarch" into a single instance.[16] In doing so, it creates a compound notion unlike anything in Dante or Petrarch: bringing together versions of Love, Death, Fame, and Time into its overarching emphasis on Life – setting aside aspects of Love, as well as Chastity and Eternity, for the "sacred few" of "Athens and Jerusalem" (128, 134) – it shows how passion and death operate simultaneously in what it depicts as a death drive, a perpetually generative/destructive erotic force, which motivates as well the desire for and at times the achievement of fame and which like time itself necessarily obliterates the subject it inhabits. The poem's depiction of this process of erotic wreckage has unmistakable overtones of Lacanian jouissance, especially in the narrator's initial depiction of the "maniac dance" surrounding the chariot of Life – the dance of those who "Mix with each other in tempestuous measure / To savage music," who, "tortured by the agonizing pleasure," "Oft to new bright destruction come and go," until "the fiery band which held / Their natures, snaps" and the chariot passes over them – only to consign them to the fate of those who "Limp in the dance and strain with limbs decayed" to participate in a frenzy now lost to them (110, 141–2, 143, 154, 157–8, 167). Evidently, an imperative compels the dancers to "live on" in a ghostly or vampiric state, in the mode of an uncanny, mindlessly insistent will to agonizing pleasure.[17] Accordingly, one might call that imperative the *undead drive*, giving it a name more precisely attuned to its Shelleyan deployment.[18] Insofar as the poem melds a range of Petrarchan figures into a single destructive force that also displaces the deity of Ezekiel, it suggests that the drive is a leading aspect of what wrecks transcendence from within – of an Undeath hollowing out the apparent triumph of Life.[19] In this respect, the poem confirms and extends a construction that appears in a somewhat different form in a text of which Shelley was unaware, in Wordsworth's depiction of his crossing the Alps, finding once again an aspect of the uncanny in the formation of a deathless, disastrous subjectivity.

To provide such an uncanny depiction of human life is indeed to depart from any typical account of ordinary experience. The poem's refiguration of disastrous transcendence as what one might call a disastrous immanence also leads to a wholesale redescription of human life itself; in effect, the poem carries out several transformations simultaneously. It is no surprise that shortly before it plunges into its vision of Life, it accentuates a strategy of defamiliarization, extending and partly inverting the aesthetic intervention Shelley proposes in "A Defence of Poetry," suggesting that what it provides arises in a moment of déjà vu, whereby the narrator knows that he had "felt the freshness of that dawn" and "sate as thus upon that slope of lawn" on some previous occasion (34, 36) – and that in consequence, precisely through its entranced mode of apprehension, it sees the unsuspected, uncanny dimensions of what previously appeared to ordinary waking consciousness.[20] As William A. Ulmer comments, the world the narrator enters "is the mirrored inverse of the life-world, a repository of prophetic and retrospective shadows of earthly events, like Freud's atemporal unconscious."[21] In effect, "The Triumph" suggests that it can provide access to the undead logic of ordinary life only through the medium of an uncanny vision – that is, through an unsettling counterpart of the prophetic insight of Dante or Milton.

The poem's recasting of disaster, theophany, and the moral hierarchy implicit in the genre of triumph already goes far. But it takes its broad interest in conflating love, life, and death much further in its virtually endless fusions of apparently opposed terms. It carries out in a poetic guise a seemingly ruthless exposure of the radical finitude of thought and its articulations, hinting that the notion of the undead drive is only one in a long series of similarly devastating reconceptions. Interweaving morn and eve, light and dark, pleasure and pain, power and subjection, wisdom and contagion, knowledge and ignorance, personhood and anonymity – to name a few – it suggests that no conceptual or metaphorical framework by which one might attempt to apprehend its themes remains undisturbed in its most basic functioning, that the very attempt to interpret it must be infected by the same radical negativity depicted in its central scenario.[22] If on one level it maps out themes that psychoanalytic thought elaborates long after, it also enacts with stunning cogency the critique of signification which poststructuralist theory – or rather what Rajan has taught us to consider as post-phenomenological theory – brings about in a more recent period as well.[23]

But the poem also extends this concern with the radical instability of figuration, long of concern in deconstructive readings of the poem, into further, less familiar registers. "The Triumph of Life" invokes a series of themes from the *De Rerum Natura* of Lucretius, a signal predecessor that similarly writes aspects of atomistic thought in a poetic medium. The poem's use of Lucretius works well with its celebration of Francis Bacon, who drew on ancient atomism as he opened the way for early modern empiricism (269–73), as well as its use of recent natural philosophy; the key findings of Herschel, Erasmus Darwin, or Georges Cuvier, as Hugh Roberts points out, "can all be read as extrapolations from the chaotic errancy of Lucretian venereal creativity."[24] The poem frequently alludes to aspects of the Lucretian epic: Vicario suggests that the pageant may well allude to Lucretius's denunciation of the frenzied, violent celebration of the Great Mother in book 2 of his epic, and Roberts points out that the "perpetual flow" of a "great stream / Of people" (298, 44–5), their appearance "like atomies that dance / Within a sunbeam" (446–7), their spinning in the "rapid whirlwinds" around the chariot (144), the "silent splendour" dropping "veil by veil" from Lucifer, the morning star (413), and the extensive passage on the exuding of shadows, or simulacra, which fall from the figures surrounding the chariot (482–535), all show that the poem's imagery is pervasively Lucretian.[25] Moreover, the strange sequences in the poem, the discontinuities that "always leave a residue of continuity," hint at a Lucretian sense of chaos congruent with that of recent chaos theory – that is, as Roberts argues, drawing in part on Michel Serres's reading of Lucretius, a sense not merely of turbulence or disorder but of a "flux" that is "as much creative as it is destructive," a disorder from which order can emerge.[26]

Attending closely to the poem's capacity to marshal its Lucretian motifs across all these registers, Amanda Goldstein argues that "The Triumph of Life" deploys "an extraordinary concurrence" within Lucretius "of vital, rhetorical, and historical eventfulness," drawing on the classical poet's capacity to "cast *figuration* as the inalienable activity and passion of matter in general, without thereby casting matter as either alive or a product of its verbal representation."[27] In her view, Shelley's poem evokes a materialist poetics which, like Bruno Latour's later argument, can break down "modern partitions of knowledge" that "render" various dimensions of reality "mutually unrepresentable," creating a poetic counterpart of what she, following Monique Allewaert, calls "materialist figuration."[28] In deploying such a sense of figuration, Goldstein suggests, "The Triumph" also dissents from a triumphalist rendition of "life" in the period's vitalist debates, a tendency to accentuate life's difference from its "particular mortal embodiments": the poem's sense of life shifts from the formulations on view in the leading protagonists in those debates towards those available in Lucretius, who sees life as "an obsolescent and transitive expression between bodies that multiplies their relations and exacerbates their contingency."[29] For the latter, life is not ontologically distinct from the inorganic, since both arise alike from "the atoms' intricate, accidental concrescences."[30]

The poem's treatment of these themes broaches even further aspects of radical materiality that another feature of recent thought helps make visible. Alluding to the chariots of Necessity that appeared in *The Daemon of the World* and *Hellas*, "The Triumph of Life" suggests that its own chariot of Life is a further instance of such Necessity – and accordingly that materialist figuration constitutes the preconditions for *any* embodiment, including that of human beings. The complex, embedded machinery of Life thus hints at the necessity of contingency, the unsurpassable status of chaos itself.[31] Here the poem evokes a stance that has returned in our own time in speculative realist thought, especially in that of Quentin Meillassoux, who argues that one must posit "*the necessity of contingency, or in other words … the omnipotence of chaos.*"[32] It does so, moreover, not by invoking the notion of an arche-fossil, as does Meillassoux, or the death of the sun, as does Ray Brassier, but by relocating a disastrous materiality from the distant past or future into an ongoing temporality, effectively radicalizing the eventual stance of speculative realism itself.[33] Moreover, by folding such a prospect into the domain of human subjectivity, it brings the operations of an inhuman materiality into human subjectivity as well, sketching a position that has not yet been fully articulated even in contemporary thought.

The poem's work on all these aspects of its central scenario might inspire us to return to themes even closer to its surface, its concern with the mode of power embedded in the notion of triumph. The practice of the Roman triumph, it suggests, emerged "When Freedom left those who upon the free / Had bound a yoke which soon they stooped to bear" (115–16) – when the free capacity to conquer the free hints at the prospect that those in the conquering force will lose their freedom as well. In these lines, the poet suggests that to conquer others is to be conquered by the violence of longing for power over others. Those who succeed in their quest for power do not succeed, but fail. Moreover, the poem's critical depiction of the Roman triumph resonates with its sense of Napoleonic military might and thus of the fate of the French Revolution; this echo suggests that the attempt to instantiate ethical ideals – or human freedom – in the forms of the modern state only carries forward what the Roman triumph reveals.

"The Triumph" does not make this suggestion lightly; on the contrary, it does so with unmistakable force precisely because it alludes to the French Revolution, and the broader philosophical, political, social, and military histories of which it is a part, far more extensively than has been proposed – in a series of evocations well worth tracing briefly here. Orrin Wang suggests that the maniac dance near the chariot, which features "women foully disarrayed" (165), recalls Burke's depiction of the actions of the women who surround the monarchs taken captive during the October days.[34] The poem's evident allusion in this respect, however, reaches back through that phobic account to the October days themselves, which in turn derive, as Colin Lucas has demonstrated, from an older interplay between monarch and collective central to the popular legitimacy of the French state. That interplay, in turn, shares much with reciprocity in the British tradition to which the poem gestures in its use of the term "jubilee" (111), a reference to the jubilee celebrations of George III in 1810 and, more cryptically, to a contrary, millennial deployment of the term among British radicals.[35] The symbolic exchange between monarch and populace recalls the local interplay between gentry and plebeians in what E.P. Thompson has called the "moral economy of the English crowd," the reciprocity of which went far towards establishing the relations between social ranks in England throughout the early modern era.[36] These references further evoke the rituals in various European cities featuring the juxtaposition of officializing processions with the festive energies of the urban crowd – a conjunction captured well in an image that, as Nancy Moore Goslee points out, "Shelley would have seen frequently from 1820 on," "the Campo Santo frescoes at Pisa," which "combine Petrarch's triumphs with a dance of death" – and ultimately all the way back to the interplay of power that operated in Rome itself.[37]

Such echoes resonate with a long series of further practices in France and elsewhere during and after the Revolution, too extensive to list here, which amplify and extend the traditional interplay of crowd and power. As Goslee argues, "With David's and Robespierre's revival of the triumph in the French Revolution, many of these spatially directional, temporally processional, and ekphrastic elements reappeared, with sculpted figures, *tableaux vivants*, or cohorts of marching groups who carried labels."[38] Such a broader pattern of activity easily includes practices that appear in the poem's more cryptic, less noted allusions. One festival especially popular in the early days of the Revolution, for example, featured the ritual planting of trees of liberty, one of which we might find in the "old chestnut" (25) so closely associated with "what was once Rousseau." (The image of the "old root" [182] recalls the etymology of "radical," a link pervasive throughout the period and quite relevant to these rituals of replanting.) The gesture whereby sacred processions are echoed in revolutionary pageants is reprised ironically in events such as *la nuit de Varennes*, when the monarch and his family attempted to escape revolutionary France in the royal carriage only to be discovered and brought back to Paris in a scenario echoing aspects of the October days – an event framed shortly thereafter by a further iteration of the revolutionary pageant in the vast public procession installing the remains of Voltaire in the newly instituted Panthéon.[39] The practice of that pageant finds a parallel as well in processions that occurred within the mass radical movement in post-Waterloo Britain: a leading example would be Henry "Orator" Hunt's triumphal return to London in

September 1819, shortly after the Peterloo Massacre, significant because of its Christological and counter-monarchical resonances and its twist on the themes of the "Mask of Anarchy," a poem written in response to Peterloo and whose staging of the parade of "Anarchs" reappears in "The Triumph" as well.[40] Thus the poem's staging of the triumph ultimately invokes a sequence of developments in France, Britain, and elsewhere in the late eighteenth and early nineteenth centuries, which moves from an initial understanding of the interplay of power and counterpower, through its reformulation in revolutionary and counterrevolutionary versions, to its reinterpretation in the practices of Napoleonic empire and British protest – one that reinscribes an initial practice across a second, third, and possibly fourth level of self-conscious revision.

The range of the poem's allusions to these developments in Romantic-era political practice might lead one to think that its central pageant speaks primarily of this history, that it thematizes most urgently specific, recent events. But as the poem's broader field of allusions makes clear, that pageant ultimately speaks of a series of impositions that have taken place "since the world begun [*sic*]" (146), from the very dawn of European political life. In its view, no specific historical reference has any pride of place, for each is only an instance of the endless iteration of a phenomenon allegorized in the figure of Life. The French Revolution, or the promise of *any* subsequent revolution – along with any restoration following a revolution – now appears as one more instance of a logic that dissolves every potentially oppressive – and liberating – transformation into a moment within an interminable, chaotic process.[41]

As I suggested above, "The Triumph" reinforces this displacement by depicting the triumph not of power itself but of that figure who conquers those who exercise power. It features not a political history but rather the pageant of an ethical failure in which such a history is embedded. In the poem's terms, the apparent achievement of those who exercise power reveals their submission to a will to power that infests human history with a wholesale logic of imposition. The poem extends this displacement, already crucial enough, when it incorporates even philosophers and poets into its critique. Among those who wear "[m]itres and helms and crowns," it places those who wear "wreathes of light, / Signs of thought's empire over thought" (210–11), suggesting that those of supreme intellectual achievement have also been conquered by Life and thus by the specious attempt to subjugate the world.[42] In a move that cuts especially close to home, the poem proposes that the "great bards of old" who, unlike Rousseau, "inly quelled / The passions which they sung" (274–5) nevertheless enacted their version of that will to power; even if – or rather, precisely because – "their living melody / Tempers its own contagion to the vein / Of those who are infected with it" (276–8), they are supremely effective in spreading that contagion, in extending the disastrous sway of undead Life. And since the poem suggests that Rousseau, in practising no such ethical constraint on articulating his passions, is even less admirable than they, placing him at least two degrees from the practice of virtue, it raises even further doubts regarding recent literary achievement, as if to hint at an utter ethical failure on display in Romantic-era literature.

The poem's emphasis on the fraudulence of all those who seek or exercise power across various domains clearly cuts through the shared sense in early nineteenth-century culture that the period participates in the formation of a progressive, developmental history – that events might build on themselves and lead to enlightenment and liberation for all. Indeed, "The Triumph" undermines this sense several times over. The depiction of the temporal threshold in the fusion of old and new moon in the figure of Life, the staging of Life's indifferent, tempestuous movement, and the poem's mocking reference to the chariot's "progress since the morn" (193) erase any such promise, any hope that power might operate in another mode or that its movement might actually *go* somewhere. That depiction provides instead a sharply critical comment on the attempt to gain ascendancy through the assertion of dominance over the past and future, a dominance in effect over time. Those on display in the pageant, seeking to be among the "unforgotten" (209) or to exert "thought's empire over thought" (211), hope to impose their sway over future memory – much as Rousseau himself, echoing Shelley in "Ode to the West Wind," claims that "there rise / A thousand beacons from the spark I bore" (206–7) – only to find that they are now subject to public indifference, for their "name[s] the fresh world thinks already old" (238), their claim to ascendancy effaced under the claims of still others. The new is not so new, only a further instance of the temporality of evanescence operating through the fascination with novelty that has obsessed mortals since the world began.

Accordingly, the poem's narrator – turning away from "the spent vision of the times that were / And scarce have ceased to be" (233–4), from the "spoilers spoiled" who so recently ruled the world (235) – cries out, "Let them pass," for they did not make the world "so much more glorious than it was / That [he] desire[d] to worship those who drew / New figures on its false and fragile glass / As the old faded" (243, 245–8). In these lines, the poem indicates that in the domain of the chariot, the very medium of articulation dissolves what appears there, making visible not only a deconstructive or materialist figuration but also figuration as disappearance. As if already forgetting his reference to the thousand beacons, Rousseau extends the narrator's thoughts in this regard: "Figures ever new / Rise on the bubble, paint them how you may; / We have but thrown, as those before us threw, / Our shadows on it as it past away" (248–51). Alluding to the bubbles of the late stanzas of *Childe Harold's Pilgrimage*, canto 4 and accentuating further aspects of their fragile movement, this passage treats its bubble not only as a sign of history's nullity but also as the surface on which the shadows of a vanishing present perpetually appear and disappear. In Rousseau's view, the inscription of a figure requires nothing more than the mere passage of a mortal through life; the great and small, the prolific and the silent, all cast their shadows for a moment on the translucent surface encircling sheer nothingness, on the "bubble" that has never ceased to float on the movement of its "foam" (162, 163; cf. 458).

If all this is the case, how can the poem conceive of any alternative? If the operation of materialist figuration, accidental vitality, necessary contingency, undead eroticism, conceptual and metaphorical deconstruction, and the evanescence of all attempts to gain ascendancy – to mention a few instances – exemplify the workings of a disastrous anti/transcendence, how might any *non*-disastrous possibility arise? The poem underlines this difficulty when it folds Shelley's prior metaphors for transcendence into its depiction of Life, when aspects of the Power of *Mont Blanc* reappear in attributes of her destructive movement, or when the darkness visible of Demogorgon is discernible once again in the shadowy glare of her form.[43] The domain beyond the phenomenal world seems to have appeared within it, as if the poem wishes to bring a representation of the final cause into that of a self-erasing temporality. Such a prospect appears yet again when Rousseau asks the shape, "Shew whence I came, and where I am, and why – / Pass not away upon the passing stream" (398–9). Hoping to secure her from the effects of time and, by gaining a definitive knowledge of his origin and end, to overleap the constraints of time in his own right, he enters the scene of perpetual self-erasure instead. It is as if the poem hints that what Rousseau sought can only be found in *this* knowledge, that *this* is the form an eternal wisdom must take. Although in "A Defence of Poetry" Shelley insisted that poetry "makes us the inhabitants of a world to which the familiar world is a chaos" (533), "The Triumph" does nearly the opposite, plunging into a chaos so bright that anything promising to exceed it virtually disappears.

But this poem does not utterly erase any domain beyond that of Life's triumph. Even on its initial level, which I have sketched so far, it incorporates the ethical teaching of the Epicurean tradition, according to which human beings may overcome the turbulence of the passions and attain a state of serenity. In its vision of the stream of people who spin in "rapid whirlwinds" around the chariot (144) and appear "like atomies that dance / Within a sunbeam" (446–7), for example, the poem does not depict the movement of atoms but uses the latter as a metaphor for the activity of human beings.[44] Its focus is not on a materialist figuration per se but on how those in the dance have submitted to the self-destructive frenzy of their passions.[45] Moreover, through the narrator's opening description of how some in the "mighty torrent" were "flying from the thing they feared and some / Seeking the object of another's fear," while others "mournfully within the gloom / Of their own shadow walked, and called it death ... / And some fled from it as it were a ghost" (53, 54–5, 58–60), the poem reinforces Lucretius's insistence that erotic passion, as well as ambition of every kind, arises from the fear of death – a fear that the ethical subject may overcome by accepting the transience of life.[46] Insofar as it adopts this ethical teaching, the poem holds out the prospect that the ethical will may overcome such fear. In lines well known to Shelley, Lucretius affirms that "so picayune / Are the traces of those natural faults which reason / Can't clear away" – faults arising from the power of atomic movement to disturb the soul – "that nothing hinders us / From leading calm lives worthy of the gods."[47] As David Konstan remarks, for the Epicurean tradition, the sage is thus "independent of chance," for his soul's "pleasure is static, wants nothing from time, and is in this sense divine and immortal." Human beings may attain peace if "they see and give assent to the ever-changingness of the cosmos, and do not seek there a lastingness that cannot be."[48]

The poem expands on this Lucretian ethics in many of its features. Its depiction of the great figures of history, for example, endorses the Lucretian repudiation of political ambition – and implicitly of other forms of excessive desire – as arising from the fear of impermanence and death.[49] In this regard, the poem participates in an ethical critique of the political, emphasizing the delusions inherent in seeking power; as Timothy Clark points out, in a letter from 1815 Shelley writes that "even the men who hold dominion over nations fatigue themselves by the interminable pursuit of emptiest visions; the honour and power which they seek is enjoyed neither in acquirement, possession or retrospect."[50] The quasi-erotic terms of this passage hint that for Shelley erotic and political delusions speak of the same restlessness, a conjunction evident as well in the appearance of both forms of delusional pursuit among those conquered by Life. Sexual and political desire, private and public disturbance, arise from the same matrix – from what Shelley calls, in one of his letters, "the delusions of an imagination not to be restrained."[51]

Shelley's repudiation of the attempt to escape death through such delusions shows how much he inherits from the Epicurean tradition; his resistance to the impositions of power in the name of what one might call peace is especially germane in this regard.[52] But he departs from it as well. The depiction of contingency in that tradition has a paradoxical feature: if one assents to such contingency, one is released from its capacity for disturbance; by accepting chaos, one undoes its disturbing power. In contrast, although Shelley accepts a broadly atomic theory of the physical world, he invokes what Lucretius does not, the notion of a final cause, and thus stakes his position not on the sage's serenity but in an orientation to humanity's true destination. As we have seen, in his view "man ... disclaim[s] alliance with transience and decay"; accordingly, while he accepts the sway of contingency over the material world, and thus to some degree over his own mortal embodiment, he looks beyond the operation of that turbulence to a final cause yet to be realized, sustaining an allegiance to a collective good.

The poem reinforces this orientation when, imitating the single-canto sequence in Dante, it invokes the prospect that just as Dante eventually surpasses his guide, Virgil, so also will the poem's narrator eventually move beyond the possibilities represented in Rousseau.[53] Its simultaneous evocations of a Lucretian and a Dantean ethics point towards an implicit argument: the poem's narrator must overcome Rousseau's flawed response to chaos, discover a more credible relation to the final cause, and thereby attain insight.[54] An extensive critical tradition on the poem argues that Rousseau's invention of the "shape all light" (352) out of details in the scene along the "gentle rivulet" (314) and his response to her reveal an ideological failure, a flawed attempt to seize a knowledge of his origins and ends from an aesthetic figure, when he should better have renounced all such questions, accepted the limits placed on mortal knowledge, and embraced the sway of contingency over human finitude.[55] The poem's ethical fidelities suggest instead that this encounter points to the task of seeing through temporal figuration towards the enduring good that lies beyond it, to a final cause that neither poetic figuration nor philosophical knowledge can capture but that nevertheless must remain their ultimate telos. But because Rousseau is a negative exemplum, even if his role is to serve as a guide to the narrator, "The Triumph" places a more difficult burden on its narrator than that placed on Dante. Although Rousseau has seen much, he does not know how to *read* his experience; through his narrative, he challenges the narrator – and through him, the reader – to find a cogent interpretation of his confessions and by that means to discover an appropriate response to Life's triumph.[56]

The absence of a reliable guide in this process, however, indicates that for Shelley, the labour of interpretation has no guarantee of success. While Rousseau can now look at those whirlwinds in retrospect, and the narrator is stationed at some distance from them, neither has secure access to a domain beyond them. Nevertheless, both figures know full well that they need not consider the figure of Life as definitive: her status as a displaced version of Power or of Demogorgon, and thus her claim to constitute the unsurpassable principle of experience, may be sheer imposture, a performance that may capture only an apparent primacy. As a result, both Rousseau and the narrator hesitate between *two* versions of Power: one that flows by under the blinding, incomprehensible glare of Life and another that endures outside the pageant in the realm of eternity.

At first the poem's strategy for positioning its protagonists between these two realms is unclear. As many readers have noted, it sustains its orientation to an eternal brightness at the same time that its figures for that brightness derive from phenomena in time; accordingly, it might seem that it does not firmly establish that eternity actually transcends the realm of time. How is it that the "sacred few" of "Athens and Jerusalem" "as soon / As they had touched the world with living flame / Fled back like eagles to their native noon" (128, 134, 129–31) if elsewhere the poem suggests that the pageantry of Life, which began in the "morn" and proceeds towards the "night," passes through its own version of noon – a phase without shadows when its light is apparently at its zenith (193, 195, 444–5)? How is it that "Gregory and John and men divine" create an "eclipse" of "the true *Sun*" if they exemplify the activity whereby the "car's creative ray / Wrought all the busy phantoms that were there / As the *sun* shapes the clouds" (288, 290, 292, 533–5; emphases added)? The very terms by which the poem attempts to capture what lies beyond (the noon, the sun) may instead exemplify the self-erasing figurations of Life.[57]

But any reading that reduces what lies beyond time to an aspect of time soon fails.[58] If there is no true sun because all metaphors of the sun point back to the movement of temporality, then how might Gregory and John eclipse its light, exemplifying a power that "was given / But to destroy" (292–3)? If the native noon to which the sacred few return is the same noon that appears in ordinary temporality, from what world have they fled? One must conclude that the poem does not operate on a single level of articulation; it deploys the same metaphors on two levels at once temporality and eternity, ethical failure and the sacred. The poem thus insists that Rousseau and the narrator are indeed caught between two versions of Power – or rather makes clear that Power abides in eternity while Life displays only a fraudulent echo of that abiding, unknowable force. Yet at the same time, the passages I have been considering greatly complicate this bivocal poetics, for they clearly accentuate the fact that the poem's metaphors for eternal principles are borrowed from temporality's domain. It follows that the poem deliberately mobilizes figures of temporality to suggest both what passes and what endures, and thereby to suggest that those who live in time may have no access to eternity except through the perspectives provided by temporality. Depicting whatever lies beyond figuration must rely on what is afforded by figuration itself. Yet in a further twist, through its persistent use of such terms as "the true Sun," the poem suggests that ethical and temporal finitude perpetually indexes what surpasses it, that the very mobility of figuration endlessly hints at what does *not* pass and what is *not* subject to self-erasure.

"The Triumph" deploys its bivocal use of temporal figures in an especially telling passage, where it describes how the "lore" of the "great" "Taught them not this – to know themselves; their might / Could not repress the mutiny within, / And for the morn of truth they feigned, deep night / Caught them ere evening" (209, 211, 212–15). These lines clearly indicate that the poem is using metaphors of time on two levels at once: the opposite of the "morn of truth" – presumably the night of falsehood – catches the "great" before they reach the end of their mortal day. Evidently, night can fall before nightfall: the vertical axis of truth/falsehood interrupts the horizontal axis of life's passing. A version of transcendence thus endures in this poem beyond finitude, in a good it places at the heights. In that case, in its ethical register the poem suggests that the pageant of Life does not display the unsurpassable truth of finitude, the internal limit of the Real, but rather what transpires when ethical subjects fail "to know themselves." The apparently dazzling light of the Real is only a fraudulent eclipse of what remains in the beyond.

The poem indefinitely expands on this theme of imposture when it indicates, in a stunning irony, that the barely visible light of the new moon of Life manages to outbid the sun, that the dimly lit movement through humanity's collective day eclipses the morn of truth (77–85). Does it follow that the true sun shines in the poem's opening lines, before the narrator enters his trance? On the contrary, the strict analogies between that sun's impositions on all mortal things, the shape all light's tramplings, and the disfiguring movements of Life – analogies the poem emphasizes when it holds that the "cold glare" of Life "obscured with [ ] light / The Sun as he the stars" (77–9) – suggests that the opening scene already narrates in capsule form the dramatic scenarios to come, indicating, as I argued above, that the trance provides an uncanny, more penetrating insight into the logic of temporality than is available to the narrator's waking consciousness. The true sun is not that of imposition, not the sort that obscures the stars (79) or, like the figure of Life, makes the star of dawn "unseen" (417): it is rather a figure free from all such contests for power, all such attempts to assert a mighty but evanescent dominion over the visible world.[59]

The poem's use of divergent orders of light is confirmed in a closely related bitonal poetics through which it mobilizes two kinds of melody at once. Invoking Dante's "wondrous story / How all things are transfigured, except Love," it holds that "deaf as is a sea which wrath makes hoary / The world can hear not the sweet notes that move / The sphere whose light is melody to lovers" (475–6, 477–9). This passage's celebration of "Love" contrasts with the earlier statement that Life "conquered the heart" of "[a]ll that is mortal of great Plato" "by love," for "[t]hat star that ruled his doom was far too fair" – the star of the youth Aster (258, 254, 256). The poem suggests that the mortal part of Plato "[e]xpiates the joy and woe his master knew not" (255), for in his love for the youth he acted on a sexual passion that his master Socrates overcame; as a result, it points to the divergence between Plato's consummated "love" for Aster and Dante's unconsummated "Love" for Beatrice (echoed in Petrarch's love for Laura).[60] In the same vein, the poem indicates that the noisy passage of Life's tempest – the "sea which wrath makes hoary," which enacts in its own way the movement of the "sweet tune" to which moves the shape all light (382) – deafens that higher, untransfigured music. In doing so, it also hints that the latter constitutes a heavenly counterpart both of the shape all light and of Life's chariot, for it is a moving sphere of brightness whose light "is melody to lovers," to those who can move to the more-than-sensual appeal of Love.

The near similarity of these two levels of melodious brightness indicates that the poem offers its readers competing versions of the same metaphors as exemplars of contrasting premises.[61] In doing so, it takes further the poetics of *Adonais*, which, as Earl R. Wasserman demonstrates, alters a set of metaphors across its three sections, reconceiving of its key terms twice over and absorbing previous formulations into more capacious versions until in its last stanzas it provides what it depicts as a final, definitive articulation.[62] "The Triumph of Life," which could have deployed its metaphors through a similar sequence – in a series of triumphs, for example – instead presents contrasting states simultaneously. In adopting this strategy, it suggests that while a sequential transformation of metaphor may be appropriate to the genre of elegy, which classically moves through several phases, it is appropriate in another context to juxtapose temporality directly with the eternal, with what is at once simultaneous with and superior to time. In effect, this bitonal poetics makes evident the contrast between those who, submitting to their passions, fall prey to falsehood or lust and those who remain faithful to a virtue that transcends time. Such a contrast expands and reinforces the contrast intrinsic to Shelley's intellectual system – the bifurcation between the domain of contingency and that of the final cause.[63]

This turn towards an ethical finality in contrast to the temporality of Life, however, raises a pressing question, one in which we might hear an echo of the Kantian inquiry with which this book began: How might that final cause ever be realized in time? If indeed it is a final cause, the telos for virtuous action, does the poem conceive of how such action might lead to a collective good? The poem's harshly negative answer to this question places its entire ethical structure in jeopardy and indeed undermines its own deep premises in Shelley's intellectual system. Although in other texts, most notably "A Philosophical View of Reform" (1819), Shelley is surprisingly pragmatic, accepting a largely incrementalist view of the eventual adoption of universal suffrage, at no point in "The Triumph of Life" does he suggest that the chariot of Life might be dissolved in the distant future, that a collective ethical labour might eventually overcome its sway.[64] The stark disjunction between the false and true suns suggests instead that their divergence is a perpetual fact, that it will extend as far into the future as it does into the past. If "man is a being of high aspirations 'looking both before and after,' whose 'thoughts that wander through eternity,' disclaim alliance with transience and decay" ("On Life," 506), in this poem all four faces of Life's charioteer are banded, looking neither before nor after, as if to parody a being with high aspirations – while the poem depicts the alternative as an ability not to look before or after but to look above, to apprehend a native noon or true sun. The poem thus invokes eternity's triumph over the *entire sweep of human history*, past, present, or future, forestalling the eventual arrival of the collective good, which endures purely in a domain beyond temporality. In doing so, it erases the promise inherent in the notion of a final cause, the sense that ethical action is grounded in a purposeful invocation of a good to come.

The strong bifurcation between a benighted temporality and bright eternity may seem to represent a significant departure from Shelley's prior stance. But in fact it may only take that stance more seriously. Shelley's orientation to the final cause had always recognized the constitutive limits of human perception or achievement; as we have seen, in *Mont Blanc* the poet suggests that human beings cannot attain certain knowledge of earthly origins or ends. On the basis of that position, the poem holds that the mountain's voice calls for an ethical labour to repeal fraud and woe, to destroy erroneous constructions of transcendence and undo the impostures that still dominate within human history. But it is not clear how such a labour might ever construct a better alternative, for attempts to realize superior versions of the final cause would still be temporal interpretations of the eternal, human constructions of what must remain beyond all such mediations. The sense of this divergence thus inscribes in a Shelleyan idiom a counterpart of the structural impasse that framed Kant's rather modest conception of the sign of history: to attempt to realize the final cause in time by definition forces the eternal into the constraints of temporality and thereby creates another version of imposture. Shelley's scepticism about any finite knowledge comprehending Power may thus lead to an equally sharp scepticism regarding the human ability to fulfil the final cause.

"The Triumph of Life" hints at points in this regard on several occasions. In the very passage that celebrates Dante's "wondrous story / How all things are transfigured, except Love," it speaks of how he "returned to tell" this story "[i]n words of hate and love" (475–6, 474–5), suggesting that in his very articulation of a higher Love the poet blended it with its opposite. Just as metaphors for eternity must be borrowed from the temporal domain, any attempt to represent a higher possibility must be articulated in a medium that mixes imposture with splendour, evil with good. Elsewhere the poem radicalizes this point, putting the very privilege of eternal Love at stake. In its lines on Plato's love for Aster, it hints that such a love was not entirely in error, for in the pageant Plato "[e]xpiates the joy and woe his master knew not" (255), in which case the consummation of desire brings a joy denied to the sacred few. Here temporality is not merely an obstacle to an entire compliance with the final cause; in some respects Plato's consummated love for Aster might be preferable to the unconsummated Love Socrates felt for Alcibiades. In such a moment, the poem comes close to suggesting that the higher Love might be joyless, that it might require too great a sacrifice of what makes life worth living. But in that case, for a moment it reveals a fidelity not to the final cause but to the consolations of finitude, to the partial realizations that embodiment, and thus temporality, make possible.

The poem does not entirely endorse this latter possibility; after all, in these lines the poem also suggests that such joy requires expiation and that Socrates, in refusing the love that causes it, remains the master – just as, in the lines on Dante, it holds that his poetry, even if in "words of hate and love," tells of "How all things are transfigured, except Love." These passages complicate a structure that they nevertheless leave in place. But they already hint at an insight that troubles Shelley's ethical system. If human attempts to realize the final cause inevitably mix evil with good, then it is not clear how efforts in this regard will ever have an effect: the poem's premises point to a radical asymmetry between means and ends, between what human beings might achieve and the eternity towards which they aim. The poem considers this asymmetry on several occasions. At one point, for example, it suggests that "Gregory and John" enable an "eclipse" to be "worshipped by the world o'er which they strode / For the true Sun it quenched" (288, 290, 291–2), whereas that true sun, far from outshining such an eclipse, is simply quenched. Evidently eternity is only an ethical ideal, something that might *call* for ethical action but can do nothing to bring it about. It provides ends but no means to realize them. Thus where Gregory and John may act, the true sun does not, remaining immaculate in a zone beyond history. The splendour of the true sun may shine beyond the domain of all possible achievement.

At one point, the problem of this asymmetry becomes explicit in a discussion between Rousseau and the narrator. Rousseau states that Napoleon wished for "more / Of fame and peace than Virtue's self can gain" (219–20). Much as this comment suggests that Napoleon's career highlights a virtue to which he cannot lay claim, it also proposes that "Virtue's self" may never secure a sufficient measure of fame or peace, that it can never become truly effective in the temporal world. Such a thought soon comes to the narrator, who ponders "how power and will / In opposition rule our mortal day – / And why God made irreconcilable / Good and the means of good" (228–31), finding in this mismatch a potentially ineradicable obstacle to virtue's agency. While it might be tempting to argue that these are the thoughts of a narrator who by definition cannot see the broader framework of the poem or that these words bring into play the dubious suggestions of the Furies in act 1 of *Prometheus Unbound* (625–6), in fact these lines articulate an understanding of means and ends that, as we have seen, often crop up elsewhere in the poem.[65] No doubt there is an element of optimism even in this passage: if this comment deplores the "means of good," it hints that the will may seek good – and accordingly that the will is not irrational or blind but rather akin to what Thomas Aquinas defines as a rational appetite oriented to the good.[66] But at the same moment, the poem also suggests that insofar as the will hopes to implement the good in actual history through the "means of good," it must resort to the logic of imposition that is contrary to the good. By repudiating the means of good in this way, the poem makes explicit the intractable impasse at the heart of its split orientation to eternity and temporality.

In doing so, the poem reworks themes visible in one of its closest intertexts, *Prometheus Unbound*. In a moment that echoes the epistemological scepticism of *Mont Blanc*, in act 2 of *Prometheus Unbound* Asia discovers that the deep truth is imageless – and liberates time from its submission to the false transcendence of Jupiter and makes possible the arrival of history's long-awaited consummation. Yet in a sign that such a transformation is not so straightforward as it might seem, act 3 narrates how Demogorgon, the personification of what lies beyond time, dethrones Jupiter in an act that speciously conflates an unknowable beyond with historical agency. It fuses something in the domain of pure ends, the final cause, with something in the realm of means. The poem thus brings into view the theme of means and ends, calling to mind Walter Benjamin's musings in "Critique of Violence" and indicating as does Benjamin that the central problem lies in the attempt to link the two, to realize ends through means. Benjamin opts for a politics of pure means best realized in divine violence, an absolute act that cuts through all forms of state or legal violence.[67] Act 3 displays a similar preference, for it shows a divine violence in Demogorgon's dethronement of Jupiter. But in doing so, it directly contradicts the nonviolence of act 1. It seems that for Shelley, what lies beyond temporality can intrude into time only through a hyperbolic imposition that cuts through temporal forms of power altogether. Eternity may have no agency outside of divine violence. Yet the sharp contradiction of such an act with the poem's nonviolent premises suggests that this form of violence is ethically illegitimate; rather than fulfilling the final cause, Demogorgon's act ironically destroys it.

In that case, *Prometheus Unbound* may tacitly repudiate the notion that eternity should take action of any kind. But Shelley's intellectual system goes further: since he holds that mind "cannot create, it can only perceive" ("On Life," 508), that there can be no "*creative* Deity," only a "pervading Spirit co-eternal with the universe," he disallows the prospect that a divine agency might bring about apocalypse and recreate the world. For him, eternity simply cannot intervene into temporality, which is evidently the domain in which creation may be found (as the poem suggests in its reference to the "car's creative ray" [533]). Thus the depiction of Demogorgon dethroning Jupiter is not merely utopian, one of the "beautiful idealisms of moral excellence" of which the preface speaks (209), but an ontological and conceptual impossibility.

The critique of divine violence in the dramatic poem, however, may leave open an alternative possibility. Although the sequence of acts implies that the nonviolent gesture of act 1 (whereby Prometheus renounces his curse against Jupiter) somehow leads to the breakthroughs of acts 2 and 3, the contradiction traced above suggests instead that there can be no such sequence. As Rajan writes, "the play, rather than unfolding as a linear plot, occurs in disconnected segments," creating a "montage of supplementary spaces" in which "Prometheus's attempt to renounce hatred is simply not consistent with Demogorgon's violently Jovian overthrow of Jove."[68] In that case, Prometheus's refusal to engage in violence, rather than setting in motion the eventual dethroning of Jupiter, may constitute instead a form of divine passivity, an undoing of means. But such a gesture would leave Jupiter, the master of means, in place. Thus a return to the purely nonviolent ethos of act 1 leads to a further conclusion: to refuse violence, even divine violence, in the name of the final cause leaves that cause unrealized. *Prometheus Unbound* ultimately suggests that both divine responses to the field of human impositions collapse: they either take the form of an infinitely violent act or, through the renunciation of action, leave fraudulent forms of power in place. *Divine action and divine passivity both fail.*

While these implications remain tacit in the dramatic poem, hovering below the surface in its various doubts and contradictions, "The Triumph of Life" makes them explicit, as if to suggest that the poet is now fully aware of the limitations of his ethical system and willing to articulate the consequences of such a self-critique. The poem's rejection of any prospect that something might interrupt the endless "progress" of Life's chariot across time makes clear that it repudiates any appeal for divine violence, any hope for eternity's intrusion into time. But it lingers for a moment longer over the alternative – over the potential ethics of enacting an absolute nonviolence for the sake of the good. Its reference to the "sacred few" of "Athens and Jerusalem" (128, 134), ostensibly Socrates and Jesus, apparently celebrates those who, in the name of the good, suspend all means to the good and thus must nonviolently accept a violence committed against them. But the poem immediately qualifies such an apparent celebration. Although in their refusal of violence these figures "Fle[e] back like eagles to their native noon" (131), in doing so they leave the field of temporality to the sway of Life and its impositions. Here even the willingness to die for the sake of the final cause fails to make a difference; it merely enables the sacred few to escape human history, to leave it behind them in their eagle-like flight back to the true sun. In this moment the poem exposes the failure of any ethics that proposes that one die for the sake of truth; such an act, however greatly it remains faithful to the good, even in defiance (for example) of a lethal sovereign akin to that which appears in Kant's ethical tale, leaves Life's triumph in place. A total compliance with eternity's demands allows a radically destructive process to continue unabated. Ironically, then, in a logic contrary to that in Petrarch, the poem suggests that eternity's apparent triumph over Life actually allows Life to triumph instead. On this level, the poem follows through on similar insights already broached in *Mary: A Fiction*, *Manfred*, and *Prometheus Unbound*, insights suggesting that an ethics of self-sacrifice and/or of defiance must be found wanting.

If divine action and passivity both fail, does "The Triumph" turn back towards the realm of human action and endorse it instead? Does it find a way to affirm a version of ethical finitude – the partial realization of the final cause within time? The most telling moment in this regard arises when the poem briefly considers a form of virtue closely akin to that of the sacred few – the virtue of "those who put aside the diadem / Of earthly thrones or gems" (132–3), who refused the temptations of power or wealth and thus made possible the self-governance of city-states such as "Athens and Jerusalem" (134).[69] The absence of such figures in the pageant suggests that unlike all those conquered by Life, these exemplars of virtue enacted a good distinct from mere imposition, governing such cities through wisdom rather than power. Yet that absence also suggests that their achievement is so exceptional, so rare, that it cannot interrupt the main flow of history. Such mediations are possible, the poem submits, but because they take place only in specific times and places, in historical moments that must pass, they are not enough: the will to power is otherwise too dominant to give way. To alter that force would require a far more daring imposition, the equivalent of a divine violence.

Does the poem thus envision the possibility of affirming the scene of ethical failure itself, of embracing what is revealed in Life's passage? In its depiction of the maniac dance, it hardly gives us much hope. Things hardly look better at a slight remove from that tempest – in the story of Rousseau's entry into its whirlwinds. In the space of a few lines, Rousseau claims both that he "among the multitude / Was swept" and that "among / The thickest billows of the living storm / [He] plunged" (460–1, 465–7), as if to blend activity and passivity, assertion and self-destruction. This fusion takes the conflations already familiar to the reader – between life and death, conquering and being conquered – and brings them into a radically distinct ethical register, suggesting that the very category of the ethical will is now mixed with what submits that will to the undead drive. Indeed, the absence of any explanation for Rousseau's actions hints that they are contingent, that they merely reveal the subjective equivalent of atomic unpredictability. Elsewhere Rousseau suggests that he "was overcome / By [his] own heart alone" (240–1), hinting that he persisted in his desire in the face of all challenges, including that of "the tomb" (242), as if he enacted what amounts to an ethics of desire. But such is not the case. When an intangible hint of the shape all light accompanies Rousseau as he moves with Life's tempest along the wilderness, it represents for him something "forever sought, forever lost" (431) – the object of desire. Yet Rousseau admits that when he took the plunge, nothing detained him, not even "the falling stream's Lethean song" or "the phantom of that early form / Which moved upon its motion," the shape all light (463, 464–5) – that is, no form of his desire: his plunge thus enacts his submission not to desire but to the drive, showing that he acceded to what eclipses the subject, even the subject of desire, and that this plunge immerses him in the turbulence of the drive itself.

Accordingly, the poem proposes (as does Lacanian theory) that there can be no ethics of the drive, for the ethical subject in such a domain is destroyed from within: whatever it chooses dissolves the illusion of active agency behind such a choice, undoing the notion of mastery or achievement.[70] Moreover, because Rousseau embraces the undead drive, he becomes in some sense undead; although he has "died" (200), he still endures as a "grim Feature" akin to Milton's Death, surviving as what seems to be an old root but is in fact a large, distorted skull covered in hair (182–8). One who encounters him, then, seems to confront an instance of one's *own* drive, in a logic much like that of Lacanian anamorphosis: to speak with Rousseau is in some sense to listen to the anonymous speech of the drive, to the articulation of a radical unknowing.[71] Such a position appears to retain a certain agency; insofar as Rousseau can claim that he "suffered what [he] wrote, or viler pain" (279), and that he is "one of those who have created, even / If it be but a world of agony" (294–5), he suggests that to articulate suffering is to create a world, to transform pure affect into the space for a shared mode of being. Such a possibility might seem to verge on an ethics of creativity. But when the poem refers to the "car's creative ray," it reminds the reader that in the chariot's domain, creation and destruction go together, at once producing and erasing life. To create a world of agony is to replicate the logic evident in the triumph of Life itself, to participate in its own activity of endlessly reinscribing its sway.

Thus the poem does not only outline a stunning depiction of radical finitude in the triumph of Life; in an even more devastating move, it also proposes that *there is no viable ethical response to that triumph*. To embrace the triumph, to articulate it, to articulate what lies beyond it, to mediate it in virtuous action, to choose eternity, or to imagine that eternity can interrupt time: all possible options fail. As a result, all options for an ethically based politics fail as well. Although the poem is incomplete, its interwoven deployment of all its levels of concern – its evocation at once of the triumph, the demand for an ethical response to it, and the impossibility of finding any such orientation – suggests that it already articulates a stance that informs its details throughout and that would have shaped even its final gestures. Thus the poem enacts something new for Shelley, a radical step that cuts to the heart of his enterprise: the *destitution of the ethical subject*. The poem does so not because it merely ramifies further the deconstructive treatment of finitude evident on its first level of articulation; on the contrary, it takes up a sharply distinct set of concerns, the poet's orientation to the final cause, which throughout his career he has distinguished from the domain of mutability, mortality, and epistemological uncertainty. Indeed, his position in "The Triumph of Life" derives in part from an entirely distinct set of considerations: for the divine to bring about the universal telos, it must contradict that very telos, revealing *a contradiction internal to the good*. Moreover, as the examples of divine violence or sacred passivity suggest, in the poem, will as rational appetite enacts something other than the good when it seeks to realize the good; it thus falls prey to a logic of self-defeat and self-erasure like that visible in the maniac dance, replicating in a different form aspects of the undead drive. Will as rational appetite, it turns out, is not entirely unlike the irrational will that swirls in Life's tempest: it too participates in Life's triumph even when, or especially when, it seeks to overcome it. *As a result, it is defeated not by submitting to Life's passage but when, in resisting that passage, it enacts or leaves in place a logic of imposition akin to what is allegorized in that passage itself.* The poem's most radical act is not to suggest that the logic of finitude imposes itself without reserve, but to indicate that *imposition inhabits the ethical will itself, even where it seeks the good*. Life triumphs because on another level it allegorizes a contradiction that infests even the sacred.[72]

This position outlines a logic arising within a conception of the good in what is for Shelley an ethical tradition extending over millennia. Such an ethical destitution clearly sets Shelley well apart from his contemporaries. For one thing, as we have seen, in his overall intellectual system he refuses to identify the cancellation of creation or apocalypse with the cancellation of transcendence, folding the knowledge of natural disaster intrinsic to earthly existence into a framework that leaves an ethical telos intact. His approach thus remains distinct from those proposed by Wordsworth or Byron. Furthermore, because he does not consider the counterfactual scenario whereby a human being achieves the impossible – a scenario writ large in Godwin's *St Leon* and Mary Shelley's *Frankenstein* – but ponders instead what might transpire when *immortal* agents transcend time (in the final pages of *Prometheus Unbound*, act 3), he also does not conclude, with such counterfactual tales, that the impossible must be prohibited. As a result, he does not directly construct a fictional counterpart of the Real.

Thus the poem suggests that one apprehend the triumph of Life with no ethical recourse, not even an ethics of the Real – that is, with no capacity to call upon any principle to defend against or subsume onto another level what that triumph reveals. If that triumph displays the ongoing disaster of human life, the poem in effect brings about a *second* disaster unweaving the prospect of incorporating the first into a higher intentional act that would affirm, negate, or sublate it. The poem's destitution operates in a mode that disallows the emergence of anything like the ethics appearing in *Manfred*, anything that would in this case permit one to affirm the infinite subject's capacity to destroy its own finitude. On the contrary, within this poem ethical destitution, like the disaster theorized by Maurice Blanchot, "ruins everything, all the while leaving everything intact."[73] Utterly exposed, the narrator has little choice but to apprehend all that transpires in a state of dismayed astonishment. Without any legitimate ethical response to what he witnesses, unable to overcome the challenge it poses to him, he can only tarry with it in a state of radical unknowing. But he is not alone in this state; insofar as he endures the scene only because at its start "a Vision on [his] brain was rolled" (40), the poem considers him as an instance of what he must share with every reader of the poem, indeed every witness of Life's triumph, who by virtue of that witnessing partakes in, and becomes subject to, that spectacle.

Thus the poem, stunned by what it depicts, finds itself caught in a state Blanchot has thematized as worklessness, in which the efficacy of every effort of articulation, response, or inscription is disabled in advance. Yet here, as perhaps in Blanchot, this state may emerge out of the even more primordial condition of eventlessness, in which the possibility of the arrival of the end is sustained in relation to "its non-occurrence," an arrival that takes place, as it were, only in its absence. The prospect of such an end is so effaced, so evacuated, that it cannot be assumed through any ethical gesture but can only transpire through a severe *non*-assumption, what in Blanchot is a passivity so great that it renders one into a "*subjectivity without any subject*." If in Kant and Byron one witnesses the prospect of an ethical act that may take place within the space of a subjectivity beyond the subject, beyond what any finite ethical agent might carry out, in "The Triumph" one witnesses a contrary prospect, that of an ethical destitution so great that it produces a state in which the ethical subject has been obliterated, where it endures, if at all, in a state of erasure and absence.[74]

Yet where one might expect the poem to cultivate an aesthetics of the barest impoverishment, one finds instead that through the beauty of its terza rima and its deployment of the capacity to find in such a scene a horrific "wonder worthy of [Dante's] rhyme" (480), it invites its readers to find within the violence of such destitution the possibility of an infernal transport.[75] The poem thus takes its share in articulating a poetics of disaster – one that, as Jacques Khalip and I have argued elsewhere, "ultimately hopes not to evade what it sees in disaster but to dwell with it, bear with it, and thus to find in this very abiding its own mode of impossible consolation."[76]

Coda. Melting the Sublime

Disastrous Objectivity in the Era of Climate Change

So far this book has attended to a central cultural transformation taking place in Romantic-era Britain. The new awareness of the history of the earth, undoing the notion of a transcendental origin or end to the world, made that world radically vulnerable to a disastrous transcendence capable of disrupting it at any time – or more radically of inhabiting the field of its own ongoing creative and destructive forces. At the same time, the new sense that political institutions, far from being grounded in eternal verities, were products of a human history made them equally subject to disruptions transforming them from within. The emergence of the internal limit of the Real in both domains allowed each to become a metaphor for the other, especially in texts featuring a subjectivity capable of incorporating the Real into its political, ethical, and spiritual orientations. The linkage between these developments is also evident in Kant's critical philosophy, where the demand for an infinite justice intersects with the aesthetics of the sublime, each revealing aspects of the subject not evident in empirical reality but deriving from its transcendental capacities. Such developments helped shape the premises of an overall ensemble in the West that has ever since regarded itself as modernity, the architecture of the societies in which we still live.

Yet if one takes into account the full dimensions of the present moment, one cannot help but notice how a new awareness of the human impact on the preconditions of life severely undercuts the premises of that modernity. While the current perspective retains the sense that human beings live in a biosphere that is the product of a material history, it is also becoming clear that such a history is not the only framework for life. Under the pressure of anthropogenic climate change, in the midst of bringing about the sixth great extinction event in earth's history – under the sign, that is, of human actions – humanity can no longer be confident that it will continue to flourish on this planet a century or two hence, nor certain that in its current form it is anything other than a force for massive destruction.[1] These developments necessarily challenge the accommodations to disaster reached in Romantic-era writing. As a result, there may be no clearer way to trace the contours of a subjectivity proper to our moment than by reinterpreting the disastrous subjectivity inherent in modernity – by reworking the stances on view so far in this book.

The conceptual stakes of the current transformations in the biosphere become evident almost immediately if one turns to discourses key to the emergence of that modernity, the Kantian analytic of the sublime and its Romantic intertexts. In Kant's account of the formal contours of sublime experience, the natural scene that provokes such an experience is necessarily found in a domain indifferent to human activities. Kant writes that a sublime object must be "absolutely great," great beyond comparison, for we "do not allow a suitable standard for it to be sought outside of it, but merely within it. It is a magnitude that is equal only to itself."[2] He goes on to show that such greatness can never be a property of any object in nature, since the mind can always compare that object with something greater or smaller and thus become aware that sublimity finally inheres in itself. Yet he also insists that for the mind to embark on such an activity and confront its own sublime grandeur, it must be moved by an object whose magnitude seems absolutely great to the senses. A similar aesthetic is on display in Shelley's *Mont Blanc*, one of the most canonic instances of the sublime in Romantic poetics. The poem depicts the mountain's capacity to devastate any landscape hospitable to humankind, to breach the boundary between the "dead and living world" through physical forces that "scorn ... mortal power," forcing the "race / Of man [to fly] far in dread."[3] Here the glaciers that descend from the heights of that mountain exemplify an absolute magnitude proper to the dynamical sublime – a force utterly superior to any human mode of dwelling, absolutely indifferent to human flourishing.[4]

But today, the glaciers of the Alps, subject to a much warmer climate over the past several decades, are rapidly diminishing and have in some cases disappeared entirely. Their fate reveals that human activities can indeed modify natural processes, indirectly forcing immense icy masses to vanish. Those scenes now perpetually speak of the difference history makes, a difference that is registered in our conscious or unconscious comparison between the Alps before and after the melting of the glaciers, or between the Alpine scene today and what it will be a few years hence. No doubt the climate of the Alps has had a long and storied history over the millennia, but what we experience today is in fact unprecedented, subjecting the Alps, not to mention countless other natural phenomena, to a human influence with an intensity and on a planetary scale they have not previously endured. Thus today, that scene, if measured by itself, as Kant demands, shows that climate change has opened up a split within it between a formerly absolute magnitude and what that magnitude has now become.

Such features of that scene bear on further aspects of sublime aesthetics as well. In Kant's account, our encounter with an absolutely great magnitude could take place only if it suspended other faculties of mind in favour of an aesthetic judgment: "A pure judgment on the sublime ... must have no end of the object as its determining ground if it is to be aesthetic and not mixed up with any judgment of the understanding or of reason."[5] In much the same vein, *Mont Blanc* does not directly identify the destructive/creative processes that apparently take place on the mountaintop with eternity, or Power, itself. As I argued in chapter 5, within the terms of that poem, Power lies beyond all cognition, even beyond the constructions of geological knowledge. Such a distinction, however, ultimately highlights the aesthetics of the sublime; like Kant's analytic, the poem suspends a cognitive grasp of those processes to emphasize instead an aesthetic apprehension of what necessarily lies beyond such cognition. Thus the poem treats the operation of an inhuman, infinite force not as something to be understood through the discourse of geology but as a trigger for an aesthetic response to what structurally exceeds understanding. Moved by the glacier's force, dazzled by the destructive processes at work in the mountain scene, the speaker orients his response to that which exceeds physical survival and human understanding both – to what he calls Power.

In viewing the scene near Mont Blanc today, however, the understanding unquestionably comes into play as one contemplates the relation between those glaciers and the contingent causes of a warmer climate, as well as the place of both within a global atmospheric system. Gazing at the valleys in which mighty glaciers once flowed, one is moved by the grandeur of the scene but at the same time reminded of many other concerns, such as the level of carbon dioxide in the atmosphere, changes to the water cycles across the planet, and rising levels of the seas worldwide. Rather than displaying phenomena that vastly exceed humanity in scale or force, the Alpine scene has become a symptom of the potential consequences of the era of fossil fuel consumption in which the viewer is implicated, complete with its inventions, material practices, and characteristic political impasses. It no longer simply inspires the mind's pleasure or displeasure in confronting phenomena too large for the faculty of imagination to comprehend; rather it calls upon that mind's power to measure the difference history makes upon the bare surface of the magnificent object itself. In short, thanks to climate change, the understanding perpetually interferes in what might otherwise have been proper to aesthetic judgment.

This scene of the melting sublime is, of course, not unique. A similar shift in status can extend indefinitely to other contexts – for example, to hurricanes, tornadoes, floods, fires, and vast winter storms, potential instances of Kant's dynamical sublime, the intensity of which, we now know, have in the aggregate increased and will continue to increase as a result of climate change. Virtually all potentially sublime scenes now bristle with implicit references to quotidian functions within the earth's biodynamic systems.

That fact is quite relevant as one examines a key moment later in Kant's exposition. In the final portion of the "Analytic of the Sublime," in the "General remark on the exposition of aesthetic reflective judgments," Kant proposes a further refinement to his argument, suggesting that one should take only certain attributes of a natural object into account when calling it sublime. We should not "take the sight of the ocean as we **think** it," he writes, "enriched with all sorts of knowledge ... for example ... as the great storehouse of water for the evaporation which impregnates the air with clouds for the benefit of land ... for this would yield merely teleological judgments; rather, one must consider the ocean merely as the poets do, in accordance with what its appearance shows," such as "when it is turbulent, an abyss threatening to devour everything."[6] One might, in short, separate those aspects of the ocean that we treat as objects of knowledge from the aesthetic effect of its immediate appearance. With this argument, the philosopher seems to provide us with a method of retaining the sublime even in the midst of climate change, for one could set aside one's knowledge of transformations to planetary systems while taking in a natural scene in all its immediacy. But insofar as aesthetic judgment responds to the dynamical magnitude of a given appearance, that is, to its superhuman force, in our time it cannot easily disentangle its apprehension of that dynamism from the causes of its force; the magnitude of the appearance itself, we now know, may well derive from the effect of climate change on the intensity of all earth's atmospheric disturbances. The distinction on which Kant relies in this moment of his argument is wearing away.

These developments bear as well on further aspects of the overall orientation of Kant's critical philosophy and of Shelley's poetics. The poem links its apprehension of Power with a certain political confidence; as I discussed in chapter 5, it holds that the mountain has a "voice … to repeal / Large codes of fraud and woe" – a voice whose effect can undermine the ideological bases of traditional oppression.[7] Insofar as the aesthetics of the sublime enacted by the poem emphasizes the gap between human cognition and Power, it gestures as well to a counterpart in the domain of justice, a gap between contingent political institutions and a collective good. As seen in chapter 1, Kant discusses this gap in his *Conflict of the Faculties*, suggesting that human beings may at times justify their hopes for an eventual realization of universal justice on the basis of signs that erupt into the flow of history. For Kant, one such sign is the nearly universal enthusiasm shown in response to certain events in France. While Kant articulates this confidence in a separate text, not directly linking the sublime to political hope, *Mont Blanc* juxtaposes them outright, directly associating the overall structure of the sublime and the formal contours of political enthusiasm. Both accounts, then, deduce from the mind's response to a certain absolute magnitude a sense of a transcendental destination for the mind as well as the idea of a universal justice.

The melting of the glaciers thus destabilizes more than the aesthetics of the sublime; it threatens to erase the transcendental destination at the culmination of sublime experience, as well as the prospect of a universal good associated with that destination.[8] One may deduce as much from the loss of absolute magnitude in the Alpine landscape. But such a conclusion also follows directly from an awareness that anthropogenic climate change threatens to erase a viable future for the biosphere, an awareness that is the precondition for the long work of attempting to realize the Idea of a universal justice. Human actions are not merely altering the climate; if one calls upon the terms relevant in Shelley's poetics, they verge on destroying the very prospect of a final cause that for millennia has oriented the search for justice.[9]

Working through the distinctive intellectual projects of the Romantic era in the context of the present environmental crisis thus almost inevitably raises devastating questions. What happens to an entire conceptual architecture if the Alpine glaciers melt, shrink, and indeed disappear – and if, as a result, that landscape no longer bodies forth a truly inhuman nature? The logic of Kant's critical philosophy, as well as of Shelley's poem, suggests that we must now speak of the end of a certain transcendence that loomed beyond the reach of empirical experience, human cognitive capacity, or ethical and political endeavour. Of course, if we choose to do so, we may respond to environmental catastrophe itself as an instance of another sort of sublime, one presumably to be found in futuristic scenarios of the world's cataclysmic end, and thereby attempt to sustain some version of transcendence on radically different terms. Yet insofar as such a catastrophic sublime would necessarily abandon any reference to the Idea of an eventual justice, it would merely codify the undoing of the sublime on view in Kant and Shelley – a sublime that still retained some element of political hope. Moreover, since this apparent alternative, this even more catastrophic sublime, capable of wrecking not only the villages beneath Mont Blanc but all human dwellings, speaks of biophysical forces responding in part to human activities rather than of an absolute magnitude, it too falls prey to the subtle unworking of sublimity I have sketched above; it provides no genuine alternative but another rendition of the same. This anthropogenic undoing of the sublime thus adds a further twist to the theme of disaster I have been exploring in this book: insofar as the catastrophic violence that operates in *Mont Blanc* does so through its glaciers, which are rapidly melting away and which have either disappeared entirely or will soon, we are witnessing a catastrophe for this sublime rendition of catastrophe – *a disaster for the very logic of disastrous transcendence itself.*

This shift from one level of disaster to another is so sharp that it not only cancels the sense of absolute magnitude, as we have seen, but even invades what once figured that magnitude, in effect reversing the direction of sublime imposition. Confronted with the shrinking glaciers of the Alps, we might realize that the cumulative effect of *human* actions now breaches the boundary between "the dead and living world," interfering into the processes visible in the mountain landscape and inverting the logic traced in *Mont Blanc*. Today, the "works and ways of man" once threatened by the glaciers threaten them in turn, causing them, as it were, to fly far in dread.[10] It does not follow, of course, that humanity is now the dominant force, that nature is now somehow subjected to human will; on the contrary, the climatological changes we have unleashed function in a complex dynamic well beyond human control. Yet the fact remains that aspects of human action have prodded that dynamic into a new pattern that is reshaping the preconditions for every aspect of the planet's biosphere. Human actions have altered what once seemed absolutely great, even if it continues to exceed what humanity can master.

This eclipse of one disaster by another – of earth's history by anthropogenic catastrophe – alters the basic premises of the literature I have been exploring in this book. That eclipse marks a severe shift from the awareness of deep time to a new sense of the geological import of human time. It displaces the sense of an absolute magnitude outside us by a growing knowledge that certain human actions now constitute a singular threat to the biosphere's continued flourishing. Where an older etymology once imagined that those experiencing "disaster" had been abandoned by their star, and where Lord Byron proposed that Manfred lived under the sign of a "bright deformity on high, / The monster of the upper sky," we sense that *human* actions now constitute this abandoning star, this cruel force condemning the biosphere to a cruel fate: the premises encoded in the word "disaster" are woefully inadequate to what we face.[11] Unlike Wollstonecraft, who concluded *Mary: A Fiction* with her protagonist seeking a redemption beyond the reach of the "world in ruins" in which she lived, we endure within an incomplete history *without* a beyond, in ruins to which there is no future alternative. Where the erasure of the rainbow covenant once led Wordsworth to see the world as a blend of creation and destruction, eternity and apocalypse, and to propose that the imagination participates in a similarly uncanny and endless process, our new awareness brings about a second-order erasure of history itself, plunging us into a futile process without destination and without hope. Furthermore, where the Romantic sublime on view in Kant and Shelley produced the sense of a supersensible destination for all human endeavour, anthropogenic disaster deletes any such destination, bringing into view the rather different prospect of human extinction and the eclipse of the telos of all ethical purposes. If the future is disappearing, the notion of a credible final cause for ethical and political labour, a telos for humanity, is endangered as well.

These wide-ranging, devastating transformations have taken place in part because modern societies put the new understanding of earth's history to use in developments that contrast sharply to those on view in this book. Industrial civilization emerged thanks to the wholesale exploitation of fossil fuels – first of coal, whose more intensive mining and use, coordinated by capitalist industry in mid-nineteenth-century Britain, powered an extraordinary increase in productive capacity; then of oil, whose emergence as an energy source in the mid- to late nineteenth century has made possible the enormous increase in productive capacity around the globe over the course of the twentieth and early twenty-first centuries.[12] Thus while Romanticism responded to the awareness of geological disaster in one way – through an aesthetics and ethics of disastrous subjectivity – capitalism reworked such a response in another medium, using geological knowledge to extend its sway over the physical resources of the earth, find and exploit ever new oil reserves, and create the framework for the seemingly indefinite expansion of population, economic productivity, and cultural transformation that have taken place ever since.[13] While these developments provided the context for the elaboration of Western liberal democracy, including aspects of the disastrous subjectivity that emerged in Romantic-era writing, they also subsumed the question of a subjective response to deep time into a literal use of what geological history provides, enacting within the mode of appropriation and production a telling counterpart of the limitlessness on view in modern subjectivity itself.[14] Modern unlimited productivity, apparently casting aside any ethical, political, or aesthetic reinterpretation of what deep time reveals, creates a *disastrous objectivity* bereft of any human orientation – except for the orientation encoded in the demand for, and subjective participation and enjoyment in, this form of productivity in the first place.[15] What we now see is a Romantic sublime detached from its initial literary articulation and realized instead in an entire cultural history, a capitalist sublime of indefinitely expanding, and destructive, abundance. Such a version of the sublime in effect revises the Wordsworthian version, transforming the uncanny persistence of imaginative desire into the infinite process of production and consumption in global capitalism.

This shift to an infinite exploitation of disastrous objectivity has its cost for the ethical subject: the possibility that earth's geological history is only an objective fact the knowledge of which capitalism may exploit ad infinitum, even at the cost of humanity's future, suggests that for capitalism, the question of a collective telos, or indeed of individual ethical purpose, may safely be subsumed into the question of collective material abundance. But this projection of subjective infinity onto a limitless *material* process makes clear that modernity's gambit with the internal limit – its attempt to locate infinity within the finite contours of the biosphere – creates a process that must eventually wreck that biosphere, obliterating its own conditions. When it is implemented in the context of a material appropriation of the forms of life, the internal limit – that is, the destruction of any external limit on, or any ethical telos for, an endless productivity – has catastrophic results for the conditions of life. As we can now see, the indefinite elaboration of productivity across time and space smashes through every conceivable boundary, revealing that once it is literalized, the internal limit becomes a material limitlessness, a logic that ramifies beyond any conceivable rationality or usefulness. It thus becomes capable of threatening the continued existence of everything on which it seems to rely – planetary resources, human productivity, political and social context, and even economic productivity itself.

While this limitless process may thus articulate aspects of Romantic subjectivity in objective form, foregrounding the consequences of modernity's gambit, it ultimately has far more severe consequences than any disastrous subjectivity, for it threatens to destroy even the logic of the internal limit itself. Despite its affiliation with disastrous subjectivity, then, this process is finally distinct from it, operating on other terms and with other consequences. This contrast may be clearest if one traces how the operation of a terminal capitalism wrecks even the scenario visible in that seemingly most negative of poems, "The Triumph of Life." At first one might wish to argue that the pageantry of a blind, undead, vastly creative-destructive force enacts the process whereby fossil fuel capitalism endlessly generates a maniac dance of annihilating consumption. In such a rendition, the poem would show how the fossil fuel economy, creating abundance out of dead life, de-sublimates Shelley's speculative insight into a material counterpart, the triumph of undead capitalism. Yet such a reading rapidly modulates into another: since the "progress" of undead capitalism destroys the material basis for such undead flourishing, producing such changes in the biosphere that even endless useless productivity will cease, it opens up the prospect that *the chariot may incinerate itself*. The triumph of capitalism threatens the extension of its own ruinous conquest: it takes shape for a moment, only to dissolve before long into a ghostly scenario and then disappear. It thus not only constitutes a materially enforced instance of ethical destitution *but also erases the preconditions for ethical destitution itself*.

It seems that the very prospect of a human future, as well as all possible realizations of the good, are in eclipse. Under this pressure, modern ethics collapses; an act in the Real, an act of infinite singularity, disappears into irrelevance. One might think that an ethics that recognizes from the start the alterity of the future, as well as of the biosphere, might aspire to a real purchase on our condition. Yet even that ethics is in abeyance, its telos fading into darkness. As a result, the stance of last resort, the most minimal ethics of which one can conceive – that of Derridean survival, which in the words of Jacques Khalip lacks "any capacity to fully possess or know the event" – dissolves, for in our time even the thought of survival begins to fade away.[16] Only one gesture remains: one whereby the ethical subject, through a *negative* judgment, accepts its part in a vast ethical and political failure. Such an act would refer to a sense of the good that will not be realized and would thus remain faithful to a telos now in eclipse; it would register the gap between history and its final cause not out of a sense that such a gap might be overcome but to mark out precisely where it will not be, taking upon itself the impress of what is now impossible. For such an act to be viable, it would have to accept the task of attempting despite all odds of realizing the good even today, to participate in a politics that would challenge the sway of global catastrophe.[17] But such an effort would take its failure into account from the start; it would enact, even within its own terms, the symbolic exchange of a ruined agent with a devastated alterity. In such a gesture, in this last remnant of what was once ethics, one might incorporate into a subjectivity truly of our time the full weight of a final, unsurpassable disaster.

Notes

Introduction

1 Jean-François Lyotard, *Enthusiasm: The Kantian Critique of History*, trans. Georges Van Den Abbeele (Stanford, CA: Stanford University Press, 2009), 11.
2 Immanuel Kant, *The Conflict of the Faculties*, in *Religion and Rational Theology*, trans. Allen W. Wood and George Di Giovanni (Cambridge: Cambridge University Press, 1996), 300–4.
3 Immanuel Kant, *The Critique of Practical Reason*, 3rd ed., trans. Lewis White Beck (Upper Saddle River, NJ: Prentice Hall, 1993), 129.
4 Lewis White Beck, *A Commentary on Kant's "Critique of Practical Reason"* (Chicago: University of Chicago Press, 1960), 270. Here I follow aspects of the argument in Alenka Zupančič, *Ethics of the Real: Kant, Lacan* (New York: Verso, 2000), 79–80.
5 Kant, *The Conflict of the Faculties*, 305, 300.
6 Lyotard, *Enthusiasm*, 30.
7 Kant's willingness to allow aspects of his architecture to remain incomplete – or, more radically, for him to demonstrate that within the limits of reason alone they *must* remain incomplete – testify to what one must regard as a severe modesty, a daring refusal to attempt to complete reason's totality. Such a refusal manifests an ethical courage in its own right. For an exemplary treatment that places Kant's critical philosophy in "the tradition of aporetic philosophy," see Howard Caygill, *Art of Judgement* (Oxford: Basil Blackwell, 1989), 2. For a treatment that sees Kant's third critique as a "work in progress," that points to "a sense of development and mutation" in Kant's thought and that values the third critique's capacity to bring certain contradictions to the surface, see Michael Wayne, *Red Kant: Aesthetics, Marxism, and the Third Critique* (London: Bloomsbury, 2014), 8, 25, 30. For a capacious and lucid rendition of these aspects of

Kant, see many discussions in Lyotard, including several moments in his masterwork, *The Differend: Phrases in Dispute*, trans. Georges Van Den Abbeele (Minneapolis: University of Minnesota Press, 1988), especially xiii, 61–5, 118–27, 130–5, 161–71; *Lessons on the Analytic of the Sublime*, trans. Elizabeth Rottenberg (Stanford, CA: Stanford University Press, 1994); and *Enthusiasm*.

8 Timothy Michael similarly takes up the theme of a "Kantian Romanticism" in his *British Romanticism and the Critique of Political Reason* (Baltimore, MD: Johns Hopkins University Press, 2015), 3; cf. 35. He does so by building his analyses on what he takes to be the self-consistent, praiseworthy endeavour of enlightening reason, throughout his work aligning Kant and the Romantics with a project he too endorses. As a result, however, he leaves out of view the aporias and impasses of critique, especially in Kant's critical philosophy and in the key political arguments he analyses; moreover, through his identification with enlightenment he sets aside the question of modernity's place in the larger tradition.

9 It is beyond the scope of this study to delve into the contours of post-Kantian idealism, particularly in the work of Fichte, Schelling, and Hegel. The debate regarding whether Hegel's dialectic is open or closed, for example, is vast, and bears directly on whether he accepts or rejects crucial aspects of the internal limit as I describe it here. Insofar as Hegel sublates the breach in the subject as the site for the subject's self-consciousness, he radicalizes aspects of modernity in his dialectic. Insofar as he repudiates what he calls "spurious infinity" in favour of the infinity of the circle, he turns away from incompleteness or radical openness, seeks to resolve the aporia of the internal limit, and in effect revives the notion of an infinity that can be totalized, thereby evading – or in his view repudiating – the scandal of a Kantian infinity: see G.W.F. Hegel, *Hegel's Science of Logic*, trans. A.V. Miller (Atlantic Highlands, NJ: Humanities Press, 1969), 139, 149. The fact that both Hegels figure in the work of such a thinker as Jacques Derrida shows how unstable this question may be; for a treatment of the open Hegel endorsed by Derrida, see Catherine Malabou, *The Future of Hegel: Plasticity, Temporality, and Dialectic*, trans. Lisabeth During (New York: Routledge, 2005), and on how the notion of the circle resonates across the entire history of philosophy – from Aristotle through Hegel to Heidegger – apparently placing Hegel within the tradition of a totalizing philosophy, see Jacques Derrida, "*Ousia* and *Gramme*: Note on a Note from *Being and Time*," in *Margins of Philosophy*, trans. Alan Bass (Chicago: University of Chicago Press, 1982), 29–67.

10 *Oxford English Dictionary*, 3rd ed., s.v. "apocalypse"; accessed 24 January 2016.

11 Claude Lefort, *Democracy and Political Theory*, trans. David Macey (Minneapolis: University of Minnesota Press, 1988), 17–19. For Laclau's most

recent articulation of this stance, see Ernesto Laclau, *On Populist Reason* (New York: Verso, 2005).

12 Joan Copjec, *Imagine There's No Woman: Ethics and Sublimation* (Cambridge, MA: MIT Press, 2002), 94, 95–6. The notion of the "internal limit" here is meant in part to displace or even reverse the familiar rendition of the "internal" and of "internalization" one finds both in certain Romantic texts and in critical readings of those texts; this book thus bears on the argument whereby Hegel, marking the shift from "symbolic" to "romantic," traces the displacement of an external with an internal basis for art – see Hegel, *Hegel's Aesthetics: Lectures on Fine Art*, trans. T.M. Knox, vol. 1 (New York: Oxford University Press, 1975), 517–29 – and is also in dialogue with a major treatment of these themes in Joshua Wilner, *Feeding on Infinity: Readings in the Romantic Rhetoric of Internalization* (Baltimore, MD: Johns Hopkins University Press, 2000).

13 Paolo Rossi, *The Dark Abyss of Time: The History of the Earth & the History of Nations from Hooke to Vico*, trans. Lydia G. Cochrane (Chicago: University of Chicago Press, 1984), alluding to *The Tempest*, 1.2.49–50: "What seest thou else / In the dark backward and abysm of time?" William Shakespeare, *The Complete Works of Shakespeare*, 3rd ed., ed. David Bevington (Glenview, IL: Scott, Foresman, 1980), 1501.

14 Reinhart Koselleck, *Futures Past: On the Semantics of Historical Time*, trans. Keith Tribe (New York: Columbia University Press, 2004), 22.

15 For a discussion that places the Heideggerian thematic within the context of historical temporalization sketched by Koselleck, see the introduction to Thomas Pfau, *Romantic Moods: Paranoia, Trauma, and Melancholy, 1790–1840* (Baltimore, MD: Johns Hopkins University Press, 2005), 1–26.

16 Copjec, *Imagine There's No Woman*, 96.

17 Kant, *Critique of Practical Reason*, 30. As Eckart Förster suggests, this tale is probably modelled on a story Diogenes Laertius tells of the philosopher Zeno of Elea. Having plotted against the tyrant Nearchus, only to be arrested and interrogated, Zeno refused to implicate any of his friends, denouncing the supporters of the tyrant instead. Citing Antisthenes, Laertius writes that Zeno said to bystanders, "I marvel at your cowardice, that, for fear of any of those things which I am now enduring, you should be the tyrant's slaves." In the end, Zeno bit off his own tongue and spat it in the face of Nearchus, "and his fellow-citizens were so worked upon that they forthwith stoned the tyrant to death." See Förster, *The Twenty-Five Years of Philosophy: A Systematic Reconstruction* (Cambridge, MA: Harvard University Press, 2012), 116n; Laertius, *Lives of Eminent Philosophers*, trans. R.D. Hicks (New York: Putnam's, 1925), 2:435, 437.

18 For one formulation of this paradox, as well as a summary of his attempt to resolve it, see Bertrand Russell, *Introduction to Mathematical Philosophy*

(New York: Macmillan, 1919), 135–6; for an accessible account of Lacan's use of the same, see Bruce Fink, *The Lacanian Subject: Between Language and Jouissance* (Princeton, NJ: Princeton University Press, 1995), 29–30. For a discussion of related elements in Kant, see Lyotard, *The Differend*, 60.

19 See Tilottama Rajan, *Deconstruction and the Remainders of Phenomenology: Sartre, Derrida, Foucault, Baudrillard* (Stanford, CA: Stanford University Press, 2002).

20 Michel Foucault, "Language to Infinity," in *Language, Counter-Memory, Practice: Selected Essays and Interviews*, ed. Donald F. Bouchard, trans. Donald F. Bouchard and Sherry Simon (Ithaca, NY: Cornell University Press, 1977), 59, 60, 65.

21 Jacques Derrida, *Writing and Difference*, trans. Alan Bass (Chicago: University of Chicago Press, 1978), 289.

22 Gilles Deleuze, *Difference and Repetition*, trans. Paul Patton (New York: Columbia University Press, 1994), 41.

23 On the impasses that arise when one attempts to interpret society by examining it in its own right, see Brian C.J. Singer, *Society, Theory, and the French Revolution: Studies in the Revolutionary Imaginary* (New York: St Martin's Press, 1986).

24 On the absent cause, see Louis Althusser, *Reading Capital*, trans. Ben Brewster (New York: Verso, 1979), 188. That cause is "absent," Althusser argues, not because of its "exteriority" to what it causes but because "it is the very form of the interiority of the structure, as a structure, in its effects" – and thus an exemplary instance of the internal limit. For an influential discussion of Althusser in the Anglo-American Marxist tradition, see Fredric Jameson, *The Political Unconscious: Narrative as a Socially Symbolic Act* (Ithaca, NY: Cornell University Press, 1981), 23–58. On Althusser's rejection of telos, see his dictum that "[h]istory is a process without a *telos* or subject," quoted in Jameson, *Political Unconscious*, 29. For a Lacanian reading of Spinoza quite relevant in this context, see A. Kiarina Kordela, *$urplus: Spinoza, Lacan* (Albany: SUNY Press, 2007).

25 The emphasis on "unreason" is evident in the use of the term throughout the text; see Michel Foucault, *History of Madness*, ed. Jean Khalfa, trans. Jonathan Murphy and Jean Khalfa (New York: Routledge, 2006).

26 See Charles Shepherdson, "History and the Real," in *Rhetoric in an Antifoundational World: Language, Culture, and Pedagogy*, ed. Michael Bernard-Donals and Richard R. Glejzer (New Haven, CT: Yale University Press, 1998), 293–317. The passage in Copjec on which I am building here complements Shepherdson's argument, for her discussion of the internal limit arises in a passage that, invoking Deleuze's reading of Foucault, provides a Lacanian rereading of Foucault's theory of power – a reading in which she proposes the theory of power, freedom, and the internal limit on which I touched above; see Copjec, *Imagine There's No Woman*, 94–6, 102–3.

27 Fredric Jameson, *A Singular Modernity: Essay on the Ontology of the Present* (New York: Verso, 2002), 34.

28 Pursuing an even more rigorous argument, Nicholas Halmi shows that the term "Romanticism" has a status at least as difficult as "the modern"; in his examination of the former, he shows how the concept can be contained fully "neither within a scheme of historical periodization nor within one of formalist categorization." The various attempts to categorize Romanticism, he argues, may never converge on any single definition or account, but they share "a common challenge: reconciling a sense of historical temporality with the systematization of knowledge." Moreover, by a certain paradox, "as a result of the temporalization of history" near the end of the eighteenth century, "the past becomes at once more elusive and more available to the present, more elusive in its very availability." Halmi, "Romanticism, the Temporalization of History, and the Historicization of Form," *MLQ* 74 (2013): 365, 367, 384. Halmi's approach exemplifies the mode of intellectual history with which this study has most in common: a mode that, without skewing its account to advocate for or against modernity, traces changes in the assumptions that underlie representative discourses, changes that may never be articulated directly in them. Such an approach foregrounds gaps in renditions of Romanticism and modernity alike, gaps with which we are only beginning to contend. As I outline below, this book differs from Halmi's investigation primarily by attempting to isolate a specific set of impasses from a much larger mass and to pursue the implications of that set across an array of closely associated articulations.

29 Bruno Latour, *We Have Never Been Modern*, trans. Catherine Porter (Cambridge, MA: Harvard University Press, 1993).

30 Gil Anidjar holds this argument in solution with several others in "Secularism," a chapter in *Semites: Race, Religion, Literature* (Stanford, CA: Stanford University Press, 2008), 39–63. Anidjar's pivotal discussion of the mutual relations between Judaism, Christianity, and Islam goes far towards illuminating what one might mean by "the West" in the context of the present argument. Stathis Gourgouris, repudiating arguments that in his view "claim that secularization (in the West) is nothing but a continuation of Christianity by other means," misses the chance to engage their subtle understanding of continuity in discontinuity or to grapple with how certain aspects of the Christian tradition remain intact in the process of secularization that transpires within and beyond it. See Gourgouris, *Lessons in Secular Criticism* (New York: Fordham University Press, 2013), 29, 65.

31 For leading examples of such studies see Alasdair MacIntyre, *After Virtue: A Study in Moral Theory*, 3rd ed. (Notre Dame, IN: University of Notre Dame Press, 2007); and John Milbank, *Theology and Social Theory: Beyond Secular Reason*, 2nd ed. (Malden, MA: Blackwell, 2006). For recent books that

bring similar approaches to the study of Romanticism, see Vivasvan Soni, *Mourning Happiness: Narrative and the Politics of Modernity* (Ithaca, NY: Cornell University Press, 2010); and Thomas Pfau, *Minding the Modern: Human Agency, Intellectual Traditions, and Responsible Knowledge* (Notre Dame, IN: Notre Dame University Press, 2013).

32 Jean-Luc Nancy, *Dis-Enclosure: The Deconstruction of Christianity*, trans. Bettina Bergo, Gabriel Malenfant, and Michael B. Smith (New York: Fordham University Press, 2008), 25, 36.

33 See M.H. Abrams, *Natural Supernaturalism: Tradition and Revolution in Romantic Literature* (New York: Norton, 1971).

34 James K. Chandler, *England in 1819: The Politics of Literary Culture and the Case of Romantic Historicism* (Chicago: University of Chicago Press, 1998).

35 Jerome J. McGann, *The Romantic Ideology: A Critical Investigation* (Chicago: University of Chicago Press, 1983).

36 This book thus shares much with recent treatments of how Romanticism discloses its sense of temporal dislocation by evoking a certain futurity. For telling instances, see Emily Rohrbach, *Modernity's Mist: British Romanticism and the Poetics of Anticipation* (New York: Fordham University Press, 2016); and Christopher M. Bundock, *Romantic Prophecy and the Resistance to Historicism* (Toronto: University of Toronto Press, 2016).

37 Pfau, *Romantic Moods*, 10, 25.

38 For an exploration of the limits of Pfau's approach, especially insofar as it tends to place the interpretation of Romanticism within the framework established by Romanticism's own modernity, see my essay, "Troping Mood: Pfau, Wordsworth, and Hegel," *Literature Compass* 6 (2009): 373–83. For an essay that follows up on that exploration, especially regarding the construction of a certain historicity within Romanticism, see my "The Force of Indirection: 'Tintern Abbey' in the History of Mood," in *British Romanticism: Criticism and Debates*, ed. Mark Canuel (New York: Routledge, 2015), 409–17.

39 Anne-Lise François, *Open Secrets: The Literature of Uncounted Experience* (Stanford, CA: Stanford University Press, 2008); Jacques Khalip, *Anonymous Life: Romanticism and Dispossession* (Stanford, CA: Stanford University Press, 2009); Anahid Nersessian, *Utopia, Limited: Romanticism and Adjustment* (Cambridge, MA: Harvard University Press, 2015).

40 Rei Terada, *Feeling in Theory: Emotion After the "Death of the Subject"* (Cambridge, MA: Harvard University Press, 2001), 157.

41 Gordon E. Michalson Jr, for example, argues that although the "moral life takes narrative form … Kant's theory of ethics" by contrast "is notorious for the way it systematically seals off moral considerations from temporal influence"; *Fallen Freedom: Kant on Radical Evil and Moral Regeneration* (Cambridge: Cambridge University Press, 1990), 116. Moreover, virtue theorists such as Alasdair MacIntyre, who build narrative directly into their

sense of the ethical life, place Kant well within a failed project: see MacIntyre, *After Virtue*, 51–61, 215–23.

42 For a pivotal discussion of autonarration, see the reading of Mary Hays's *Memoir of Emma Courtney* in chapter 3 of Tilottama Rajan, *Romantic Narrative: Shelley, Hays, Godwin, Wollstonecraft* (Baltimore, MD: Johns Hopkins University Press, 2010), 82–116; for an exemplary discussion of what I am calling the deliberate differend, see chapter 2 of that study, "Shelley's Promethean Narratives," 46–81.

43 For a contrasting depiction of the relation between Kantian critical philosophy and literature, see Philippe Lacoue-Labarthe and Jean-Luc Nancy, *The Literary Absolute: The Theory of Literature in German Romanticism*, trans. Philip Barnard and Cheryl Lester (Albany: SUNY Press, 1988). These authors propose that Kantian aesthetics reaches its further development in post-Kantian literary explorations, particularly in the cultivation of the literary fragment by the Athenaeum group, especially Friedrich Schlegel. For them, such explorations remain within the purview of philosophy while realizing it in literary form; moreover, their concern with the infinite finds expression in the cultivation of the fragment (48). My argument suggests that writings in British Romanticism bear philosophical import without necessarily inheriting the Kantian mantle; these texts are adjacent to Kant, rather than succeeding from him. The works I examine consider the infinite not via the deployment of the fragment but in alternative forms; in effect this book explores a range of further possibilities for articulating the "literary absolute."

44 Zupančič, *Ethics of the Real*.

45 The appearance of the infinite in this context represents a further stage in the long encounter between early modern thought and the problem of infinity. For a classic treatment of the breaching of an external *spatial* limit on the cosmos in early modern science, see Alexandre Koyré, *From the Closed World to the Infinite Universe* (Baltimore, MD: Johns Hopkins University Press, 1957). On how the impossibility of totalizing the infinite, of reaching a final knowledge of its indefinite extension, leads to the "learned ignorance" of Nicholas of Cusa – an early modern counterpart of the limits on knowledge inscribed within modern discourse – see Koyré, *From the Closed World*, 8, 11. On the role that constructions of the infinite played within early modern mathematics and mathematical physics, see Michel Blay, *Reasoning with the Infinite: From the Closed World to the Mathematical Universe*, trans. M.B. DeBevoise (Chicago: University of Chicago Press, 1998). This history of "reasoning with" a fundamentally impossible object may well provide a model for Kant's efforts to do the same within the context of analytic thought.

46 Kant's argument gestures in this direction when it makes clear that the Idea of infinity appearing at the culmination of the mathematical sublime is an attribute not of determining but of reflective judgment; as Lyotard comments,

"sublime judgment is not determinant in relation to the object. It is reflective with regard to the state of thought when it thinks the object (tautegorical)." That is, in this context "the Idea of the absolute is not present … as a concept of reason" but only in the form of the "'soul-stirring delight' that thinking feels on the occasion of the object it judges sublime." The Idea of an infinite whole thus appears not in relation to any claim that such a whole exists but rather as an aspect of the mind's delight; Lyotard writes, "What matters is that the delight is felt to be absolute" (*Lessons*, 121). In effect, this notion does its work less as a positive claim than as a perpetual rebuke to accepting what can be presented or understood; as Lyotard comments, "The absolute is never there, never given in a presentation, but is always 'present' as a call to think beyond the 'there'" (*Lessons*, 150).

47 For a fuller discussion of these arguments, see my *Monstrous Society: Reciprocity, Discipline, and the Political Uncanny, c. 1780–1848* (Lewisburg, PA: Bucknell University Press, 2009).

1 Wollstonecraft's Shipwreck

1 Mary Wollstonecraft, *Mary: A Fiction*, in *The Works of Mary Wollstonecraft*, ed. Janet Todd and Marilyn Butler, vol. 1 (New York: New York University Press, 1989), 50–2. Further references to the novel will be given in the text.

2 Janet Todd, *Mary Wollstonecraft: A Revolutionary Life* (New York: Columbia University Press, 2000), 70–1.

3 For representative instances of this argument see Mary Wollstonecraft, *A Vindication of the Rights of Men*, in *Works*, 5:33–4; and *A Vindication of the Rights of Woman*, in *Works*, 5:95, 177–9.

4 *Vindication of the Rights of Men*, 5:16.

5 *Vindication of the Rights of Woman*, 5:95.

6 *Vindication of the Rights of Woman*, 5:184.

7 Zupančič, *Ethics of the Real*, 79–80, emphasis in original.

8 Zupančič, *Ethics of the Real*, 80–1.

9 For the key statement in this regard see Jacques Lacan, "Kant with Sade," trans. James B. Swenson Jr, *October* 51 (1989): 55–104, also available in *Écrits: The First Complete Edition in English*, trans. Bruce Fink, in collaboration with Héloïse Fink and Russell Grigg (New York: Norton, 2006), 645–68. Lacan provided a further, and somewhat different, argument on these themes in Lacan, *The Seminar of Jacques Lacan*, ed. Jacques-Alain Miller, book 7, *The Ethics of Psychoanalysis*, trans. Denis Porter (New York: Norton, 1992), 71–84, 188–203.

10 Marquis de Sade, *Juliette*, trans. Austryn Wainhouse (New York: Grove, 1968), 765–82.

11 Wollstonecraft, *A Vindication of the Rights of Men*, 5:58.

12 On this theme see Lacan, *The Ethics of Psychoanalysis*, 179–203, as well as the essays gathered in Slavoj Žižek, Eric L. Santner, and Kenneth Reinhard, *The Neighbor: Three Inquiries in Political Theology* (Chicago: University of Chicago Press, 2005).

13 At the end of section 26 of the analytic of the sublime, Kant places this statement in boldface: "That is sublime which even to be able to think of demonstrates a faculty of the mind that surpasses every measure of the senses." See Kant, *Critique of the Power of Judgment*, ed. Paul Guyer, trans. Paul Guyer and Eric Matthews (Cambridge: Cambridge University Press, 2000), 134.

14 See section 26 of Kant, *Critique of the Power of Judgment*, 134–40.

15 Lyotard, *Enthusiasm*, 30–1.

16 Jan Plug, *Borders of a Lip: Romanticism, Language, History, Politics* (Albany: SUNY Press, 2003), 37.

17 Syndy McMillen Conger no doubt captures the opinion of many others when she writes that in this passage, "sentimental discourse is at its weakest, the kind its detractors must always have in mind: strained, hyperbolic, diffuse and digressive or associative, emotionally saturated, and heavily derivative … hardly the kind of language she could use in conversation to much advantage." But this response shows the flaws in reading *Mary: A Fiction* primarily through the question of its treatment of sensibility: doing so leaves out of view how such a passage might make evident the overall structure of sensibility's orientation beyond itself – and how it might, precisely through an associative entry, capture more than narrative alone can do. See Conger, *Mary Wollstonecraft and the Language of Sensibility* (Plainsboro, NJ: Associated University Presses, 1994), 47.

18 Kant, *Critique of the Power of Judgment*, 141.

19 Kant, *Critique of the Power of Judgment*, 145.

20 Readers at times place this novel in the category of the Bildungsroman; see, for example, Conger, *Mary Wollstonecraft and the Language of Sensibility*, 39.

21 Rajan, *Romantic Narrative*, 95, 96.

22 Timothy Michael is perceptive to point out that in her *Vindication of the Rights of Men*, Wollstonecraft brings about an "inward turn" to the authority of reason per se, thereby entering a domain she shares with Kantian critique; see Michael, *British Romanticism*, 90. But it is an urgent matter in reading the Romantics to ask how one might discern a similar turn outside of political treatises – in novels, for example – a question that I take up here.

23 Kant's ethical tale includes both a question as to whether a man might satisfy his lust on pain of being hanged immediately afterward and a question as to whether he might defy the sovereign's threat of death on the gallows. Lacan argues that these two questions may not be so opposed as Kant suggests, for one might well elevate one's passion to the status of duty, as if to conceive of love in the key of an ethical idealism. He comments that "it is possible that a

partisan of passion, who would be blind enough to combine it with questions of honor, would make trouble for Kant by forcing him to recognize that no occasion precipitates certain people more surely toward their goal than one that involves defiance of or even contempt for the gallows": *Écrits*, 660. On this passage, Žižek remarks that *"true 'passion' is uncannily close to the fulfilling of one's duty in spite of the external threat to it"*: see Slavoj Žižek, *For They Know Not What They Do* (New York: Verso, 1991), 239, italicized in the original. This insight, however, may point back to the even more fundamental point, tacit within the initial ethical tale itself, that (as Žižek puts it) "the very renunciation of 'pathological' enjoyment … brings about a certain surplus-enjoyment," so that the compliance with duty, which seems to defy all such pathological satisfactions, may itself be accompanied by the "stain" of enjoyment; see Žižek, *For They Know Not*, 231; cf. Slavoj Žižek, *The Sublime Object of Ideology* (New York: Verso, 1989), 81.

24 Readers have long attended to the same-sex passion evident in the novel, following up on Mary's husband's reference to the notion of "romantic friendship" (18). One of the first to do so was Lillian Faderman, who reads the fiction in the context of Wollstonecraft's own love for Fanny Blood; see *Surpassing the Love of Men: Romantic Friendship and Love between Women from the Renaissance to the Present* (New York: William Morrow, 1981), 138–42. For a more recent treatment of these themes see Ashley Tauchert, *Mary Wollstonecraft and the Accent of the Feminine* (Houndmills, UK: Palgrave, 2002), 33–53.

25 Wollstonecraft, *Vindication of the Rights of Woman*, 5:179.

26 Lacan, "Kant with Sade," 63, 71; for an alternative translation see *Écrits*, 654, 663. Wollstonecraft captures a similar insight early in the novel when she describes Mary as the "slave of compassion" (9), as if to suggest that she has become the instrument of the jouissance of care. On the ethics of desire, see Lacan, *The Ethics of Psychoanalysis*, 319–25. His most succinct formulation of this ethics is this: "I propose then that, from an analytical point of view, the only thing of which one can be guilty is of having given ground relative to one's desire" (319).

27 In this respect, the novel anticipates much of what William Godwin brings about in *Caleb Williams*, which as Rajan argues, "puts on trial the very genre of the Novel as judgment: the very reaching of a moral decision formalized by 'deciding' or resolving the plot," a gesture that "gives literature the role of a critique of judgment": see *Romantic Narrative*, 121, 122.

28 For a passage directly on these themes, see Rajan, *Romantic Narrative*, 12–14.

2 Godwin and the Formation of the Real

1 William Godwin, *Enquiry Concerning Political Justice and Its Influence on Modern Morals and Happiness* (Harmondsworth, UK: Penguin, 1985), 236. This text is based on the third and final edition published in 1798.

Unless otherwise noted, all further quotations will be based on this edition and cited in the text. When the first version differs significantly from this edition, I will refer to the relevant passage in the text edited by J.B. Priestley, 3 vols. (Toronto: University of Toronto Press, 1946), which provides an exhaustive guide to the differences between the versions of 1793, 1796, and 1798. In this case, in the 1793 version the second sentence reads: "Reason is the only legislator, and her decrees are irrevocable and uniform": Priestley, 3:156.

2 Useful guides to these dimensions of Bentham's work may be found in Ross Harrison, *Bentham* (London: Routledge, 1983), ch. 5; and Eldon J. Eisenach, "The Dimension of History in Bentham's Theory of Law," *Eighteenth-Century Studies* 16 (1983): 290–316.

3 On this point see Zupančič, *Ethics of the Real*, 79–105.

4 This last sentence does not appear in the 1793 version of the *Enquiry*.

5 Kant, *Critique of Practical Reason*, 30.

6 Godwin entirely rewrote the chapter cited here for the 1796 edition; for the 1793 chapter see Priestley 3:294–6.

7 Lacan, "Kant with Sade," 63, 71. For an alternative translation see *Écrits*, 654, 663.

8 Godwin, *Enquiry*, Priestley 3:292.

9 On the latter blunder see Marilyn May, "Publish and Perish: William Godwin, Mary Shelley, and the Public Appetite for Scandal," *Papers on Language and Literature* 26 (1990): 502–4.

10 William Godwin, *Caleb Williams* (New York: Norton, 1977), 1. All further references to this edition will be cited in the text.

11 Tilottama Rajan, *The Supplement of Reading: Figures of Understanding in Romantic Theory and Practice* (Ithaca, NY: Cornell University Press, 1990), 185–7.

12 In this way the novel anticipates Lacan's theory of the subject. As Joan Copjec argues, "The fact that it is materially impossible to say the whole truth – that truth always backs away from language, that words always fall short of their goal – *founds* the subject." *Read My Desire: Lacan against the Historicists* (Cambridge, MA: MIT Press, 1994), 35; emphasis in original.

13 For a useful, if at times reductive, treatment of this theme, see François Flahault, *Malice*, trans. Liz Heron (New York: Verso, 2003), 89–107.

14 John Bender argues that by endorsing sympathy in this scene, the novel accepts a mode of external judgment attacked in the *Enquiry* and thus contradicts Godwin's project; see Bender, "Impersonal Violence: The Penetrating Gaze and the Field of Narration in *Caleb Williams*," in *Critical Reconstructions: The Relationship of Fiction and Life*, ed. Robert M. Polhemus and Roger B. Henkle (Stanford, CA: Stanford University Press, 1994), 115, 119, 125. But the idea that private judgment could escape external determination

buys into the fantasy that the subject could precede social articulation – the fantasy, as I argue below, that generated the mode of violent spectatorship to begin with.

15 Randa Helfield, "Constructive Treason and Godwin's Treasonous Constructions," *Mosaic* 28 (1995): 54–5.

16 See appendix 2 of Godwin, *Caleb Williams*, 337.

17 William Godwin, *The Enquirer: Reflections on Education, Manners, and Literature* (New York: Augustus M. Kelley, 1965), 26.

18 For an exploration of the "heightened sense of a possible compatibility between truth and its artful expression" via Ciceronian rhetoric in "Godwin's later revisions of the novel," see Yasmin Solomonescu, "'A Plausible Tale': William Godwin's *Things as They Are*," *European Romantic Review* 25 (2014): 603.

19 Helfield, "Constructive Treason," 45–7, 58.

20 See appendix 2 of Godwin, *Caleb Williams*, 337.

21 For the relevant passage in Sade, see *Juliette*, 769–72. The notion of the "second death" is a central part of Lacan's discussion of ethics; see *The Ethics of Psychoanalysis*, 210–17.

22 In Lacan, one works through the fantasy by recognizing that the jouissance absent from the subject is barred from the Other – from the field of signification – as well. On the lack in the Other, see Lacan, *Écrits*, 693–4; and Žižek, *Sublime Object of Ideology*, 121–4.

23 Thus, as Rajan argues, the novel puts "the very genre of the Novel as judgment" on trial and "gives literature the role of a critique of judgment": see *Romantic Narrative*, 121, 122. In this respect, it revisits a mode of narrative autocritique that, as I argued in chapter 1, took place in *Mary: A Fiction*, though it does so more explicitly in relation to a scene of trial and judgment, as well as to the public use of rhetorical appeal. In effect, Godwin takes themes already broached in Wollstonecraft's tale and gives them more explicit treatment and emphasis.

24 Kant, *Political Writings*, 2nd ed., ed. Hans Reiss, trans. H.B. Nisbet (Cambridge: Cambridge University Press, 1991), 54–60; Lefort, *Democracy and Political Theory*, 17–19.

25 Several readers argue that the unspeakable truth of the self in this novel is to be read as the secret of same-sex desire: see Alex Gold Jr, "It's Only Love: The Politics of Passion in Godwin's *Caleb Williams*," *Texas Studies in Literature and Language* 19 (1977): 135–60; Eve Kosofsky Sedgwick, *Between Men: English Literature and Male Homosocial Desire* (New York: Columbia University Press, 1985), 83–96, 116–17; and Robert J. Corber, "Representing the 'Unspeakable': William Godwin and the Politics of Homophobia," *Journal of the History of Sexuality* 1 (1990): 85–101. But the notion that a sexual secret can reveal the truth of the subject requires a prior notion that there is a singular, hidden

truth of the subject, a site for unspeakable jouissance – the very notion that the novel eventually exposes as false.

26 For a discussion of the continuity between the two novels, especially with regard to the Kantian paralogism evident in each – that is, the use of an "illogical presupposition" violating "the categories through which we experience the world" – a trope that defines both Caleb and St Leon as characters and that shapes the disputable fictional constructions in each text, see Rajan, *Romantic Narrative*, 156; cf. 153, 163–4.

27 William Godwin, *St Leon* (New York: Oxford University Press, 1994), 302. Further citations will be given in the text.

28 On the "lack of the lack," see Mladen Dolar, "'I Shall Be with You on Your Wedding-Night': Lacan and the Uncanny," *October* 58 (1991): 13.

29 Lacan, *Ethics of Psychoanalysis*, 260.

30 This passage from Sade's last testament appears in Maurice Lever, *Sade: A Biography*, trans. Arthur Goldhammer (San Diego: Harcourt Brace, 1993), 563.

31 See Thomas Malthus, *An Essay on the Principle of Population* (1798), ed. Geoffrey Gilbert (New York: Oxford University Press, 1993), 3–4, 74–87; Kenneth Smith, *The Malthusian Controversy* (London: Routledge, 1951), 122–31; and William Godwin, *Of Population: An Enquiry Concerning the Power of Increase in the Numbers of Mankind, Being an Answer to Mr Malthus's Essay on That Subject* (New York: Augustus M. Kelley, 1964).

32 On the shift from the idea of natural desire to scarcity as the premise of socially constituted needs, see Nicholas Xenos, *Scarcity and Modernity* (London: Routledge, 1989); on an account of the emergence of a mode of consumer desire very like desire as understood in Lacanian theory, see Colin Campbell, *The Romantic Ethic and the Spirit of Modern Consumerism* (Oxford: Basil Blackwell, 1987). Godwin's novels evoke the emergent sphere of serialized literary consumption, as several readers have noted: see Kristin Leaver, "Pursuing Conversations: *Caleb Williams* and the Romantic Construction of the Reader," *Studies in Romanticism* 33 (1994): 589–610; and Andrew McCann, "William Godwin and the Pathological Public Sphere: Theorizing Communicative Action in the 1790s," *Prose Studies* 18 (1995): 199–222. *St Leon* displays the close alignment of this serialized community with new conceptions in several domains, including the subject, desire, power, knowledge, scarcity, and consumption.

33 On this aspect of Bentham's project see my *Monstrous Society*, 112–17.

34 William Godwin, "Essay of History and Romance," in *Political and Philosophical Writings of William Godwin*, ed. Mark Philp, vol. 5, *Educational and Literary Writings*, ed. Pamela Clemit (London: William Pickering, 1993), 290–301; Jon Klancher, "Godwin and the Republican Romance: Genre, Politics, and Contingency in Cultural History," *Modern Language Quarterly* 56 (1995): 156, 159.

35 See Klancher, "Godwin and the Republican Romance," 164.
36 For a discussion of the link between *St Leon* and *Frankenstein* that takes up several of the themes of this chapter, see my *Monstrous Society*, 193–8.
37 According to Mark Philp, the three versions of the *Enquiry* emerged out of Godwin's evolving participation in the radical circles of London in the late 1780s and 1790s. These circles narrowed considerably in the final years of the latter decade as the possibility of radical social change dissipated. See Philp, *Godwin's Political Justice* (Ithaca, NY: Cornell University Press, 1986), 122–9, 162–4, 169–74, 219–21.

3 Undead Subjectivity in Wordsworth's Alpine Sublime

1 All quotations from Wordsworth are taken from William Wordsworth, *Major Works*, ed. Stephen Gill (Oxford: Oxford University Press, 1984). Further references to the 1805 *Prelude* will be given in the text.
2 The following argument relies on my previous treatment of this text in *Wordsworthian Errancies: The Poetics of Cultural Dismemberment* (Baltimore, MD: Johns Hopkins University Press, 1994), 180–206. On the covenantal resonances of the "analogy passage," see Mary Jacobus, *Romanticism, Writing and Sexual Difference: Essays on "The Prelude"* (New York: Clarendon Press, 1989), 277–9. On the five-book *Prelude* see Jonathan Wordsworth, "The Five-Book *Prelude* of Early Spring 1804," *JEGP* 76 (1977): 1–25; Joseph F. Kishel, "The 'Analogy Passage' from Wordsworth's Five-Book *Prelude*," *Studies in Romanticism* 18 (1979): 271–85; Robin Jarvis, "The Five-Book *Prelude*: A Reconsideration," *JEGP* 80 (1981): 528–51; and Jacobus, *Romanticism, Writing, and Sexual Difference*, 276–86. For a reconstruction of the poem see William Wordsworth, *The Five-Book Prelude*, ed. Duncan Wu (Oxford: Blackwell, 1997); for the "analogy passage" itself, see (among others) William Wordsworth, *The Prelude: 1799, 1805, 1850*, ed. Jonathan Wordsworth, M.H. Abrams, and Stephen Gill (New York: Norton, 1979), 496–9; and Wordsworth, *The Five-Book Prelude*, appendix 1.
3 For my previous discussion of "Michael," see *Wordsworthian Errancies*, 157–79.
4 Marjorie Hope Nicholson, *Mountain Gloom and Mountain Glory: The Development of the Aesthetics of the Infinite* (Ithaca, NY: Cornell University Press, 1959); Ernest Bernhardt-Kabisch, "The Stone and the Shell: Wordsworth, Cataclysm, and the Myth of Glaucus," *Studies in Romanticism* 24 (1985): 455–90; Theresa M. Kelley, *Wordsworth's Revisionary Aesthetics* (Cambridge: Cambridge University Press, 1988), 14–23, 100–8, 173–86; Alan Bewell, *Wordsworth and the Enlightenment: Nature, Man, and Society in the Experimental Poetry* (New Haven, CT: Yale University Press, 1989), 236–79; Noah Heringman, *Romantic Rocks, Aesthetic Geology* (Ithaca, NY:

Cornell University Press, 2004); and John Wyatt, *Wordsworth and the Geologists* (Cambridge: Cambridge University Press, 1995).

5 Thomas Malthus, *An Essay on the Principle of Population* (1803), ed. Donald Winch (Cambridge: Cambridge University Press, 1992), 249; Mary Shelley, *The Last Man*, vol. 4 of *The Novels and Selected Works of Mary Shelley*, ed. Jane Blumberg with Nora Crook (London: William Pickering, 1996), 325–6.

6 Jean-Pierre Mileur, *Literary Revisionism and the Burden of Modernity* (Berkeley: University of California Press, 1985), 78–191.

7 Hans Blumenberg, *The Legitimacy of the Modern Age*, trans. Robert M. Wallace (Cambridge, MA: MIT Press, 1985), 199, 206.

8 Gourgouris, *Lessons in Secular Criticism*, 65–89, argues that the secular does best to take up a stance of indifference to belief or disbelief in God, setting aside the question altogether – and thereby replicates the gesture of bracketing outlined here. But he rightly insists that in doing so one enacts "a decision that has no foundation in anything that exists prior or exterior to it" (20), "stake[s] out a position of living without presuming a content for the void of the Real" (69), and accepts the overall contours of the process of secularization, which is necessarily ongoing, unfinished (29). His stance thus exemplifies the logic of the internal limit explored in this book, though he neither discerns the direct links between aspects of his position nor accounts for the emergence of his stance at a specific juncture in the trajectory of the West.

9 José Casanova, *Public Religions in the Modern World* (Chicago: University of Chicago Press, 1994), 57–66, 211–34.

10 Mark Canuel, *Religion, Toleration, and British Writing, 1790–1830* (Cambridge: Cambridge University Press, 2002), 36.

11 Jameson, *The Political Unconscious*, 291.

12 Charles Taylor, *A Secular Age* (Cambridge, MA: Harvard University Press, 2007), 221–69.

13 Colin Jager, *The Book of God: Secularization and Design in the Romantic Era* (Philadelphia: University of Pennsylvania Press, 2007).

14 Taylor, *A Secular Age*, 322–51. See Rossi, *The Dark Abyss of Time*. For a useful overview of how this sense of the much vaster reach of time emerged over the course of early modern scientific investigation, see Martin J.S. Rudwick, *Bursting the Limits of Time: The Reconstruction of Geohistory in the Age of Revolution* (Chicago: University of Chicago Press, 2005).

15 James Hutton, "Theory of the Earth; or an Investigation of the Laws Observable in the Composition, Dissolution, and Restoration of the Land upon the Globe," *Transactions of the Royal Society of Edinburgh* 1 (1788): 304.

16 For a broader interpretation of symbolic exchange within the context of late eighteenth-century British culture, see Collings, *Monstrous Society*, 26–58.

17 E.P. Thompson, *Customs in Common: Studies in Traditional Popular Culture* (New York: New Press, 1993), 185–258.
18 Collings, *Monstrous Society*.
19 For a pivotal account of the effect of Copernicus and Galileo on the history of the West, see Hannah Arendt, *The Human Condition*, 2nd ed. (Chicago: University of Chicago Press, 1958), 257–80.
20 See Kant, *Natural Science*, ed. Eric Watkins, trans. Lewis White Beck et al. (New York: Cambridge University Press, 2012). On the "theory of the heavens," see 182–308; on the Lisbon earthquake, 327–36. On the greatness of God in the context of the inevitable decay of the known universe, see 269–73; on theodicy in the wake of the earthquake, see 362–4. For the reference to "the whole of nature" and humanity's being "in the dark," see 363.
21 For Kant's pivotal suspension of any philosophical claim to have established a link between a telos for nature and for humanity, see *Critique of the Power of Judgment*, 319; see also the entirety of §88. For a searching analysis of Kant's teleological thought, see Geoffrey Bennington, *Kant on the Frontier: Philosophy, Politics, and the Ends of the Earth* (New York: Fordham University Press, 2017), 144–97.
22 Caygill, *Art of Judgement*, 2–3.
23 Thus it simply will not do to suggest, as does Judith Butler, that because critique "inquir[es] into the conditions that make judgment possible," it follows that "critique is prior to judgment": see Butler, "The Sensibility of Critique: A Response to Asad and Mahmood," in *Is Critique Secular? Blasphemy, Injury, and Free Speech*, by Talal Asad, Wendy Brown, Judity Butler, and Saba Mahmood (Berkeley, CA: Townsend Center for the Humanities, 2009), 109. Critique is judgment's enquiry into itself – and thus necessarily falls into what Caygill describes as an aporia (*Art of Judgement*). Nor will it do to endorse the contradiction whereby Gourgouris, claiming that Kantian ethics, "putting the subject in God's place," in effect "signifies the *internalization* of transcendence" into the ethical subject (*Lessons in Secular Criticism*, 36), also argues that critique is secular (24). One does better to argue that Kant's project brings about a failed or negative internalization of transcendence – producing not the secular but rather an *aporia* in the secular.
24 Deleuze, *Difference and Repetition*, 146; emphasis in the original.
25 Lyotard translates the Kantian term *Widerstreit* (opposition, antagonism) as "differend"; see his *Lessons*, 124. For Lyotard's most extensive discussion of the differend in the analytic of the sublime, see *Lessons*, 123–46. Lyotard's analysis of Kant more broadly constitutes a major portion of his masterwork, *The Differend*; see especially xiii, 61–5, 118–27, 130–5, 161–71.
26 Lyotard, *The Differend*, xi.
27 On this moment of disidentification see Mileur, *Literary Revisionism*, 215–16.

28 John Milton, *Complete Poems and Major Prose*, ed. Merritt Y. Hughes (Indianapolis: Odyssey Press, 1957), *Paradise Lost* 11.827–9.

29 This argument relies on my discussion of related themes in *Wordsworthian Errancies*, 233–6.

30 See the classic discussion of this theme in the antinomy of pure reason in Kant, *Critique of Pure Reason*, trans. Paul Guyer and Allen W. Wood (Cambridge: Cambridge University Press, 1998), 517–30.

31 Lyotard, *Lessons*, 143–6.

32 Exemplary instances include Alan Liu, *Wordsworth: The Sense of History* (Stanford, CA: Stanford University Press, 1989), 3–31; and Simon Bainbridge, *Napoleon and English Romanticism* (Cambridge: Cambridge University Press, 1995), 54–94. These readings overlook how the passage's revision of Wordsworth's Salisbury Plain poems elaborates on the poetics of errancy introduced in them and thereby invokes the poet's understanding of cultural dismemberment following England's going to war with France; on these themes, see *Wordsworthian Errancies*, 194–9, 263n18.

33 Pfau, *Romantic Moods*, 11.

34 For the larger argument regarding Pfau's historiography on which the present remarks are based, see my "Troping Mood."

35 For a related discussion of Wordsworth's construction of historicity in "Tintern Abbey," see my essay, "The Force of Indirection."

36 Matthew Lewis, *The Monk*, ed. Howard Anderson (New York: Oxford University Press, 1973), 159–63. For a discussion of the formal significance of this episode within that novel, see Collings, *Monstrous Society*, 152–60.

37 Geoffrey Hartman, *Wordsworth's Poetry: 1787–1814* (New Haven, CT: Yale University Press, 1971), 63; for the overall discussion of these passages, see 33–69. For a key earlier discussion of the ambiguity in the Snowdon passage – the juxtaposition of harmony and formlessness, the sacramental and the mysterious – which anticipates aspects of the present argument, see David Ferry, *The Limits of Mortality: An Essay on Wordsworth's Major Poems* (Middletown, CT: Wesleyan University Press, 1959), 159, 169, 171.

38 On the rewriting of the Alpine passages in book 13, see Jager, *The Book of God*, 177–87; Collings, *Wordsworthian Errancies*, 203–4. Laurence S. Lockridge is right to point out that in *The Prelude* overall, "moral consciousness and purpose is characterized by reversals, sudden insights, strides into new states of being, gaps, surprises, and centers of indifference": see *The Ethics of Romanticism* (Cambridge: Cambridge University Press, 1989), 234. In that case, the Alpine passage is not alone in disrupting the reader's expectations of coherent narrative; indeed, as Lockridge suggests as well, the poem "*does not answer to* our need for narrative" (229). But then it is all the more suspect that the poet attempts to reverse the import of the Alpine passage in the epic's final book and on that basis to conclude in a tone of resounding certainty.

39 Here I hint that Wordsworth may step back from the implications of the Alpine passage out of a tacit preference for another relation to the world of things; on his ethical relation to that world, in which he includes human beings, see the exemplary discussion in Adam Potkay, *Wordsworth's Ethics* (Baltimore, MD: Johns Hopkins University Press, 2013), 71–89, especially 87. But a full-fledged ethics of things would accept not only the quieter mode of a poem such as "Tintern Abbey" but also the more traumatic encounter visible in the Alpine passage; a retreat from trauma in preference for the ordinary in some sense betrays what could be a truly capacious stance.
40 Zupančič, *Ethics of the Real*, 96–104.

4 Byron's Poetics of the Real

1 One must therefore be cautious in using a term such as "autonomy" to describe the destination of *Manfred*; see, for example, Frederick W. Shilstone, *Byron and the Myth of Tradition* (Lincoln: University of Nebraska Press, 1988), 153–71, especially 169. While this reading is useful, it takes for granted that Byron's key task in the poem is to rid himself of various forms of external imposition or constraint; it does not consider the possibility that rather than achieving radical self-determination, such a subject may find itself exposed to even harsher judgments it metes out upon itself, judgments from within the subject that exceed the subject per se. This aspect of Manfred's subjectivity, which I will call "singularity," thus sharply distinguishes it from the form of self-possession familiar within liberal notions of autonomy. For a discussion of how Manfred's subjectivity exceeds him as subject, see the argument later in this chapter. I will use the term "independence" to indicate the status Manfred seeks when he refuses external constraint; such independence, however, eventually gives way to singularity, a more difficult state.
2 Jonathan David Gross, *Byron: The Erotic Liberal* (New York: Rowman and Littlefield, 2001), 6–7. On Byron and negative liberty, see Peter Graham, "Byron, *Manfred*, Negativity, and Freedom," in *Liberty and Poetic Licence: New Essays on Byron*, ed. Bernard Beatty, Tony Howe, and Charles E. Robinson (Liverpool: Liverpool University Press, 2008), 50–9.
3 Alan Rawes is thus right to argue that Byron's stance includes much more than his apparent liberalism; see Rawes, "Byron's Romantic Calvinism," *Byron Journal* 40 (2012): 129–30. But it is not clear that Rawes is thus correct to place the poet's position within the Calvinist tradition; see Rawes, "Byron's Romantic Calvinism," 129–41. Although his relation to the liberal political tradition is long and complex, on occasion Foucault explicitly accepted a certain degree of liberty as a necessary precondition for his sexual ethics; see *Foucault Live: Collected Interviews, 1961–1984*, ed.

Sylvère Lotringer, trans. Lysa Hochroth and John Johnston (New York: Semiotext(e), 1996), 434.

4 For a wide-ranging argument covering much of the relevant critical tradition on Byron's scepticism, see Terence Allan Hoagwood, *Byron's Dialectic: Skepticism and the Critique of Culture* (Lewisburg, PA: Bucknell University Press, 1993), 15–33; for his discussion of scepticism in *Manfred*, see 34–47. For a key discussion of how Byron displaces philosophical scepticism through its literary articulation, see Anthony Howe, *Byron and the Forms of Thought* (Liverpool: Liverpool University Press, 2013), 15–42.

5 Hoagwood, *Byron's Dialectic*, 43.

6 Stephen C. Behrendt, "*Manfred* and Skepticism," in *Approaches to Teaching Byron's Poetry*, ed. Frederick W. Shilstone (New York: Modern Language Association, 1991), 121.

7 Emily A. Bernhard Jackson, *The Development of Byron's Philosophy of Knowledge: Certain in Uncertainty* (New York: Palgrave Macmillan, 2010), 133, 152.

8 On catastrophism in *Cain* and *Don Juan*, see Christine Kenyon Jones, "'When This World Shall Be *Former*': Catastrophism as Imaginative Theory for the Younger Romantics," *Romanticism on the Net* 24 (2001), https://www.erudit.org/revue/ron/2001/v/n24/006000ar.html; and Chris Washington, "Byron's Speculative Turn: Visions of Posthuman Life in *Cain*," *Essays in Romanticism* 22 (2015): 73–95. On Byron's use of geology see Ralph O'Connor, "Mammoths and Maggots: Byron and the Geology of Cuvier," *Romanticism* 5 (1999): 26–42; and on his impact on geological writing over the ensuing decades see O'Connor, "Byron's Afterlife and the Emancipation of Geology," in *Liberty and Poetic Licence: New Essays on Byron*, ed. Bernard Beatty, Tony Howe, and Charles E. Robinson (Liverpool: Liverpool University Press, 2008), 147–64. For a discussion of Byron within the popular geological writing in his time and after – in a book that incorporates the above essays – see O'Connor, *The Earth on Show: Fossils and the Poetics of Popular Science, 1802–1856* (Chicago: University of Chicago Press, 2007).

9 Kant, *Critique of the Power of Judgment*, 320.

10 See Kant, *Natural Science*, esp. 269–73.

11 On the Lucretian context for "Darkness," see Martin Priestman, *Romantic Atheism: Poetry and Freethought, 1780–1830* (New York: Cambridge University Press, 1999), 239. See Lucretius, *On the Nature of Things: De Rerum Natura*, ed. and trans. Anthony M. Esolen (Baltimore, MD: Johns Hopkins University Press, 1995), 5.91–9, 5.301–5, 6.43–79, 6.1089–285. Lucretius's discussion of the plague follows his account of cyclones, earthquakes, and volcanoes, all of which he attributes not to the gods but to natural causes. His materialist theory, in short, shares much with the premises of eighteenth-century

scientific investigation of natural disaster. Solar astronomy did not mature enough to provide a useful hypothesis about stellar lifetimes until the late 1910s and early 1920s, when Arthur Stanley Eddington made a signal advance in the understanding of the sun's internal constitution; see Karl Hufbauer, *Exploring the Sun: Solar Science since Galileo* (Baltimore, MD: Johns Hopkins University Press, 1991), 98–101.

12 On the Tambora volcano and "Darkness," see Gillen D'Arcy Wood, *Tambor: The Eruption That Changed the World* (Princeton, NJ: Princeton University Press, 2014), 66–9.

13 For recent philosophical discussions of solar death, see Jean-François Lyotard, *The Inhuman: Reflections on Time*, trans. Geoffrey Bennington and Rachel Bowlby (Stanford, CA: Stanford University Press, 1991), 10, 9; and Ray Brassier, Nihil *Unbound: Enlightenment and Extinction* (New York: Palgrave Macmillan, 2007), 223–5. Unfortunately, I do not have space here to take up the question of Byron's place in relation to speculative realism. For an important discussion relevant in this context, see Washington, "Byron's Speculative Turn."

14 All quotations from *Manfred* are taken from George Gordon (Lord) Byron, *Lord Byron: The Complete Poetical Works*, ed. Jerome J. McGann, vol. 4 (New York: Oxford University Press, 1986).

15 Marie-Hélène Huet, *The Culture of Disaster* (Chicago: University of Chicago Press, 2012), 3–4.

16 Percy Bysshe Shelley, *Shelley's Poetry and Prose*, 2nd ed., ed. Donald H. Reiman and Neil Fraistat (New York: Norton, 2002), *Mont Blanc*, 117–18; see 98.

17 Stephen Cheeke, *Byron and Place: History, Translation, Nostalgia* (New York: Palgrave Macmillan, 2003), 90.

18 See Lyotard, *The Inhuman*, 9–10; and Brassier, Nihil *Unbound*, 223.

19 Søren Kierkegaard, *Christian Discourses: And The Lilies of the Field and the Birds of the Air and Three Discourses at the Communion on Fridays*, trans. Walter Lowrie (Princeton, NJ: Princeton University Press, 1971), 214.

20 The poem reinforces this reading when Manfred later declares, "I dwell in my despair – / And live – and live for ever" (2.2.149–50).

21 Manfred's traumatic immortality affiliates him, of course, with the figure of the Wandering Jew, central to various strands of British Gothic fiction, although the play's ending poses a sharp contrast between Manfred and the wanderers who are not permitted to relinquish their immortality. But it is not simply a Gothic motif, for it appears in another form in Keats's *Fall of Hyperion*, whose narrator is forced to experience the slow time of immortal apprehension while still within his "own weak mortality"; for the Keatsian narrator, immortality is traumatic even though it is not a feature of his own subjectivity. See Keats, *The Poems of John Keats*, ed. Jack Stillinger (London: Heinemann, 1978), *The Fall of Hyperion*, 1.389, p. 488.

22 Kant, *Critique of Practical Reason*, 104.
23 For another discussion of the intersection of the poem's concerns with Kant's treatment of subjectivity and time, see William D. Melaney, "Ambiguous Difference: Ethical Concern in *Manfred*," *New Literary History* 36 (2005): 461–75, especially 463.
24 Cheeke, *Byron and Place*, 86, 89.
25 Alan Richardson writes, "The strategy adopted by each of the spirits whom Manfred summons lies in first granting him an appearance of the power he thirsts for, then asserting a greater power, beguiling and outfacing him in turn as they attempt to enslave him." Richardson, *A Mental Theater: Poetic Drama and Consciousness in the Romantic Age* (University Park: Pennsylvania State University Press, 1988), 46. The inability of the spirits to convey any of the knowledge Manfred seeks confirms the argument that the poem adheres to a largely sceptical stance.
26 Zupančič, *Ethics of the Real*, 85.
27 Zupančič, *Ethics of the Real*, 93–4.
28 Zupančič, *Ethics of the Real*, 120, 127.
29 Zupančič, *Ethics of the Real*, 127.
30 Frederick Garber, *Self, Text, and Romantic Irony: The Example of Byron* (Princeton, NJ: Princeton University Press, 1988), 134.
31 Along the same lines, Richardson notes that "Manfred's incest can be seen as regressively antisocial, another sign of his alienation from humankind" (*A Mental Theater*, 51–2).
32 Insofar as *Manfred* experiences a satisfaction that remains structurally foreclosed in *Alastor*, it is aligned with *Frankenstein*, which also imagines the realization of the impossible wish of *Alastor*. The structural counterpart of Manfred's consummation with Astarte is the creature's coming to life. Thus that moment of consummation, like the creature's living body, exemplifies the Real of the subject – a monstrous dimension that the subject will ordinarily do anything not to encounter. For a relevant discussion of how the creature in *Frankenstein* shatters the illusion of subjective coherence based on the mirror-stage, see my essay, "The Monster and the Maternal Thing: Mary Shelley's Critique of Ideology," in Mary Shelley, *Frankenstein*, ed. Johanna M. Smith (New York: Bedford's, 2016), 323–39.
33 On the strategy in Matthew Lewis's *The Monk* of eclipsing references to same-sex desire through heterosexual, and eventually incestuous, coupling, see Clara Tuite, "Cloistered Closets: Enlightenment Pornography, the Confessional State, Homosexual Persecution, and *The Monk*," *Romanticism on the Net* 8 (November 1997), https://www.erudit.org/revue/ron/1997/v/n8/005766ar.html. One could argue that in *Manfred* Byron pursues a similar strategy for effacing the potentially even more scandalous theme of sodomy through the theme of sibling incest.

34 Martyn Corbett, *Byron and Tragedy* (New York: St Martin's Press, 1988), 46.
35 Zupančič, *Ethics of the Real*, 96, 100.
36 Lord Byron, *"So Late into the Night": Byron's Letters and Journals*, vol. 5, *1816–17*, ed. Leslie A. Marchand (London: John Murray, 1976), 257.
37 See Lee Edelman, *No Future: Queer Theory and the Death Drive* (Durham, NC: Duke University Press, 2004), 1–31.
38 Copjec, *Imagine There's No Woman*, 96.
39 All quotations from *Childe Harold's Pilgrimage* are taken from *Lord Byron: The Complete Poetical Works*, vol. 2, *Childe Harold's Pilgrimage* (1980). Numbers refer to lines unless otherwise noted.
40 For earlier arguments that emphasize how Byron achieves a breakthrough in *Manfred* on which he builds in his later works, see Edward E. Bostetter, *The Romantic Ventriloquists: Wordsworth, Coleridge, Keats, Shelley, Byron* (Seattle: University of Washington Press, 1963), 278, 281; and Stuart M. Sperry, "Byron and the Meaning of 'Manfred,'" *Criticism* 16 (1974): 189–202. Although I shift from *Manfred* itself to the moment of its deployment shortly thereafter, my argument owes much to these assessments. The shift I outline here may have some bearing on explaining the change from the early to late phases of the Byronic career as traced by Jerome Christensen in his landmark study, *Lord Byron's Strength: Romantic Writing and Commercial Society* (Baltimore, MD: Johns Hopkins University Press, 1993).
41 This argument may also help explain why *Manfred* already contains comic elements that typify *Don Juan*: as Jerome J. McGann points out, its highly packed pun on "awful" (2.4.164) introduces an apparently inappropriate but complex resonance into the serious texture of the poem. See McGann, *Byron and Romanticism*, ed. James Soderholm (New York: Cambridge University Press, 2002), 184–5.

5 Ethical Destitution in Shelley's "The Triumph of Life"

1 All quotations from the poetry and prose of Percy Bysshe Shelley, unless otherwise noted, are taken from *Shelley's Poetry and Prose*; line numbers for the poems and page numbers for the prose writings will be given in the text.
2 On "the intellectual system," see "On Life," *Shelley's Poetry and Prose*, 507; on the pervading Spirit, see "There Is No God," a redaction of "The Necessity of Atheism" published as a note to *Queen Mab*, in Shelley, *The Complete Poetry of Percy Bysshe Shelley*, ed. Donald H. Reiman and Neil Fraistat, vol. 2 (Baltimore, MD: Johns Hopkins University Press, 2004), 263.
3 Michael A. Vicario, *Shelley's Intellectual System and Its Epicurean Background* (New York: Routledge, 2007), 63, 69. With regard to Shelley's theistic atomism, his restricted scepticism, and his criteria of truth, Vicario's study

serves as an important corrective to the account of Shelley's scepticism provided by Terence Allan Hoagwood, *Skepticism and Ideology: Shelley's Political Prose and Its Philosophical Context from Bacon to Marx* (Iowa City: University of Iowa Press, 1988). For an initial study of Shelley's scepticism, see C.E. Pulos, *The Deep Truth: A Study of Shelley's Scepticism* (Lincoln: University of Nebraska Press, 1962). For a pivotal example of theistic atomism especially influential in the British tradition, see the first chapter of Ralph Cudworth, *The True Intellectual System of the Universe* (Bristol, UK: Thoemmes Press, 1995), 1:1–99.

4 The notion that things exist only as perceived appears several times in William Drummond, *Academical Questions*, vol. 1 (London: Bulmer, 1805), though it is meant to apply to phenomena or to mental distinctions applying to phenomena, rather than to such entities as God or a divine cause. For an instance of this notion see 77; on the final cause, in a passage that declares the "doctrine of Epicurus" to be "monstrous," see 336. On Drummond's revival of the classical fourfold causal theory and his maintaining only efficient and final causes, see Vicario, *Shelley's Intellectual System*, 157, 172. While Drummond hardly wishes to return to the positions of Aristotle or Aquinas, his revival of the final cause nevertheless strongly undercuts the nominalist positions at the inception of modernity. His work on the restrictions on divine power (Vicario, *Shelley's Intellectual System*, 168–73) has a similar import. His writing thus constitutes an important challenge to central features of the modern philosophical tradition. For a discussion of the devastating effects of the nominalism of William of Ockham – both in his suspending the notion of the final cause and in placing God above any ethical relation to his creation – see Pfau, *Minding the Modern*, 160–82.

5 On the consistency of this passage with Drummond's position, see Vicario, *Shelley's Intellectual System*, 154.

6 Thus Colin Jager is right to locate *Mont Blanc* "after atheism," that is, in a position that resists the imposition of secularism (or, for that matter, of belief) by the state. See Jager, *Unquiet Things: Secularism in the Romantic Age* (Philadelphia: University of Pennsylvania Press, 2015), 224–43, especially 242. The argument that follows is in extended dialogue with Jager's account, for it aims in part to suggest that Shelley is even more resistant to the radical Enlightenment and the claims of secularism than Jager suggests.

7 For a reading of *Mont Blanc* that ties its use of "vacancy" to that which appears in the essay, see Christopher Hitt, "Shelley's Unwriting of Mont Blanc," *Texas Studies in Literature and Language* 47 (2005): 139–66.

8 For a representative statement along these lines well known to Shelley, see Drummond, *Academical Questions*, 153–4.

9 On Gilbert Wakefield's reconstruction of Lucretius's attack on superstition in an edition of *De Rerum Natura* that influenced Shelley, see Vicario, *Shelley's Intellectual System*, 108–19.

10 While Shelley in some ways may appear to be a political liberal, as his advocacy for rights in his early "Declaration of Rights" would suggest, in fact he insists on rights as a precondition for living the ethical life: see *The Complete Works of Percy Bysshe Shelley*, ed. Roger Ingpen and Walter E. Peck (New York: Scribner's, 1928), 5:271–5. The attempt to draw a sharp distinction between such ethical labour and the demands of liberalism, visible throughout contemporary virtue theory – especially in such founding texts as Alasdair MacIntyre, *After Virtue* – fails to take into consideration the basic political and social agency necessary for a subject to embark on living such a life. For a discussion of liberalism as a precondition for ethical living, see Michel Foucault, *Foucault Live*, 434.

11 Shelley, *The Letters of Percy Bysshe Shelley*, ed. Frederick L. Jones (Oxford: Clarendon, 1964), 1:499; P.M.S. Dawson, "'The Mask of Darkness': Metaphor, Myth, and History in Shelley's 'The Triumph of Life,'" in *History & Myth: Essays on English Romantic Literature*, ed. Stephen C. Behrendt (Detroit: Wayne State University Press, 1990), 240.

12 For a discussion of Shelley's response to the effects of the Tambora volcano on the glaciers surrounding Mont Blanc, see Gillen D'Arcy Wood, *Tambor*, 152; on the prospect of an indefinite expansion of those glaciers, see Shelley, *Letters*, 1:499.

13 Quoted in Carl Grabo, *A Newton among Poets: Shelley's Use of Science in "Prometheus Unbound"* (1930; repr., New York: Gordian, 1968), 51, 84; see also Hugh Roberts, *Shelley and the Chaos of History: A New Politics of Poetry* (University Park: Pennsylvania State University Press, 1997), 244. But as Grabo soon points out, in June 1818 Herschel read a paper announcing his sense that the universe was much larger than he previously anticipated, and thus may have a much longer duration as well, taking a position of which Shelley may never have become aware; see Grabo, *A Newton among Poets*, 85–6, 165.

14 Harold Bloom, *Shelley's Mythmaking* (New Haven, CT: Yale University Press, 1959), 232–6. Bloom discusses as well the poem's place within the broader evocations of the *merkabah* in the New Testament, Dante, and Blake; see 232–44.

15 Alan M. Weinberg, *Shelley's Italian Experience* (New York: St Martin's Press, 1991), 206–7, 213, 216.

16 Weinberg, *Shelley's Italian Experience*, 218–19.

17 Here I allude to the essay in which Jacques Derrida addresses *The Triumph of Life*: "Living On," in *Deconstruction and Criticism* (New York: Seabury, 1979), 75–176. His title alludes to the sentence that appears in Shelley's essay "On Life": "We live on, and in living we lose the apprehension of life" (506).

18 For the reconception of the Freudian death drive in the late Lacan, see Slavoj Žižek, *The Ticklish Subject: The Absent Centre of Political Ontology* (New York: Verso, 1999), 290–7.

19 The poem thematizes the undead drive as well in its faster, more decentred deployment of the terza rima, as well as the reckless forward movement of its composition. On its disrupted use of terza rima, see Jerrold E. Hogle, *Shelley's Process: Radical Transference and the Development of His Major Works* (New York: Oxford University Press, 1988), 337; cf. Weinberg, *Shelley's Italian Experience*, 209–11; on the "compulsive and nearly regressive energy" of the poem's use of that stanza, see Joel Faflak, "The Difficult Education of Shelley's 'Triumph of Life,'" *Keats-Shelley Journal* 58 (2009): 74, 75; and on how the poem's manuscript "encourages us to read the poem as a palimpsest of traces, as the site of its own constant displacement," see Rajan, *Supplement of Reading*, 341.

20 On defamiliarization, see Shelley, "A Defence of Poetry," in *Shelley's Poetry and Prose*, 517, 533. On the poem's displacement of the experiential through its radical critique of consumption, see Arkady Plotnitsky, "All Shapes of Light: The Quantum Mechanical Shelley," in *Shelley: Poet and Legislator of the World*, ed. Betty T. Bennett and Stuart Curran (Baltimore, MD: Johns Hopkins University Press, 1996), 161–80.

21 William A. Ulmer, *Shelleyan Eros: The Rhetoric of Romantic Love* (Princeton, NJ: Princeton University Press, 1990), 161.

22 For an exemplary reading of the poem along these lines, see J. Hillis Miller, *The Linguistic Moment: From Wordsworth to Stevens* (Princeton, NJ: Princeton University Press, 1985), 114–79.

23 See Rajan, *Deconstruction and the Remainders of Phenomenology*.

24 Roberts, *Shelley and the Chaos of History*, 472–3. In a similar vein, John Mason Good, in the "Life of Lucretius" that appears in his translation of *De Rerum Natura*, argues that the doctrine of Lucretius "was perfectly coincident with the creed of almost every modern geologist": see Good, *The Nature of Things: A Didactic Poem* (London, 1805), lxxx. For a discussion of the place of Good's translation in Shelley's reception of Lucretius, see Vicario, *Shelley's Intellectual System*, 121–52.

25 Vicario, *Shelley's Intellectual System*, 190, referring to Lucretius, 2.599–643; Roberts, *Shelley and the Chaos of History*, 398.

26 Roberts, *Shelley and the Chaos of History*, 222, 251. Roberts works extensively with the reading of Lucretius provided by Michel Serres, translated as *The Birth of Physics*, ed. David Webb, trans. Jack Hawkes (Manchester: Clinamen Press, 2000). In an argument that extends the sense of chaos outlined by Roberts, Arkady Plotnitsky, noting how Paul de Man finds the poem's transitions "brusque and unmotivated," suggests that they may rather be "both motivated and unmotivated, discrete and continuous, causal and acausal – in short, complementary in all their aspects," in which case the

poem "tells us that the power of death – and of life – is always a Democritean play of complementary chance and necessity, multiplicity and oneness, centering and decentering": see Plotnitsky, "All Shapes of Light," 168–9; Paul de Man, "Shelley Disfigured," in *The Rhetoric of Romanticism* (New York: Columbia University Press, 1984), 117.

27 Amanda Goldstein, "Growing Old Together: Lucretian Materialism in Shelley's 'Poetry of Life,'" *Representations* 128 (2014): 62, 63.

28 Goldstein, "Growing Old Together," 63, 64; see Monique Allewaert, "Toward a Materialist Figuration: A Slight Manifesto," *English Language Notes* 51 (2013): 61–77. For Goldstein's later and broader discussion of a Lucretian poetics in Romanticism, see her *Sweet Science: Romantic Materialism and the New Logics of Life* (Chicago: University of Chicago Press, 2017).

29 Goldstein, "Growing Old Together," 70, 71.

30 Goldstein, "Growing Old Together," 72. One might take such observations further to complicate the notion of the undead drive; insofar as the latter infects a non-triumphant rendition of life, one might call the latter an instance of the *unalive*, the operation of a radically exposed, chaotic "vitality" indistinguishable from its perpetual extinction. Given its work on these themes, it is no surprise that in its initial depiction of Life, the poem alludes to Milton's Death, including in its phrase "o'er what seemed the head" (91), a direct verbal echo of *Paradise Lost* 2.672, "what seem'd his head" – a verbal echo noted by Donald H. Reiman, *Shelley's "The Triumph of Life": A Critical Study* (Urbana: University of Illinois Press, 1965), 29.

31 On the poem's allusions to these earlier chariots of Necessity, see Kenneth Neill Cameron, *Shelley: The Golden Years* (Cambridge, MA: Harvard University Press, 1974), 453–4.

32 Quentin Meillassoux, *After Finitude: An Essay on the Necessity of Contingency*, trans. Ray Brassier (New York: Continuum, 2008), 71; emphasis in the original.

33 Meillassoux, *After Finitude*, 10; Brassier, *Nihil Unbound*, 223–5.

34 Orrin N.C. Wang, *Fantastic Modernity: Dialectical Readings in Romanticism and Theory* (Baltimore, MD: Johns Hopkins University Press, 1996), 59.

35 Colin Lucas, "The Crowd and Politics," in *The French Revolution and Modern Political Culture*, vol. 2, *The Political Culture of the French Revolution*, ed. Colin Lucas (Oxford: Pergamon, 1988), 259–85. On contexts for interpreting the 1810 jubilee, see Linda Colley, *Britons: Forging the Nation, 1707–1837* (New Haven, CT: Yale University Press, 1992), 217–28; on the millennial and radical appropriation of the jubilee in the period, see Peter Linebaugh and Marcus Rediker, *The Many-Headed Hydra: Sailors, Slaves, Commoners, and the Hidden History of the Revolutionary Atlantic* (Boston: Beacon, 2000), 287–326.

36 E.P. Thompson, "The Moral Economy of the English Crowd in the Eighteenth Century," in *Customs in Common*, 185–258; and my *Monstrous Society*, 26–58

(on reciprocity) and 59–94 (on Burke, the October days, and the crowd in the French Revolution).

37 On urban festivities, see the discussion of Leigh Hunt's 1815 essay on masques in Ulmer, *Shelleyan Eros*, 159; on the frescoes at Pisa, see Nancy Moore Goslee, *Shelley's Visual Imagination* (New York: Cambridge University Press, 2011), 190; cf. Weinberg, *Shelley's Italian Experience*, 238–9. One must take note as well of the extensive artistic and literary traditions surrounding the theme of the triumph; for a discussion of the influence of Petrarch's triumphs on Renaissance iconography and literature, see D.D. Carnicelli, ed., *Lord Morley's "Tryumphes of Fraunces Petrarcke": The First English Translation of the Trionfi* (Cambridge, MA: Harvard University Press, 1971), 38–71.

38 Goslee, *Shelley's Visual Imagination*, 191.

39 Simon Schama, *Citizens: A Chronicle of the French Revolution* (New York: Knopf, 1989), 543–66.

40 On the triumphal return of Henry Hunt, see Collings, *Monstrous Society*, 233.

41 For a relevant discussion of the indistinguishability of revolution and restoration in the first two decades of the nineteenth century, see Rei Terada, "Hegel's Bearings," in *Romanticism and Disaster*, ed. Jacques Khalip and David Collings, Romantic Circles Praxis Series, 2012, https://romantic-circles.org/praxis/disaster/index.html, especially para. 5.

42 Compare de Man, who in discussing "thought's empire over thought" refers to "the element in thought that destroys thought in its attempt to forget its duplicity": de Man, "Shelley Disfigured," 118.

43 Angela Leighton, *Shelley and the Sublime: An Interpretation of the Major Poems* (New York: Cambridge University Press, 1984), 161.

44 On how neither Lucretius nor Shelley reduces human beings to atoms, retaining an emphasis on their status as ethical agents, see Vicario, *Shelley's Intellectual System*, 31, 33.

45 Here the poem's Lucretian themes intersect with its allusions to Dante; on the Dantean echoes in the depiction of the maniac dance, see Weinberg, *Shelley's Italian Experience*, 223.

46 For an extensive discussion of these themes, see David Konstan, *A Life Worthy of the Gods: The Materialist Psychology of Epicurus* (Las Vegas: Parmenides, 2008).

47 Lucretius, *De Rerum Natura*, 3.319–22.

48 Konstan, *A Life Worthy of the Gods*, 135, 152. But consider Serres, *The Birth of Physics*, 190, who comments that the Lucretian garden, into which the sage retreats, "is closed to the plague, a high place fortified by science against floods and pandemic." At times, it seems, Lucretius imagines that one achieves the status of the sage not by accepting a disastrous contingency but by finding a definitive defence against it.

49 On this theme in Lucretius see John Colman, *Lucretius as Theorist of Political Life* (New York: Palgrave Macmillan, 2012), 95–113.

50 Shelley, *Letters*, 1:230. For a discussion of this letter in the context of the poem, see Timothy Clark, *Embodying Revolution: The Figure of the Poet in Shelley* (New York: Oxford University Press, 1989), 230–1.

51 Shelley, *Letters*, 2:406. For a discussion of how this passage bears on the overall themes of the poem, see Michael Henry Scrivener, *Radical Shelley: The Philosophical Anarchism and Utopian Thought of Percy Bysshe Shelley* (Princeton, NJ: Princeton University Press, 1982), 283–5. Throughout his reading of the poem, Scrivener emphasizes how Shelley, pursuing an ethical idealism, seeks an alternative to such imaginative disturbance. Timothy Clark, taking this reading further, argues that Shelley's career overall reveals his capacity to blend apparently private and public concerns, to understand "the most apparently introspective 'private' emotions as elements in the movements of the historical process," and thus to see insatiable erotic and political desire together: see Clark, *Embodying Revolution*, 9.

52 Compare Serres, who writes that Lucretius advocates what may be difficult to imagine, "a rigorous and exact knowledge that could have been influenced by Venus, and not by Mars, by the desire for peace, and not destruction": see Serres, *The Birth of Physics*, 115.

53 Weinberg, *Shelley's Italian Experience*, 230; cf. Bloom, *Shelley's Mythmaking*, 253, and Ralph Pite, "Shelley, Dante, and *The Triumph of Life*," in *Evaluating Shelley*, ed. Timothy Clark and Jerrold E. Hogle (Edinburgh: Edinburgh University Press, 1996), 209. By giving Rousseau such a role, the poem clearly puts him in a privileged position, treating him as among the greatest ethical agents of recent decades; for useful guides on this theme, see Reiman, *Shelley's "The Triumph of Life,"* 39–85; Bloom, *Shelley's Mythmaking*, 252–4; Edward Duffy, *Rousseau in England: The Context for Shelley's Critique of Enlightenment* (Berkeley: University of California Press, 1979), especially 113; and Roberts, *Shelley and the Chaos of History*, 203–17.

54 In this regard the poem may register Shelley's attempt to delineate the limits of the historical Rousseau's response to Lucretius. As Roberts points out, in his works Rousseau often appropriates key terms from *De Rerum Natura*, as when he speaks of plunging, the torrent, or turbulence; see Roberts, *Shelley and the Chaos of History*, 454.

55 For readings that emphasize how Rousseau falls prey to a delusive wish to gain certainty, insight, knowledge, or something outside of the flux of experience in his response to the shape all light, see David Quint, "Representation and Ideology in *The Triumph of Life*," *SEL* 18 (1978): 639–57; de Man, "Shelley Disfigured," 107–16; Scrivener, *Radical Shelley*, 312; Hogle, *Shelley's Process*, 329; John A. Hodgson, *Coleridge, Shelley, and Transcendental Inquiry: Rhetoric, Argument, Metapsychology* (Lincoln: University of Nebraska Press, 1989), 102; Clark, *Embodying Revolution*, 245–55; Rajan, *Supplement of Reading*, 336; Forest Pyle, *The Ideology of Imagination: Subject and Society in*

the Discourse of Romanticism (Stanford, CA: Stanford University Press, 1995), 115–20; and Roberts, *Shelley and the Chaos of History*, 404. My argument suggests that Rousseau errs primarily by asking ultimate questions of an aesthetic construct, which in being derived from the phenomenal realm cannot measure up to such demands.

56 Here I follow Rajan, who argues that "demystification is not the ultimate horizon of our reading but must itself be inscribed in the intertextual processes generated by the poem"; see her *Supplement of Reading*, 351.

57 For a deconstructive reading that absorbs every aspect of the poem's optics into its treatment of a self-cancelling figuration, see Miller, *Linguistic Moment*, 132–60. For a discussion of the limitations of his approach and an indication of an alternative, see Karen A. Weisman, *Imageless Truths: Shelley's Poetic Fictions* (Philadelphia: University of Pennsylvania Press, 1994), 160–1, 167.

58 For Pyle, the poet's wish to retain the notion of the "true Sun" reveals that he "shares in the delusion of the triumph": see Pyle, *Ideology of Imagination*, 127. But as I argue below, the poem retains a distinction between the true and false sun in several passages – and in its furthest reaches suggests that the attempt to retain an ethical orientation to that Sun must fail; the poet's stance here is not final, not an instance of ideology, but a stage within a more complex development.

59 The poem's treatment of this theme extends as well to its otherwise flattering depiction of Bacon, who "compelled / The Proteus shape of Nature's as it slept / To wake": see 270–2. Bacon's act here echoes that of the sun in the opening lines and thus reiterates the logic of imposition the poem seeks to undo.

60 As Weinberg points out, drawing on Dante's treatment of Beatrice and Petrarch's of Laura, "redemptive love is a matter of serenity": see Weinberg, *Shelley's Italian Experience*, 240.

61 The poem thus takes further the question of the differend that arises in much of Shelley's writing. For a pathbreaking treatment of the differend in several of Shelley's texts, see Rajan, *Romantic Narrative*, 46–81. Rajan does not discuss the overall implications of practising a poetics of the *deliberate* differend – a crucial topic critics have yet to explore. The bivocal and bitonal poetics of "The Triumph of Life" seems to go further, insofar as it may reveal a disjunction not only between two phrase regimens, as Lyotard's definition of the differend would suggest, but at times also between the domain of phrases in general and what lies beyond them: see Lyotard, *The Differend*, xi–xii.

62 Earl R. Wasserman, *Shelley: A Critical Reading* (Baltimore, MD: Johns Hopkins University Press, 1971), 462–502.

63 Some might argue that such a bitonal poetics undermines each of its two levels. A reader could show, for example, that the poem insists *both* that the chariot of Life falsely appears to be the performance of a definitive brightness

and that it forces the higher, melodious sphere to move in an inaudible and thus largely virtual domain. Ulmer suggests that the poem's "visionary disillusionment … evokes presence as the standard of meaning, but thereby raises a standard rendered unreachable by the same relational logic that erects it": see Ulmer, *Shelleyan Eros*, 175. Such a reading, however, attempts to resolve on a local, figural level the impasse structuring all of Shelley's major poems and indeed his intellectual system as a whole; for a discussion of that more devastating deadlock, see the argument below.

64 "A Philosophical View of Reform," in *The Complete Works of Percy Bysshe Shelley*, 7:3–55. The pragmatic argument appears in the final section, "Probable Means," 42–55.

65 Some readers might take the reference to "God" in this passage to encourage an ironic reading of the narrator's comment. But as Pulos points out, "in the last few years of his life he not infrequently employed the name of God in his poetry in what appears to be an orthodox and conventional manner," as in "Mask of Anarchy," 298: see Pulos, *Deep Truth*, 101–2.

66 On will as rational appetite in Aquinas, see Pfau, *Minding the Modern*, 133–59. Despite Shelley's apparent fidelity to Hume, whose theory of the will Pfau eviscerates (283–326), his insistence on an ethics of virtue and the notion of the final cause may affiliate him with certain unsuspected predecessors.

67 Walter Benjamin, "Critique of Violence," in *Walter Benjamin: Selected Writings, 1: 1913–1926*, ed. Marcus Bullock and Michael W. Jennings (Cambridge, MA: Harvard University Press, 1996), 236–52.

68 Rajan, *Romantic Narrative*, 49; cf. 75–6. In effect, the structure of the deliberate differend that Rajan traces in *Prometheus Unbound* becomes a claim of outright *opposition* in "The Triumph of Life." The latter unquestionably relies on the structure of the intentional differend throughout the poem, making it into an even more deliberate, unsettling principle than ever. Note, for example, the relation between what is given in the voice of the narrator and what is given in the voice of Rousseau – or between the shape all light and Life. Yet whereas the earlier poem holds its sense of the incompatibility of power and will in solution, indicating it through the structure of the differend, the later poem gives it a more fundamental status largely *prior* to its articulation in distinct phrases, elevating it into an outright opposition.

69 Here I follow Scrivener, who, citing these lines, suggests that they reveal Shelley's "love for the self-governing city-state by identifying the highest ethical idealism with two cities": see Scrivener, *Radical Shelley*, 308.

70 See Žižek, *Ticklish Subject*, 297.

71 On anamorphosis, see Jacques Lacan, *The Four Fundamental Concepts of Psychoanalysis*, ed. Jacques-Alain Miller, trans. Alan Sheridan (New York: Norton, 1977), 79–90. While in this text Lacan interprets anamorphosis through a reading of desire, here I extend his discussion onto the terrain

of the drive. In suggesting that the Feature gives face to and articulates an anonymous process, I follow Jacques Khalip, who argues that a key aspect of Life "cannot be properly assigned to any one person, nor rendered meaningful through constant evocation": see Khalip, *Anonymous Life*, 182.

72 In its explorations of the contradictions within attempts to realize the good, the poem articulates a position that shares much with Derrida's reflections on the impossibility of doing justice. For Derrida's discussion of the aporia at the heart of duty, see Derrida, *The Gift of Death, Second Edition, and Literature in Secret*, trans. David Wills (Chicago: University of Chicago Press, 2008), 69; for a discussion of the aporia of democracy, also relevant in this context, see his *Rogues: Two Essays on Reason*, trans. Pascale-Anne Brault and Michael Naas (Stanford, CA: Stanford University Press, 2005), 35–6. Moreover, the poem's resistance to the divine violence carried out by Demogorgon suggests that it also finds aporias in the attempt to conceive how the eternal good might be realized in time; on this score, it resonates again with the late Derrida, according to whom, in the words of Martin Hägglund, "if the impossible were to become possible … everything would become impossible, since nothing would happen." The coming of an eternal justice would undo time itself – and thus justice as well. See Hägglund, *Radical Atheism: Derrida and the Time of Life* (Stanford, CA: Stanford University Press, 2008), 122.

73 Maurice Blanchot, *The Writing of the Disaster*, trans. Ann Smock (Lincoln: University of Nebraska Press, 1986), 1.

74 On worklessness, see (among other pivotal texts) "The Absence of the Book" in Maurice Blanchot, *The Infinite Conversation*, trans. Susan Hanson (Minneapolis: University of Minnesota Press, 1993), 285–434; on the "nonoccurrence" of the messianic event, see Blanchot, *The Writing of the Disaster*, 141; on "*subjectivity without any subject*," see Blanchot, *The Writing of the Disaster*, 30. On the impossibility of the event of death, and – in the associated impossibility of assuming that absent event – the emergence instead of a radical passivity, see Blanchot, *The Step Not Beyond*, trans. Lycette Nelson (Albany: SUNY Press, 1992), 93–100, 106–10, 123–5; and *The Writing of the Disaster*, 3, 13–33, 39–40, 65–72, 117–18, 121. For key readings of the ethics of passivity in Blanchot see Jacques Derrida, *Aporias*, trans. Thomas Dutoit (Stanford, CA: Stanford University Press, 1993), 70–7; and John D. Caputo, *The Prayers and Tears of Jacques Derrida: Religion without Religion* (Bloomington: Indiana University Press, 1997), 81–7.

75 As Weinberg comments, in his reference to the "wonder worthy of [Dante's] rhyme" (480), Rousseau "identifies his own hellish experience with the Inferno, and places that experience within the context of the whole of the *Commedia*," in effect placing the pageant within a "broader and more positive framework": see Weinberg, *Shelley's Italian Experience*, 239. But in the present context, this reference evokes instead the capacity to find wonder in the

inferno itself, where one tarries with a torment without the prospect of deliverance.

76 Jacques Khalip and David Collings, "Introduction: The Present Time of 'Live Ashes,'" in *Romanticism and Disaster*, ed. Jacques Khalip and David Collings, Romantic Circles Praxis Series, 2012, https://romantic-circles.org/praxis/disaster/index.html, para. 9.

Coda

1 For an accessible discussion of the sixth extinction, see Elizabeth Kolbert, *The Sixth Extinction: An Unnatural History* (New York: Picador, 2014).

2 Kant, *Critique of the Power of Judgment*, 133–4.

3 Shelley, *Mont Blanc*, 113, 103, 117–18, in *Shelley's Poetry and Prose*.

4 As I noted in chapter 5, *Mont Blanc* captures the glacier's response to a global climate event taking place in the summer of 1816 – a cooling in many regions of the world caused by the eruption of Mount Tambora on Sumbawa Island in what is Indonesia today; see Wood, *Tambora*, 152.

5 Kant, *Critique of the Power of Judgment*, 136–7.

6 Kant, *Critique of the Power of Judgment*, 152–3; boldface in the original.

7 Shelley, *Mont Blanc*, 80–1.

8 Kant nowhere suggests that the experience of the sublime points to anything that would guarantee the realization of the *summum bonum*; on the contrary, as Caygill points out, human activity "actualizes a proportion of nature and human ends, but in a way that is prone to distortion. Instead of the achievement of the *summum bonum* … it is possible that freedom will violate this proportion." See Caygill, *Art of Judgement*, 388.

9 For a discussion of the strong likelihood that the window for appropriate action to ward off the coming of severe, irreversible climate change has closed, see chapter 3 of my *Stolen Future, Broken Present: The Human Significance of Climate Change* (Ann Arbor, MI: Open Humanities Press, 2014), 58–73; for the online version see http://www.openhumanitiespress.org/books/titles/stolen-future-broken-present.

10 Shelley, *Mont Blanc*, 92.

11 Lord Byron, *Manfred*, 1.1.122–3.

12 On the close relationship between the exploitation of coal and the emergence of capitalist production, see Andreas Malm, *Fossil Capital: The Rise of Steam Power and the Roots of Global Warming* (New York: Verso, 2016); on the mutual implication of geological knowledge and the politics of capital in the history of oil, see Brian Frehner, *Finding Oil: The Nature of Petroleum Geology, 1859–1920* (Lincoln: University of Nebraska Press, 2011).

13 For a useful summary of scholarship on the use of geological knowledge for mapping fossil fuel reserves in Britain and the British empire, see Christophe

Bonneuil and Jean-Baptiste Fressoz, *The Shock of the Anthropocene: The Earth, History and Us*, trans. David Fernbach (New York: Verso, 2016), 202–3.

14 On how the exploitation of fossil fuels makes possible the flourishing of liberal democracies, see the exemplary discussion in Timothy Mitchell, *Carbon Democracy: Political Power in the Age of Oil* (New York: Verso, 2011). For a redescription of capital that emphasizes its ever-increasing appropriation of nature not as an external resource but an element internal to its own processes, see Jason W. Moore, *Capitalism in the Web of Life: Ecology and the Accumulation of Capital* (New York: Verso, 2015).

15 For an important argument concerning the continuities between Romanticism and modern consumer desire, a form of desire helping to generate the productive scenario mentioned here, see Campbell, *The Romantic Ethic*.

16 Jacques Khalip, "Kant's Peace, Wordsworth's Slumber," in *Romanticism and the Emotions*, ed. Joel Faflak and Richard C. Sha (New York: Cambridge University Press, 2014), 199.

17 For a closely related argument on infinite responsibility in our time, see my *Stolen Future*, 136–58.

Bibliography

Abrams, M.H. *Natural Supernaturalism: Tradition and Revolution in Romantic Literature*. New York: Norton, 1971.

Allewaert, Monique. "Toward a Materialist Figuration: A Slight Manifesto." *English Language Notes* 51 (2013): 61–77.

Althusser, Louis. *Reading Capital*. Translated by Ben Brewster. New York: Verso, 1979.

Anidjar, Gil. *Semites: Race, Religion, Literature*. Stanford, CA: Stanford University Press, 2008.

Arendt, Hannah. *The Human Condition*. 2nd ed. Chicago: University of Chicago Press, 1958.

Bainbridge, Simon. *Napoleon and English Romanticism*. Cambridge: Cambridge University Press, 1995.

Beck, Lewis White. *A Commentary on Kant's "Critique of Practical Reason."* Chicago: University of Chicago Press, 1960.

Behrendt, Stephen C. "*Manfred* and Skepticism." In *Approaches to Teaching Byron's Poetry*, edited by Frederick W. Shilstone, 120–5. New York: Modern Language Association, 1991.

Bender, John. "Impersonal Violence: The Penetrating Gaze and the Field of Narration in *Caleb Williams*." In *Critical Reconstructions: The Relationship of Fiction and Life*, edited by Robert M. Polhemus and Roger B. Henkle, 256–81. Stanford, CA: Stanford University Press, 1994.

Benjamin, Walter. "Critique of Violence." In *Walter Benjamin: Selected Writings, 1: 1913–1926*, edited by Marcus Bullock and Michael W. Jennings, 236–52. Cambridge, MA: Harvard University Press, 1996.

Bennington, Geoffrey. *Kant on the Frontier: Philosophy, Politics, and the Ends of the Earth*. New York: Fordham University Press, 2017.

Bernhard Jackson, Emily A. *The Development of Byron's Philosophy of Knowledge: Certain in Uncertainty*. New York: Palgrave Macmillan, 2010.

Bernhardt-Kabisch, Ernest. "The Stone and the Shell: Wordsworth, Cataclysm, and the Myth of Glaucus." *Studies in Romanticism* 24 (1985): 455–90.

Bewell, Alan. *Wordsworth and the Enlightenment: Nature, Man, and Society in the Experimental Poetry*. New Haven, CT: Yale University Press, 1989.

Blanchot, Maurice. *The Infinite Conversation*. Translated by Susan Hanson. Minneapolis: University of Minnesota Press, 1993.

– *The Step Not Beyond*. Translated by Lycette Nelson. Albany: SUNY Press, 1992.

– *The Writing of the Disaster*. Translated by Ann Smock. Lincoln: University of Nebraska Press, 1986.

Blay, Michel. *Reasoning with the Infinite: From the Closed World to the Mathematical Universe*. Translated by M.B. DeBevoise. Chicago: University of Chicago Press, 1998.

Bloom, Harold. *Shelley's Mythmaking*. New Haven, CT: Yale University Press, 1959.

Blumenberg, Hans. *The Legitimacy of the Modern Age*. Translated by Robert M. Wallace. Cambridge, MA: MIT Press, 1985.

Bonneuil, Christophe, and Jean-Baptiste Fressoz. *The Shock of the Anthropocene: The Earth, History, and Us*. Translated by David Fernbach. New York: Verso, 2016.

Bostetter, Edward E. *The Romantic Ventriloquists: Wordsworth, Coleridge, Keats, Shelley, Byron*. Seattle: University of Washington Press, 1963.

Brassier, Ray. Nihil *Unbound: Enlightenment and Extinction*. New York: Palgrave Macmillan, 2007.

Bundock, Christopher M. *Romantic Prophecy and the Resistance to Historicism*. Toronto: University of Toronto Press, 2016.

Butler, Judith. "The Sensibility of Critique: A Response to Asad and Mahmood." In *Is Critique Secular? Blasphemy, Injury, and Free Speech*, by Talal Asad, Wendy Brown, Judith Butler, and Saba Mahmood, 95–130. Berkeley, CA: Townsend Center for the Humanities, 2009.

Byron, George Gordon (Lord). *Lord Byron: The Complete Poetical Works*. Edited by Jerome J. McGann. 7 vols. New York: Oxford University Press, 1980–93.

– *"So Late into the Night": Byron's Letters and Journals*. Vol. 5, 1816–17, edited by Leslie A. Marchand. London: John Murray, 1976.

Cameron, Kenneth Neill. *Shelley: The Golden Years*. Cambridge, MA: Harvard University Press, 1974.

Campbell, Colin. *The Romantic Ethic and the Spirit of Modern Consumerism*. Oxford: Basil Blackwell, 1987.

Canuel, Mark. *Religion, Toleration, and British Writing, 1790–1830*. Cambridge: Cambridge University Press, 2002.

Caputo, John D. *The Prayers and Tears of Jacques Derrida: Religion without Religion*. Bloomington: Indiana University Press, 1997.

Carnicelli, D.D., ed. *Lord Morley's "Tryumphes of Fraunces Petrarcke": The First English Translation of the Trionfi*. Cambridge, MA: Harvard University Press, 1971.

Casanova, José. *Public Religions in the Modern World*. Chicago: University of Chicago Press, 1994.

Caygill, Howard. *Art of Judgement*. Oxford: Basil Blackwell, 1989.

Chandler, James K. *England in 1819: The Politics of Literary Culture and the Case of Romantic Historicism*. Chicago: University of Chicago Press, 1998.

Cheeke, Stephen. *Byron and Place: History, Translation, Nostalgia*. New York: Palgrave Macmillan, 2003.

Christensen, Jerome. *Lord Byron's Strength: Romantic Writing and Commercial Society*. Baltimore, MD: Johns Hopkins University Press, 1993.

Clark, Timothy. *Embodying Revolution: The Figure of the Poet in Shelley*. New York: Oxford University Press, 1989.

Colley, Linda. *Britons: Forging the Nation, 1707–1837*. New Haven, CT: Yale University Press, 1992.

Collings, David. "The Force of Indirection: 'Tintern Abbey' in the History of Mood." In *British Romanticism: Criticism and Debates*, edited by Mark Canuel, 409–17. New York: Routledge, 2015.

– "The Monster and the Maternal Thing: Mary Shelley's Critique of Ideology." In *Mary Shelley, Frankenstein*, edited by Johanna M. Smith, 323–39. New York: Bedford's, 2016.

– *Monstrous Society: Reciprocity, Discipline, and the Political Uncanny, c. 1780–1848*. Lewisburg, PA: Bucknell University Press, 2009.

– *Stolen Future, Broken Present: The Human Significance of Climate Change*. Ann Arbor, MI: Open Humanities Press, 2014.

– "Troping Mood: Pfau, Wordsworth, and Hegel." *Literature Compass* 6 (2009): 373–83.

– *Wordsworthian Errancies: The Poetics of Cultural Dismemberment*. Baltimore, MD: Johns Hopkins University Press, 1994.

Colman, John. *Lucretius as Theorist of Political Life*. New York: Palgrave Macmillan, 2012.

Conger, Syndy McMillen. *Mary Wollstonecraft and the Language of Sensibility*. Plainsboro, NJ: Associated University Presses, 1994.

Copjec, Joan. *Imagine There's No Woman: Ethics and Sublimation*. Cambridge, MA: MIT Press, 2002.

– *Read My Desire: Lacan against the Historicists*. Cambridge, MA: MIT Press, 1994.

Corber, Robert J. "Representing the 'Unspeakable': William Godwin and the Politics of Homophobia." *Journal of the History of Sexuality* 1 (1990): 85–101.

Corbett, Martyn. *Byron and Tragedy*. New York: St Martin's Press, 1988.

Cudworth, Ralph. *The True Intellectual System of the Universe*. 3 vols. Bristol, UK: Thoemmes Press, 1995.

Dawson, P.M.S. "'The Mask of Darkness': Metaphor, Myth, and History in Shelley's 'The Triumph of Life.'" In *History and Myth: Essays on English Romantic Literature*, edited by Stephen C. Behrendt, 235–44. Detroit: Wayne State University Press, 1990.

Deleuze, Gilles. *Difference and Repetition*. Translated by Paul Patton. New York: Columbia University Press, 1994.

de Man, Paul. "Shelley Disfigured." In *The Rhetoric of Romanticism*, 93–123. New York: Columbia University Press, 1984.

Derrida, Jacques. *Aporias*. Translated by Thomas Dutoit. Stanford, CA: Stanford University Press, 1993.

– *The Gift of Death, Second Edition, and Literature in Secret*. Translated by David Wills. Chicago: University of Chicago Press, 2008.

– "Living On." In *Deconstruction and Criticism*, 75–176. New York: Seabury, 1979.

– "Ousia and Gramme: Note on a Note from Being and Time." In *Margins of Philosophy*. Translated by Alan Bass. Chicago: University of Chicago Press, 1982.

– *Rogues: Two Essays on Reason*. Translated by Pascale-Anne Brault and Michael Naas. Stanford, CA: Stanford University Press, 2005.

– *Writing and Difference*. Translated by Alan Bass. Chicago: University of Chicago Press, 1978.

Dolar, Mladen. "'I Shall Be with You on Your Wedding-Night': Lacan and the Uncanny." *October* 58 (1991): 5–23.

Drummond, William. *Academical Questions*. Vol. 1. London: Bulmer, 1805.

Duffy, Edward. *Rousseau in England: The Context for Shelley's Critique of Enlightenment*. Berkeley, CA: University of California Press, 1979.

Edelman, Lee. *No Future: Queer Theory and the Death Drive*. Durham, NC: Duke University Press, 2004.

Eisenach, Eldon J. "The Dimension of History in Bentham's Theory of Law." *Eighteenth-Century Studies* 16 (1983): 290–316.

Faderman, Lillian. *Surpassing the Love of Men: Romantic Friendship and Love between Women from the Renaissance to the Present*. New York: William Morrow, 1981.

Faflak, Joel. "The Difficult Education of Shelley's 'Triumph of Life.'" *Keats-Shelley Journal* 58 (2009): 53–78.

Ferry, David. *The Limits of Mortality: An Essay on Wordsworth's Major Poems*. Middletown, CT: Wesleyan University Press, 1959.

Fink, Bruce. *The Lacanian Subject: Between Language and Jouissance*. Princeton, NJ: Princeton University Press, 1995.

Flahault, François. *Malice*. Translated by Liz Heron. New York: Verso, 2003.

Förster, Eckart. *The Twenty-Five Years of Philosophy: A Systematic Reconstruction*. Cambridge, MA: Harvard University Press, 2012.

Foucault, Michel. *Foucault Live: Collected Interviews, 1961–1984*. Edited by Sylvère Lotringer. Translated by Lysa Hochroth and John Johnston. New York: Semiotext(e), 1996.

– *History of Madness*. Edited by Jean Khalfa. Translated by Jonathan Murphy and Jean Khalfa. New York: Routledge, 2006.

– "Language to Infinity." In *Language, Counter-Memory, Practice: Selected Essays and Interviews*, edited by Donald F. Bouchard and translated by Donald F. Bouchard and Sherry Simon, 53–67. Ithaca, NY: Cornell University Press, 1977.

François, Anne-Lise. *Open Secrets: The Literature of Uncounted Experience*. Stanford, CA: Stanford University Press, 2008.

Frehner, Brian. *Finding Oil: The Nature of Petroleum Geology, 1859–1920*. Lincoln: University of Nebraska Press, 2011.

Garber, Frederick. *Self, Text, and Romantic Irony: The Example of Byron*. Princeton, NJ: Princeton University Press, 1988.

Godwin, William. *Caleb Williams*. New York: Norton, 1977.

– *The Enquirer: Reflections on Education, Manners, and Literature*. New York: Augustus M. Kelley, 1965.

– *Enquiry Concerning Political Justice and Its Influence on Modern Morals and Happiness*. Harmondsworth, UK: Penguin, 1985.

– *Enquiry Concerning Political Justice and Its Influence on Modern Morals and Happiness*. 3 vols. Edited by J.B. Priestley. Toronto: University of Toronto Press, 1946.

– "Essay of History and Romance." In *Political and Philosophical Writings of William Godwin*, edited by Mark Philp. Vol. 5, *Educational and Literary Writings*, edited by Pamela Clemit, 290–301. London: William Pickering, 1993.

– *Of Population: An Enquiry Concerning the Power of Increase in the Numbers of Mankind, Being an Answer to Mr Malthus's Essay on That Subject*. New York: Augustus M. Kelley, 1964.

– *St Leon*. New York: Oxford University Press, 1994.

Gold, Alex, Jr. "It's Only Love: The Politics of Passion in Godwin's *Caleb Williams*." *Texas Studies in Literature and Language* 19 (1977): 135–60.

Goldstein, Amanda. "Growing Old Together: Lucretian Materialism in Shelley's 'Poetry of Life.'" *Representations* 128 (2014): 60–92.

– *Sweet Science: Romantic Materialism and the New Logics of Life*. Chicago: University of Chicago Press, 2017.

Good, John Mason. *The Nature of Things: A Didactic Poem*. London, 1805.

Goslee, Nancy Moore. *Shelley's Visual Imagination*. New York: Cambridge University Press, 2011.

Gourgouris, Stathis. *Lessons in Secular Criticism*. New York: Fordham University Press, 2013.

Grabo, Carl. *A Newton among Poets: Shelley's Use of Science in "Prometheus Unbound."* 1930. Reprint, New York: Gordian, 1968.

Graham, Peter. "Byron, *Manfred*, Negativity, and Freedom." In *Liberty and Poetic Licence: New Essays on Byron*, edited by Bernard Beatty, Tony Howe, and Charles E. Robinson, 50–9. Liverpool: Liverpool University Press, 2008.

Gross, Jonathan David. *Byron: The Erotic Liberal*. New York: Rowman and Littlefield, 2001.

Hägglund, Martin. *Radical Atheism: Derrida and the Time of Life*. Stanford, CA: Stanford University Press, 2008.

Halmi, Nicholas. "Romanticism, the Temporalization of History, and the Historicization of Form." *MLQ* 74 (2013): 363–89.

Harrison, Ross. *Bentham*. London: Routledge, 1983.

Hartman, Geoffrey. *Wordsworth's Poetry: 1787–1814*. New Haven, CT: Yale University Press, 1971.

Hegel, G.W.F. *Hegel's Aesthetics: Lectures on Fine Art*. Translated by T.M. Knox. Vol. 1. New York: Oxford University Press, 1975.

– *Hegel's Science of Logic*. Translated by A.V. Miller. Atlantic Highlands, NJ: Humanities Press, 1969.

Helfield, Randa. "Constructive Treason and Godwin's Treasonous Constructions." *Mosaic* 28 (1995): 43–62.

Heringman, Noah. *Romantic Rocks, Aesthetic Geology*. Ithaca, NY: Cornell University Press, 2004.

Hitt, Christopher. "Shelley's Unwriting of Mont Blanc." *Texas Studies in Literature and Language* 47 (2005): 139–66.

Hoagwood, Terence Allan. *Byron's Dialectic: Skepticism and the Critique of Culture*. Lewisburg, PA: Bucknell University Press, 1993.

– *Skepticism and Ideology: Shelley's Political Prose and Its Philosophical Context from Bacon to Marx*. Iowa City: University of Iowa Press, 1988.

Hodgson, John A. *Coleridge, Shelley, and Transcendental Inquiry: Rhetoric, Argument, Metapsychology*. Lincoln: University of Nebraska Press, 1989.

Hogle, Jerrold E. *Shelley's Process: Radical Transference and the Development of His Major Works*. New York: Oxford University Press, 1988.

Howe, Anthony. *Byron and the Forms of Thought*. Liverpool: Liverpool University Press, 2013.

Huet, Marie-Hélène. *The Culture of Disaster*. Chicago: University of Chicago Press, 2012.

Hufbauer, Karl. *Exploring the Sun: Solar Science since Galileo*. Baltimore, MD: Johns Hopkins University Press, 1991.

Hutton, James. "Theory of the Earth; or an Investigation of the Laws Observable in the Composition, Dissolution, and Restoration of the Land upon the Globe." *Transactions of the Royal Society of Edinburgh* 1 (1788): 209–305.

Jacobus, Mary. *Romanticism, Writing, and Sexual Difference: Essays on "The Prelude."* New York: Clarendon Press, 1989.

Jager, Colin. *The Book of God: Secularization and Design in the Romantic Era*. Philadelphia: University of Pennsylvania Press, 2007.

– *Unquiet Things: Secularism in the Romantic Age*. Philadelphia: University of Pennsylvania Press, 2015.

Jameson, Fredric. *The Political Unconscious: Narrative as a Socially Symbolic Act*. Ithaca, NY: Cornell University Press, 1981.

– *A Singular Modernity: Essay on the Ontology of the Present*. New York: Verso, 2002.

Jarvis, Robin. "The Five-Book *Prelude*: A Reconsideration." *JEGP* 80 (1981): 528–51.

Jones, Christine Kenyon. "'When This World Shall Be Former': Catastrophism as Imaginative Theory for the Younger Romantics." *Romanticism on the Net* 24 (2001). https://www.erudit.org/revue/ron/2001/v/n24/006000ar.html.

Kant, Immanuel. "The Conflict of the Faculties." In *Religion and Rational Theology*. Translated by Allen W. Wood and George Di Giovanni. Cambridge: Cambridge University Press, 1996.

– *The Critique of Practical Reason*. 3rd ed. Translated by Lewis White Beck. Upper Saddle River, NJ: Prentice Hall, 1993.

– *Critique of Pure Reason*. Translated by Paul Guyer and Allen W. Wood. Cambridge: Cambridge University Press, 1998.

– *Critique of the Power of Judgment*. Edited by Paul Guyer. Translated by Paul Guyer and Eric Matthews. Cambridge: Cambridge University Press, 2000.

– *Natural Science*. Edited by Eric Watkins. Translated by Lewis White Beck et al. New York: Cambridge University Press, 2012.

– *Political Writings*. 2nd ed. Edited by Hans Reiss. Translated by H.B. Nisbet. Cambridge: Cambridge University Press, 1991.

Keats, John. *The Poems of John Keats*. Edited by Jack Stillinger. London: Heinemann, 1978.

Kelley, Theresa M. *Wordsworth's Revisionary Aesthetics*. Cambridge: Cambridge University Press, 1988.

Khalip, Jacques. *Anonymous Life: Romanticism and Dispossession*. Stanford, CA: Stanford University Press, 2009.

– "Kant's Peace, Wordsworth's Slumber." In *Romanticism and the Emotions*, edited by Joel Faflak and Richard C. Sha, 192–214. New York: Cambridge University Press, 2014.

Khalip, Jacques, and David Collings. "Introduction: The Present Time of 'Live Ashes.'" In *Romanticism and Disaster*, edited by Jacques Khalip and David Collings. Romantic Circles Praxis Series, 2012. https://romantic-circles.org/praxis/disaster/index.html.

Kierkegaard, Søren. *Christian Discourses: And The Lilies of the Field and the Birds of the Air and Three Discourses at the Communion on Fridays.* Translated by Walter Lowrie. Princeton, NJ: Princeton University Press, 1971.

Kishel, Joseph F. "The 'Analogy Passage' from Wordsworth's Five-Book *Prelude.*" *Studies in Romanticism* 18 (1979): 271–85.

Klancher, Jon. "Godwin and the Republican Romance: Genre, Politics, and Contingency in Cultural History." *MLQ* 56 (1995): 145–65.

Kolbert, Elizabeth. *The Sixth Extinction: An Unnatural History*. New York: Picador, 2014.

Konstan, David. *A Life Worthy of the Gods: The Materialist Psychology of Epicurus*. Las Vegas: Parmenides, 2008.

Kordela, A. Kiarina. *$urplus: Spinoza, Lacan*. Albany: SUNY Press, 2007.

Koselleck, Reinhart. *Futures Past: On the Semantics of Historical Time*. Translated by Keith Tribe. New York: Columbia University Press, 2004.

Koyré, Alexandre. *From the Closed World to the Infinite Universe*. Baltimore, MD: Johns Hopkins University Press, 1957.

Lacan, Jacques. *Écrits: The First Complete Edition in English*. Translated by Bruce Fink in collaboration with Héloïse Fink and Russell Grigg. New York: Norton, 2006.

– *The Four Fundamental Concepts of Psychoanalysis*. Edited by Jacques-Alain Miller. Translated by Alan Sheridan. New York: Norton, 1977.

– "Kant with Sade." Translated by James B. Swenson Jr. *October* 51 (1989): 55–104.

– *The Seminar of Jacques Lacan*. Edited by Jacques-Alain Miller. *Book 7, The Ethics of Psychoanalysis*, translated by Denis Porter. New York: Norton, 1992.

Laclau, Ernesto. *On Populist Reason*. New York: Verso, 2005.

Lacoue-Labarthe, Philippe, and Jean-Luc Nancy. *The Literary Absolute: The Theory of Literature in German Romanticism*. Translated by Philip Barnard and Cheryl Lester. Albany: SUNY Press, 1988.

Laertius, Diogenes. *Lives of Eminent Philosophers*. Translated by R.D. Hicks. 2 vols. New York: Putnam's, 1925.

Latour, Bruno. *We Have Never Been Modern*. Translated by Catherine Porter. Cambridge, MA: Harvard University Press, 1993.

Leaver, Kristin. "Pursuing Conversations: *Caleb Williams* and the Romantic Construction of the Reader." *Studies in Romanticism* 33 (1994): 589–610.

Lefort, Claude. *Democracy and Political Theory*. Translated by David Macey. Minneapolis: University of Minnesota Press, 1988.

Leighton, Angela. *Shelley and the Sublime: An Interpretation of the Major Poems*. New York: Cambridge University Press, 1984.

Lever, Maurice. *Sade: A Biography*. Translated by Arthur Goldhammer. San Diego: Harcourt Brace, 1993.

Lewis, Matthew. *The Monk*. Edited by Howard Anderson. New York: Oxford University Press, 1973.

Linebaugh, Peter, and Marcus Rediker. *The Many-Headed Hydra: Sailors, Slaves, Commoners, and the Hidden History of the Revolutionary Atlantic*. Boston: Beacon, 2000.

Liu, Alan. *Wordsworth: The Sense of History*. Stanford, CA: Stanford University Press, 1989.

Lockridge, Laurence S. *The Ethics of Romanticism*. Cambridge: Cambridge University Press, 1989.

Lucas, Colin. "The Crowd and Politics." In *The French Revolution and Modern Political Culture*. Vol. 2, *The Political Culture of the French Revolution*, edited by Colin Lucas, 259–85. Oxford: Pergamon, 1988.

Lucretius. *On the Nature of Things: De Rerum Natura*. Edited and translated by Anthony M. Esolen. Baltimore, MD: Johns Hopkins University Press, 1995.

Lyotard, Jean-François. *The Differend: Phrases in Dispute*. Translated by Georges Van Den Abbeele. Minneapolis: University of Minnesota Press, 1988.

– *Enthusiasm: The Kantian Critique of History*. Translated by Georges Van Den Abbeele. Stanford, CA: Stanford University Press, 2009.

– *The Inhuman: Reflections on Time*. Translated by Geoffrey Bennington and Rachel Bowlby. Stanford, CA: Stanford University Press, 1991.

– *Lessons on the Analytic of the Sublime*. Translated by Elizabeth Rottenberg. Stanford, CA: Stanford University Press, 1994.

MacIntyre, Alasdair. *After Virtue: A Study in Moral Theory*. 3rd ed. Notre Dame, IN: University of Notre Dame Press, 2007.

Malabou, Catherine. *The Future of Hegel: Plasticity, Temporality, and Dialectic*. Translated by Lisabeth During. New York: Routledge, 2005.

Malm, Andreas. *Fossil Capital: The Rise of Steam Power and the Roots of Global Warming*. New York: Verso, 2016.

Malthus, Thomas. *An Essay on the Principle of Population*. 1798. Edited by Geoffrey Gilbert. New York: Oxford University Press, 1993.

– *An Essay on the Principle of Population*. 1803. Edited by Donald Winch. Cambridge: Cambridge University Press, 1992.

May, Marilyn. "Publish and Perish: William Godwin, Mary Shelley, and the Public Appetite for Scandal." *Papers on Language and Literature* 26 (1990): 489–512.

McCann, Andrew. "William Godwin and the Pathological Public Sphere: Theorizing Communicative Action in the 1790s." *Prose Studies* 18 (1995): 199–222.

McGann, Jerome J. *Byron and Romanticism*. Edited by James Soderholm. New York: Cambridge University Press, 2002.

– *The Romantic Ideology: A Critical Investigation*. Chicago: University of Chicago Press, 1983.

Meillassoux, Quentin. *After Finitude: An Essay on the Necessity of Contingency*. Translated by Ray Brassier. New York: Continuum, 2008.

Melaney, William D. "Ambiguous Difference: Ethical Concern in *Manfred*." *New Literary History* 36 (2005): 461–75.

Michael, Timothy. *British Romanticism and the Critique of Political Reason*. Baltimore, MD: Johns Hopkins University Press, 2015.

Michalson, Gordon E., Jr. *Fallen Freedom: Kant on Radical Evil and Moral Regeneration*. Cambridge: Cambridge University Press, 1990.

Milbank, John. *Theology and Social Theory: Beyond Secular Reason*. 2nd ed. Malden, MA: Blackwell, 2006.

Mileur, Jean-Pierre. *Literary Revisionism and the Burden of Modernity*. Berkeley: University of California Press, 1985.

Miller, J. Hillis. *The Linguistic Moment: From Wordsworth to Stevens*. Princeton, NJ: Princeton University Press, 1985.

Milton, John. *Complete Poems and Major Prose*. Edited by Merritt Y. Hughes. Indianapolis: Odyssey Press, 1957.

Mitchell, Timothy. *Carbon Democracy: Political Power in the Age of Oil*. New York: Verso, 2011.

Moore, Jason W. *Capitalism in the Web of Life: Ecology and the Accumulation of Capital*. New York: Verso, 2015.

Nancy, Jean-Luc. *Dis-Enclosure: The Deconstruction of Christianity*. Translated by Bettina Bergo, Gabriel Malenfant, and Michael B. Smith. New York: Fordham University Press, 2008.

Nersessian, Anahid. *Utopia, Limited: Romanticism and Adjustment*. Cambridge, MA: Harvard University Press, 2015.

Nicholson, Marjorie Hope. *Mountain Gloom and Mountain Glory: The Development of the Aesthetics of the Infinite*. Ithaca, NY: Cornell University Press, 1959.

O'Connor, Ralph. "Byron's Afterlife and the Emancipation of Geology." In *Liberty and Poetic Licence: New Essays on Byron*, edited by Bernard Beatty, Tony Howe, and Charles E. Robinson, 147–64. Liverpool: Liverpool University Press, 2008.

– *The Earth on Show: Fossils and the Poetics of Popular Science, 1802–1856*. Chicago: University of Chicago Press, 2007.

– "Mammoths and Maggots: Byron and the Geology of Cuvier." *Romanticism* 5 (1999): 26–42.

Pfau, Thomas. *Minding the Modern: Human Agency, Intellectual Traditions, and Responsible Knowledge*. Notre Dame, IN: Notre Dame University Press, 2013.

– *Romantic Moods: Paranoia, Trauma, and Melancholy, 1790–1840*. Baltimore, MD: Johns Hopkins University Press, 2005.

Philp, Mark. *Godwin's Political Justice*. Ithaca, NY: Cornell University Press, 1986.

Pite, Ralph. "Shelley, Dante, and 'The Triumph of Life.'" In *Evaluating Shelley*, edited by Timothy Clark and Jerrold E. Hogle, 197–211. Edinburgh: Edinburgh University Press, 1996.

Plotnitsky, Arkady. "All Shapes of Light: The Quantum Mechanical Shelley." In *Shelley: Poet and Legislator of the World*, edited by Betty T. Bennett and Stuart Curran, 161–80. Baltimore, MD: Johns Hopkins University Press, 1996.

Plug, Jan. *Borders of a Lip: Romanticism, Language, History, Politics*. Albany: SUNY Press, 2003.

Potkay, Adam. *Wordsworth's Ethics*. Baltimore, MD: Johns Hopkins University Press, 2013.

Priestman, Martin. *Romantic Atheism: Poetry and Freethought, 1780–1830*. New York: Cambridge University Press, 1999.

Pulos, C.E. *The Deep Truth: A Study of Shelley's Scepticism*. Lincoln: University of Nebraska Press, 1962.

Pyle, Forest. *The Ideology of Imagination: Subject and Society in the Discourse of Romanticism*. Stanford, CA: Stanford University Press, 1995.

Quint, David. "Representation and Ideology in 'The Triumph of Life.'" *SEL* 18 (1978): 639–57.

Rajan, Tilottama. *Deconstruction and the Remainders of Phenomenology: Sartre, Derrida, Foucault, Baudrillard*. Stanford, CA: Stanford University Press, 2002.

– *Romantic Narrative: Shelley, Hays, Godwin, Wollstonecraft*. Baltimore, MD: Johns Hopkins University Press, 2010.

– *The Supplement of Reading: Figures of Understanding in Romantic Theory and Practice*. Ithaca, NY: Cornell University Press, 1990.

Rawes, Alan. "Byron's Romantic Calvinism." *Byron Journal* 40 (2012): 129–41.

Reiman, Donald H. *Shelley's "The Triumph of Life": A Critical Study*. Urbana: University of Illinois Press, 1965.

Richardson, Alan. *A Mental Theater: Poetic Drama and Consciousness in the Romantic Age*. University Park: Pennsylvania State University Press, 1988.

Roberts, Hugh. *Shelley and the Chaos of History: A New Politics of Poetry*. University Park: Pennsylvania State University Press, 1997.

Rohrbach, Emily. *Modernity's Mist: British Romanticism and the Poetics of Anticipation*. New York: Fordham University Press, 2016.

Rossi, Paolo. *The Dark Abyss of Time: The History of the Earth and the History of Nations from Hooke to Vico*. Translated by Lydia G. Cochrane. Chicago: University of Chicago Press, 1984.

Rudwick, Martin J.S. *Bursting the Limits of Time: The Reconstruction of Geohistory in the Age of Revolution*. Chicago: University of Chicago Press, 2005.

Russell, Bertrand. *Introduction to Mathematical Philosophy*. New York: Macmillan, 1919.

Sade, Marquis de. *Juliette*. Translated by Austryn Wainhouse. New York: Grove, 1968.

Schama, Simon. *Citizens: A Chronicle of the French Revolution*. New York: Knopf, 1989.

Scrivener, Michael Henry. *Radical Shelley: The Philosophical Anarchism and Utopian Thought of Percy Bysshe Shelley*. Princeton, NJ: Princeton University Press, 1982.

Sedgwick, Eve Kosofsky. *Between Men: English Literature and Male Homosocial Desire*. New York: Columbia University Press, 1985.

Serres, Michel. *The Birth of Physics*. Edited by David Webb. Translated by Jack Hawkes. Manchester: Clinamen Press, 2000.

Shakespeare, William. *The Complete Works of Shakespeare*. 3rd ed. Edited by David Bevington. Glenview, IL: Scott, Foresman, 1980.

Shelley, Mary. *The Last Man*. Vol. 4 of *The Novels and Selected Works of Mary Shelley*, edited by Jane Blumberg with Nora Crook. London: William Pickering, 1996.

Shelley, Percy Bysshe. *The Complete Poetry of Percy Bysshe Shelley*. Edited by Donald H. Reiman and Neil Fraistat. Vol. 2. Baltimore, MD: Johns Hopkins University Press, 2004.

– *The Complete Works of Percy Bysshe Shelley*. Edited by Roger Ingpen and Walter E. Peck. 10 vols. New York: Scribner's, 1926–30.

– *The Letters of Percy Bysshe Shelley*. 2 vols. Edited by Frederick L. Jones. Oxford: Clarendon, 1964.

– *Shelley's Poetry and Prose*. 2nd ed. Edited by Donald H. Reiman and Neil Fraistat. New York: Norton, 2002.

Shepherdson, Charles. "History and the Real." In *Rhetoric in an Antifoundational World: Language, Culture, and Pedagogy*, edited by Michael Bernard-Donals and Richard R. Glejzer, 293–317. New Haven, CT: Yale University Press, 1998.

Shilstone, Frederick W. *Byron and the Myth of Tradition*. Lincoln: University of Nebraska Press, 1988.

Singer, Brian C.J. *Society, Theory, and the French Revolution: Studies in the Revolutionary Imaginary*. New York: St Martin's Press, 1986.

Smith, Kenneth. *The Malthusian Controversy*. London: Routledge, 1951.

Solomonescu, Yasmin. "'A Plausible Tale': William Godwin's *Things as They Are*." *European Romantic Review* 25 (2014): 591–610.

Soni, Vivasvan. *Mourning Happiness: Narrative and the Politics of Modernity*. Ithaca, NY: Cornell University Press, 2010.

Sperry, Stuart M. "Byron and the Meaning of 'Manfred.'" *Criticism* 16 (1974): 189–202.

Tauchert, Ashley. *Mary Wollstonecraft and the Accent of the Feminine*. Houndmills, UK: Palgrave, 2002.

Taylor, Charles. *A Secular Age*. Cambridge, MA: Harvard University Press, 2007.

Terada, Rei. *Feeling in Theory: Emotion After the "Death of the Subject."* Cambridge, MA: Harvard University Press, 2001.

– "Hegel's Bearings." In *Romanticism and Disaster*, edited by Jacques Khalip and David Collings. Romantic Circles Praxis Series, 2012. https://romantic-circles.org/praxis/disaster/index.html.

Thompson, E.P. *Customs in Common: Studies in Traditional Popular Culture*. New York: New Press, 1993.

Todd, Janet. *Mary Wollstonecraft: A Revolutionary Life*. New York: Columbia University Press, 2000.

Tuite, Clara. "Cloistered Closets: Enlightenment Pornography, the Confessional State, Homosexual Persecution, and *The Monk*." *Romanticism on the Net* 8 (November 1997). https://www.erudit.org/revue/ron/1997/v/n8/005766ar.html.

Ulmer, William A. *Shelleyan Eros: The Rhetoric of Romantic Love*. Princeton, NJ: Princeton University Press, 1990.

Vicario, Michael A. *Shelley's Intellectual System and Its Epicurean Background*. New York: Routledge, 2007.

Wang, Orrin N.C. *Fantastic Modernity: Dialectical Readings in Romanticism and Theory*. Baltimore, MD: Johns Hopkins University Press, 1996.

Washington, Chris. "Byron's Speculative Turn: Visions of Posthuman Life in *Cain*." *Essays in Romanticism* 22 (2015): 73–95.

Wasserman, Earl R. *Shelley: A Critical Reading*. Baltimore, MD: Johns Hopkins University Press, 1971.

Wayne, Michael. *Red Kant: Aesthetics, Marxism, and the Third Critique*. London: Bloomsbury, 2014.

Weinberg, Alan M. *Shelley's Italian Experience*. New York: St Martin's Press, 1991.

Weisman, Karen A. *Imageless Truths: Shelley's Poetic Fictions*. Philadelphia: University of Pennsylvania Press, 1994.

Wilner, Joshua. *Feeding on Infinity: Readings in the Romantic Rhetoric of Internalization*. Baltimore, MD: Johns Hopkins University Press, 2000.

Wollstonecraft, Mary. *Mary: A Fiction*. In Wollstonecraft, *Works*, 1:1–73.

– *A Vindication of the Rights of Men*. In Wollstonecraft, *Works*, 5:1–77.

– *A Vindication of the Rights of Woman*. In Wollstonecraft, *Works*, 5:79–266.

– *The Works of Mary Wollstonecraft*. 7 vols. Edited by Janet Todd and Marilyn Butler. New York: New York University Press, 1989.

Wood, Gillen D'Arcy. *Tambor: The Eruption That Changed the World*. Princeton, NJ: Princeton University Press, 2014.

Wordsworth, Jonathan. "The Five-Book *Prelude* of Early Spring 1804." *JEGP* 76 (1977): 1–25.
Wordsworth, William. *The Five-Book Prelude*. Edited by Duncan Wu. Oxford: Blackwell, 1997.
– *Major Works*. Edited by Stephen Gill. Oxford: Oxford University Press, 1984.
– *The Prelude: 1799, 1805, 1850*. Edited by Jonathan Wordsworth, M.H. Abrams, and Stephen Gill. New York: Norton, 1979.
Wyatt, John. *Wordsworth and the Geologists*. Cambridge: Cambridge University Press, 1995.
Xenos, Nicholas. *Scarcity and Modernity*. London: Routledge, 1989.
Žižek, Slavoj. *For They Know Not What They Do*. New York: Verso, 1991.
– *The Sublime Object of Ideology*. New York: Verso, 1989.
– *The Ticklish Subject: The Absent Centre of Political Ontology*. New York: Verso, 1999.
Žižek, Slavoj, Eric L. Santner, and Kenneth Reinhard. *The Neighbor: Three Inquiries in Political Theology*. Chicago: University of Chicago Press, 2005.
Zupančič, Alenka. *Ethics of the Real: Kant, Lacan*. New York: Verso, 2000.

Index